Rumsfeld's Rules

ALSO BY DONALD RUMSFELD

Known and Unknown: A Memoir

Rumsfeld's
Rules

DONALD
RUMSFELD

BROADSIDE BOOKS
An Imprint of HarperCollins*Publishers*
www.broadsidebooks.net

HarperCollins books may be purchased for educational, business, or sales promotional use. For information, please e-mail the Special Markets Department at SPsales@harpercollins.com.

Broadside Books™ and the Broadside logo are trademarks of HarperCollins Publishers.

Grateful acknowledgment is made for permission to reprint the images on the following pages: Pages xi and 250: Courtesy of the Gerald R. Ford Library. Pages 13 and 92: Eric Draper, courtesy of the George W. Bush Presidential Library. Page 29: David Hume Kennerly. Page 33: Cherie A. Thurlby/Department of Defense. Page 57: Dirck Halstead/Getty Images. Pages 146 and 184: OSD Historical Office, Photograph Collection. Page 161: Department of Defense official photo by Robert D. Ward. Pages 171 and 214: Rumsfeld Collection. Page 280: Win McNamee/Getty Images.

FIRST EDITION

Library of Congress Cataloging-in-Publication Data has been applied for.

ISBN 978-0-06-227285-0

13 14 15 16 17   OV/RRD   10 9 8 7 6 5 4 3 2 1

To those whose insights make up the
rules contained in these pages—from Confucius to
Clausewitz to Churchill to Sun Tzu—and who made
me wiser than I had any right to be.

CONTENTS

Contents

INTRODUCTION:
THE BENEFITS OF
BORROWED WISDOM

As we journey through life many of us come across something interesting or wise from time to time and think to ourselves, "I should write that down." Well, I've had a tendency to do just that for as long as I can remember. I probably owe that habit to my schoolteacher mother. She encouraged me to jot down unfamiliar words and look up their meanings later. Eventually I found myself keeping track not only of words, but also of various phrases, expressions, and snippets of advice, and putting them in a shoe box.

For example, while my dad was stationed aboard an aircraft carrier during World War II, I wrote a letter telling him I was thinking of quitting the Boy Scouts to spend more time playing sports with my friends. Weeks later, I received his reply on the thin onionskin paper then popularly known as "V-mail" ("V" for "Victory"). Dad wrote that the decision to quit was my call. But he went on to say, "Once you quit one thing, then you can quit something else, and pretty soon you'll get good at being a quitter." That advice found its way into my shoe box.

Some years later, while I was in naval flight training in Pensacola, Florida, I noted some pithy advice in the manual for the SNJ, a single-engine propeller aircraft I was learning to fly: "If you are lost: climb, conserve, and confess." "Climb" meant that the pilot should gain altitude so that he could see a greater distance, get his bearings, and if necessary, glide without power to a safe landing. "Conserve" meant reducing airspeed and "leaning out" the fuel mixture to conserve fuel and have more time to figure out where he is. And "confess" meant getting on the radio promptly and announcing to all who might be listening, "I'm lost and I need help!"

"Climb, conserve, and confess" turns out to be sound advice for anyone who is lost or adrift, as happens to all of us from time to time. If you find yourself meandering aimlessly in a difficult spot, step back to get some perspective, slow down, and take a deep breath. And if you're still feeling lost, face up to it, and don't hesitate to ask for help.

Decades later, when I was working in the administration of President Richard Nixon, I spent a good deal of time with Nixon's top domestic advisor Daniel Patrick Moynihan, a brilliant talent who had earlier served under Presidents Kennedy and Johnson. I always came away from a conversation with Pat having learned something new and feeling good about life. Rare was the subject, no matter how great or small, that escaped his interest. In one conversation, seemingly out of nowhere, Moynihan said, "Don, only buy black socks." I gave him a quizzical look. "You can wear them with anything," he said. I took this to mean that in a busy world, it is best to make things easier by simplifying certain habits and decisions. Then again, he may have just been giving me wardrobe advice.

When he became president in 1974, Gerald Ford—a friend from our days together in the U.S. Congress—urged me to serve as White House Chief of Staff. He was grappling with the sizable chal-

When President Ford learned I had a file of quotes and observations about management in government, he asked to see them. So I gave a copy to him. He promptly labeled them "Rumsfeld's Rules."

lenges of suddenly becoming President after Richard Nixon's stunning resignation. During one of his first days in the Oval Office, I happened to mention one of the "rules" I'd collected. When he learned I had a file of other quotes and observations about management in government, he asked to see them.

So I asked my longtime assistant, Leona Goodell, to type them up and, after some polishing, I gave a copy to the President. He promptly labeled them "Rumsfeld's Rules" and asked me to give a copy to each of the senior members on the White House staff. Since then they have been read by presidents, government officials, business leaders, diplomats, members of Congress, and a great many others. Indeed, they seem to have taken on a life of their own.

It's worth noting that "Rumsfeld's Rules" are not all Rumsfeld's. Nor are they all rules. Many are life lessons and pieces of wisdom I've gathered from others. Truth be told, I don't know if I've had a truly original thought in my life. I enjoy being around people smarter than I am, who know more than I do, and who have done things I haven't done. I generally figure out what I think about a tough issue by discussing it with others. It turns out that a great many of those individuals happened to be some of the ablest leaders in business, the military, politics, government, and global affairs. Much of what is distilled in these pages is credited to them. The rest of the rules are mainly observations I have heard, read, or gained through experience over eight decades of an unusually fortunate life.

A word about the format of the rules. I have tried to attribute quotes to the source where known. The rules that originated with me and those where the source is unknown—I suppose you might call them "known unknowns"—are left in the text without attribution.

I think the reason these maxims have proved useful is that they are insights into human nature—timeless truths that have survived the changes in our culture and even the many efficiencies enabled by modern technology. Most have broad applicability and can be useful whether you aspire to be a leader in government, church, business, sports, or the military. They convey distilled wisdom that can be called upon in daily life, add insights to conversations and meetings, illustrate a point more persuasively, or serve as guideposts in decision-making.

The original rules were compiled in 1974, but they were never conceived as a static list. I've updated and changed them whenever I learned something new—which happens almost every day. It's safe to say that in the intervening four decades a whale of a lot has happened, both in my life and in history. I would go on to serve in other posts in government and as chief executive officer of two Fortune 500 companies.

What I learned in the private sector affected me as much as or more than my time in government, and the rules reflect that. They have been enhanced by continued note-taking, and in this book, they are augmented with stories and anecdotes. In some cases, Rumsfeld's Rules are the product of errors I've seen others make; others are lessons learned the hard way from mistakes of my own. As such, they represent a unique and personal distillation of wisdom gathered over the course of a lifetime.

A favorite rule of mine, and one worth keeping in mind as you turn the pages of this book, is "All generalizations are false—including this one." The point here is that rules cannot be a substitute for judgment. That's what makes leadership so difficult and truly outstanding leaders so rare. Tough decisions involve weighing not just benefits and risks, but also competing principles and sometimes even conflicting rules. Indeed, there are times when the received wisdom and prevailing ways of doing things must be challenged and the rulebook thrown out altogether. General Douglas MacArthur once said, "Rules are mostly made to be broken and are too often for the lazy to hide behind." MacArthur overstated the case—it was, after all, his breaking of the rules and disregard of orders from the commander in chief that led President Harry Truman to fire him during the Korean War. But there are certainly occasions when the judgment of exceptional leaders can and should trump the rules. There is no step-by-step guidebook or road map to life, no algorithm that can be relied upon for fail-safe answers to the tough questions, no rules that will fit every conceivable circumstance.

The rules are intended for people at various stages of their lives and careers. Some may be applicable to your current situation. Others might prove more valuable in the future, as you move up the ladder and take on more responsibility.

The book is arranged not in chronological order, but by subject area. The book can be used any way you like—reading it from cover to cover or skipping around to find topics of particular interest to you. At a minimum, I hope that at least a few of the rules will bring a smile to your face.

As a naval aviator, a congressman, White House Chief of Staff, U.S. Ambassador, Cabinet officer, special presidential envoy, secretary of defense, chief executive officer, corporate board member, husband, father of three, and grandfather of seven, I've often turned to these rules for guidance and continue to do so even today. I hasten to confess, however, that I haven't always followed them. For example, one of my favorites is: "If you develop rules, never have more than ten."

Rumsfeld's Rules

CHAPTER ONE

STARTING AT THE BOTTOM

Unless your last name is famous—like Rockefeller, Kennedy, Vanderbilt, or Bush—you don't start life with a boost up the ladder. The rest of us start closer to the bottom. When I was young, during the Great Depression and World War II, I delivered ice, sandwiches, and newspapers; sold magazines; mowed lawns; and worked as a construction worker, a janitor, and a rug cleaner to make money. Xerox's Ursula Burns, the first African American female CEO of a Fortune 500 company, started out at the company as a summer intern. NFL commissioner Roger Goodell was an intern and driver for Pete Rozell. Jim Skinner, McDonald's CEO, began as a restaurant manager trainee. Jack Welch arrived at GE in 1960 as a junior engineer. In all of these cases, they worked hard, surrounded themselves with smart people, and moved up.

When starting at the bottom, be willing to learn from those at the top.

It is easy for someone starting out in a career to look at those at the senior levels and think they somehow got there by luck or magic, or by having some special skill that the rest of us don't have. That is usually not the case. Most of the successful folks I know started with close to nothing. They had talent, to be sure, but they also worked hard and learned from those around them. Whether they knew it or not, they all followed some rules that can help guide others from an entry- or midlevel position to a senior post.

When one of our daughters was a college senior, she asked me for some career advice. Come to think of it, I can't remember if she asked me or if I volunteered my opinion—either was just as likely. Like many young people, she wondered whether she might work in this industry or whether she should live in our hometown of Chicago, in Washington, D.C., or somewhere else. My view was that the question with potentially the most importance was one she hadn't yet asked: not *where* she should work, but rather with *whom*.

Throughout my career, I've been fortunate to find myself associated with some of the finest minds in our nation and indeed in the world. I watched, listened, and learned. It made me a better staff person and ultimately a better leader as well. It also offered a considerably more interesting life than I had ever contemplated when I came off active duty in the Navy in 1957 at the age of twenty-five with a wife, a child, no money, no connections, and no job.

I got my first job after leaving the Navy by contacting the job placement office at Princeton, the university I attended on scholarship. As it happened, David Dennison, a U.S. congressman from Warren, Ohio, had written to the university looking for candidates to serve as his administrative assistant. I'd always had an interest in politics and government, so I raced from Chicago to Washington, D.C., for an interview.

Dave Dennison perfectly matched my picture of what a congressman should be. He was a thoroughly decent man who felt privileged to represent the people of his district in northeastern Ohio. When he offered me a position as his assistant, I was elated.

But the thrill of being able to work on Capitol Hill was tempered by the fact that I didn't have a clue about how to do my job. I was as green as grass. I'd never worked in an office, any office, in my life. Since college I had been a naval aviator—period. Trying to keep up with the volume and variety of work—tracking legislation, dealing with constituent correspondence, drafting speeches, and arranging radio programs—seemed next to impossible. The pace of the job coupled with my inexperience left me feeling drained at the end of each long day. I'd return home with my stomach in knots.

Throughout my career, I benefited from being in the orbit of smart, experienced people. After working for Dennison, for example, I worked for an energetic young congressman from Michigan named Robert P. Griffin, who later was elected to the U.S. Senate. In a way, my involvement with Griffin helped change history. When I won my first race for Congress, Griffin recruited me to join him in a reformers' revolt against the entrenched Republican House leadership even before I had been sworn in. The candidate he was backing to be chairman of the House Republican

Conference was his friend and fellow Michigander Gerald R. Ford. My subsequent friendship with Ford, which began in 1962, would change the course of my life—and, in a sense, his. Indeed, it's safe to say that Richard Nixon would not have selected Ford as vice president eleven years later had we not persuaded Ford to run for House Minority Leader in 1964.

As a young member of the House Science and Astronautics Committee in Congress, I came to know the brilliant scientist and former German rocket expert Wernher von Braun. Once known as "Hitler's rocketeer," Dr. von Braun was one of the designers of the V-2 rocket, which killed many hundreds of Britons during World War II. At the end of the war, he was recruited by the Soviets but came to the United States instead and was instrumental in the success of the U.S. space program. Von Braun was an influence on my interest in ballistic missiles—the threat they posed, as well as the opportunities they offered. Years later I came to champion a missile defense system for the United States in part because of those early experiences.

After Richard Nixon was elected in 1968, he urged me to give up my seat in the U.S. Congress to join his administration. I turned him down more than once. Ultimately, however, I accepted, and my experiences in the executive branch proved enormously enriching. I paid close attention to Daniel Patrick Moynihan, who had profound, interesting, and often delightful things to say. I learned from economists such as George Shultz, Arthur Burns, Herb Stein, and Milton Friedman. And I learned from President Nixon himself, who well understood the importance of immersing himself in the knowledge and expertise of the accomplished minds he recruited to his administration.

The harder I work, the luckier I am.
—*Stephen Leacock*

Looking back, I can see that my advice to my daughter applies as well to young people starting out today. Focus less on the salary, title, location, or the view from your office window. Those things will take care of themselves if you work hard, do well, and find ways to work with talented people in the first place. If you want to be a football coach, you'll be a heck of a lot better off spending a year as a junior assistant to a Bill Belichick or an intern to John or Jim Harbaugh then as a senior aide to a lesser figure. If you want to be an actor, take any position with a Meryl Streep or Clint Eastwood, even if it means getting them coffee, making photocopies, and starting at the very bottom of the ladder. Do whatever it takes to fit into that person's universe. If you learn from the best, and closely observe the talented people around them, it will be time well invested.

Dick Cheney, whom I hired as my assistant back in the Nixon administration, likes to say that I responded to good work by piling on more. That is true. When a boss finds someone who is capable, has initiative, and has a good attitude, he looks for incentives to keep that person around and help them advance. One of the best ways to do that is to give them even more responsibility.

When I first hired Dick Cheney, he was twenty-eight years old. He was a serious young man. I'm sure he had ambitions and goals, but he didn't press them on me, and I doubt that they included one day becoming Vice President of the United States. I never heard Dick complain about his salary, or ask for a better office, or angle for a promotion. Instead he put his head down, took on more and more responsibility, offered sound advice, didn't bother me with every little thing, and did the work asked of him. More than that, he did work that wasn't asked of him but that he knew needed to be done. If you do your best at what you have been assigned, whether you like the particular task or not, you will be surprised how quickly those around you take notice.

Learn from those who have been there.

When I worked for a time as a stockbroker in Chicago in the early 1960s, I'd start at the top floor of a building and knock on every door before I made my way down to the next one. I also made a point of visiting with the front office people in the companies I called on. I quickly learned that the folks in the front office, who at that time were usually women, were the first line of defense. They could help get people in the door to see their bosses or, just as easily, keep people out. They were a font of information and could be of enormous assistance if they wanted to be.

Congressman Dennison's office similarly was run by several women who made it function smoothly. Helen Wangness, Anne Drummond, and Fran Minter each had many years' experience on Capitol Hill. They taught me the ropes. Together we made the office work.

These key people can be found in any organization. In a hospital, it's the nurses who often end up teaching interns and residents many of the important practical lessons of caring for patients. In a manufacturing company, it may be the foremen. In the military, it is the chief petty officers and the sergeants. They have seen managers come and go. They are the repository of institutional knowledge, and more often than not, they are willing to share it.

Among the many things I learned from them, the most important is this: Whatever your position, reach out to those who know more than you do, and have been around longer than you have. Find those people. Listen carefully. And learn.

Don't begin to think you're the boss. You're not.

Humility and discretion are two valued qualities in an employee. Regardless of the position you hold, keep in mind that you represent your boss to the outside world. What you say and do reflects on the boss and on the entire organization. When you speak for the boss or the company, be sure you are representing them accurately.

In the execution of the boss's decisions, work to be true to his views in both fact and tone.

During the time I worked for Congressman Dennison, for example, a constituent or a journalist would ask me for the congressman's views or sometimes even my own views on a subject. I knew they didn't give a fig about my opinions. If I had any doubt about that, all I had to do was resign and see if those people were still interested in asking me questions. I knew well that I wasn't the one who had been elected to represent the interests of the several hundred thousand people in his district. Sometimes staff members, especially those with strong opinions, can forget that. An employee must quickly learn to cleanse themselves of such delusions, or else the boss will do it for him.

If a matter is not a decision for the boss, delegate it.

I've been in meetings where I have been told things I already knew or engaged in a discussion about an issue I didn't need to entertain. I expect those who did so discerned from my gaze that I was not particularly interested. An effective boss works hard. He doesn't have time to deal with every issue that crosses the organization's radar screen. That's why he has a staff to assist him. Staff members ought not to bring things to the boss simply to get face time.

The senior military and civilian assistants at the Department of Defense form a valuable staff network in the Pentagon. Most of them are seasoned upper- and midlevel officers—Air Force, Army, and Marine colonels and Navy captains—who manage the schedules and paper flow for the senior uniformed and civilian officials. The vast, largely decentralized web of elements in the Department of Defense couldn't function smoothly without them. Those who worked with me at the Pentagon became highly skilled at knowing when to ask for guidance and when to handle a matter themselves. Because they paid attention to my patterns and views, they knew they were empowered to pass along my guidance to senior civilian and military leaders. In any organization, a boss tends to appreciate those around him who pay close attention to his views and policies and pass them along down the chain. Before bringing an issue to the bosses' attention they ask themselves: Is this something that someone else could and should handle?

If in doubt, move decisions up to the boss.

If there is a legitimate question as to whether an issue merits a supervisor's time, bring it to his or her attention. Failing to get his or her views on an important matter may result in your providing guidance at variance with what the boss actually thinks. Asking the boss the right question can save a lot of time and trouble later.

When you do go to the corner office for guidance, try to pose questions in such a manner that the response can be used to deal with similar issues in the future. Instead of asking, for example, whether an individual should be allowed to get overtime for performing a certain task, you might ask, "In what instances is overtime appropriate?"

When you approach the boss for direction, try to speak accurately, and succinctly, and then be gone. You don't want to be the person who causes the boss to groan when he sees you come into the office. Another lesson a smart staff member quickly learns is to always carry a pen and some paper when meeting with the boss. Otherwise it's a bit like being in a restaurant when the waiter doesn't write down complicated orders for eight people. You just know he will forget something. Most people have a low tolerance for being asked to repeat things. When the boss calls you to his office, he most likely wants to do more than exercise his vocal cords. He undoubtedly will have something to communicate. It is best to do him the courtesy of being prepared to write it down, so he doesn't have to say it twice.

If you foul up, tell the boss and correct it fast.

When it was first announced at a press conference in Baghdad in January 2004 that the U.S. military had opened an investigation into prisoner abuse, it passed without much notice—in the press, with the public at large, and in the Pentagon. It was one of the thousands of routine investigations that take place every year in the 3-million-person Department of Defense and received in that context. It was known that there had been abuse of some Iraqi detainees during the midnight shift at a prison called Abu Ghraib. Some soldiers had taken photographs, which had been found and were being held as part of the investigation.

Three months later, I was told that a television program had obtained copies of some of the photographs and would be airing a story about them. I asked to see the photos so that I could inform the President and Congress and have some idea of how the Defense Department should respond. What I saw was appalling. These were images that could undermine our military's efforts in Iraq, mobilize the enemy in protest, and diminish the American people's support for the war. Seeing for the first time the sadistic behavior of a few prison guards wearing U.S. military uniforms left me feeling as if I'd been punched in the gut. Had I been told about the abuse the photos depicted when the investigation was first initiated, the Pentagon would have informed the President and congressional leaders and been prepared with a more effective response. Instead we were blindsided.

It was unfortunate that I and the senior uniformed leadership had not been made aware of the nature of the abuse earlier. I felt that I had let the President and the American people down. I brought the issue to the President's attention, but too late to prepare him for the shock. In the following days, I gave President Bush my letter of resignation—twice. He refused to accept it.

Mistakes can usually be corrected if the organization's leaders are made aware of them, and they are caught early enough and faced honestly. Bad news doesn't get better with time. If you have fouled up something, it's best to tell the boss fast.

Don't blame the boss. He has enough problems.

In 1977, as I was preparing to leave my post as Secretary of Defense, Admiral Hyman Rickover, the widely heralded father of the Navy's nuclear submarine program, came to see me in my office. Rickover had become an institution in the Navy and would serve sixty-three years on active duty, becoming the longest-serving naval officer in our country's history. His was so forceful a personality that—in a bit of dark humor—some who served under him nicknamed him "the kindly old gentleman." Rickover, who was anything but, was accustomed to having his recommendations accepted, without exception, by everyone, including a succession of Secretaries of Defense. And over his tenure, he had served in one capacity or another under each of the first fifteen to hold that office.

That formidable flag officer was apparently unhappy that one of his proposals had not been approved for what he considered to be *his* nuclear submarine force. He assumed the reason was that my senior military assistant, Rear Admiral Staser Holcomb, had not passed his suggestion on to me. He apparently couldn't imagine that a Secretary of Defense would not approve something he recommended, and Holcomb bore the brunt of his unhappiness. Holcomb was respectful, polite, and never let on that the individual blocking his proposal was not him, but Rickover's boss, the Secretary of Defense—which is to say, me.

Several weeks later, Rickover came to my office, unhappy about Holcomb's supposed audacity. I interrupted him mid-sentence. "Admiral, Staser was not responsible. He passed on each of your recommendations and the ones I agreed with, I approved. The ones I did not agree with, I disapproved." Rickover was surprised and I can't say all that happy, but at least he knew straight from me that Holcomb was not to blame.

This illustrates the rule that a good employee sticks up for his boss and protects him, even when he isn't asked to do so. But that also works two ways. A responsible boss stands up for his employees as well.

Keep the boss's options open. He is the one faced with the toughest decisions. The easier ones are generally made at lower levels. Don't make his job harder by making decisions that could limit his flexibility.

Agreement can always be reached by increasing the generality of the conclusion; when this is done, the form is generally preserved but only the illusion of policy is created.

Soon after I became Secretary of Defense for the second time, in 2001 in the George W. Bush administration, I found that the National Security Council was operating in a way that placed a priority on finding a consensus on tough issues, as opposed to sharpening options from which the President could choose his

Preserve the boss's options. He will need them.

desired course of action. From my perspective this could be problematic when it came to thorny issues where there were differing views. I had seen firsthand that President Bush was fully capable and willing to make decisions when presented with clearly defined options. I knew he didn't need to be shielded from tough choices. I felt that by trying to blend or merge distinctly different approaches, the NSC risked ending up with policies that could be internally contradictory—such as when there were differences over whether to isolate North Korea or continue to pursue negotiations. Each President has his own preferred approach. President Nixon, for example, liked to consider all possible alternatives to tough problems, and ruminate on them alone or with a few key advisors. I can still picture him sitting in his private office, his feet propped up on an ottoman, with a yellow pad in hand and a pen sticking out of his mouth as he considered one option, then another, working his way methodically through a difficult issue. I think leaders benefit from having the opportunity to weigh a range of options, considering the pros and cons of each. If a decision turns out to be a poor one, at least the President will know that he had carefully considered the full range of views and that all of his key advisors had an opportunity to present their case.

Don't let the urgent crowd out the important.

In a high-pressure operation there is always a danger that the urgent will crowd out the important. As Secretary of Defense, I considered it my responsibility to bring to the President's attention critical matters that might be off his radar screen. I did so usually in the form of a memo that I copied to the other members of the National Security Council.

In 2006, our national security apparatus was appropriately focused on the immediate tasks of the Afghanistan and Iraq wars and fighting global terrorism. Yet I was convinced, and remain so today, that we also needed to give thought and effort to reforming, and in some cases possibly replacing, institutions that no longer served us well in the twenty-first century. I proposed that approach in a memo to the President and hoped there would be time for a focused discussion. To my regret, a more fundamental rethinking of America's national security apparatus has still not occurred.

One of the more famous innovations of World War II began with a similar memo. In 1937, Marine 1st Lieutenant Victor Krulak witnessed the Japanese amphibious attack on Shanghai. Some twenty years after the World War I disaster at Gallipoli, where thousands of Allied forces had been killed in a misguided attempt to storm the Turkish coast, the idea of an amphibious landing was considered suicidal, so Krulak observed the assault with some interest. He noticed the Japanese had engineered boats with retractable ramps that allowed men and vehicles to off-load on the shore. He secretly took pictures from a nearby tugboat and sent a memo back to Washington that the Japanese landing craft were remarkably successful and perhaps worthy of being replicated in some form. The memo was filed away in the recesses of the War Department. A note supposedly labeled the report "the work of some nut in China."

But Krulak stuck with the idea when he returned to America. He met with an eccentric boatbuilder in New Orleans named Andrew Higgins, and together they designed a boat with retractable ramps based on the Japanese design. Eventually the Marine Corps recognized the need for a vessel that could make amphibious landings. Several years later, the so-called Higgins boat became perhaps the single most essential U.S. military vehicle in all of World War II. From the Normandy landings to the island assaults in the western Pacific, Higgins boats delivered and unloaded tens of thousands of Allied troops and massive amounts of equipment that would enable our forces to eventually win the war and free millions of people.

Disagreement is not disloyalty.
—Curtis E. Sahakian

One of the more important—and difficult—tasks for a staff member is to tell the boss when he might be wrong. With some bosses this can be a daunting prospect. But it is helpful to remember that if he or she has placed enough trust in you to have you there every day to assist him, then he most likely is willing to hear your opinion on key issues, even if it may not be what he thinks he wants to hear. Because of your proximity, you have an obligation to give it to him straight. All of us have been wrong on occasion—often more than we care to recall.

Good leaders don't have much patience for yes-men. You have probably seen the type—he turns up in an organization, praising the boss's wisdom, even his choice of necktie, and seems to agree with whatever the boss has to say. Such a person can be a hazard in an organization because he or she may cloud the boss's judgment or distort what is really going on.

Anyone who has met my wife, Joyce, knows that she is not one to hide her opinions. She has a way of putting things in perspective and, when it is needed, offering useful guidance. Once Joyce was asked how she could stay married to a guy like Rumsfeld for fifty-eight years. Without a smile, she replied, "He travels a lot."

If you have objections or think the boss may be going about something in the wrong way, try posing questions: "Have you considered this aspect of the problem?" "What if it were approached this way?" or "Have you talked to Mike about it?" You don't need to be confrontational or disrespectful. And if you still disagree with his decision, you owe it to him to state your differences privately.

Among President Ford's close friends in Congress was the Democratic Speaker of the House Tip O'Neill, a deft legislator and gregarious Irishman who loved to regale presidents and friends with good stories. In December 1974, the Speaker had invited his friend and former colleague in the House of Representatives, Gerald Ford, to his sixty-second birthday party.

Ford had been President less than four months and was still settling in to the responsibilities of the office. One of my duties as White House Chief of Staff was to have the scheduling office gather all the details on a function—where it would be, how long it would last, who would be attending, and the like.

The scheduler reported the details back to me and added that the party was being hosted by a South Korean lobbyist named Tongsun Park. I remembered the name from the newspapers and didn't feel comfortable having the President attend a function hosted and paid for by a man known to be a foreign lobbyist with dubious ties to various members of Congress.

"Mr. President, I think you should reconsider your decision to go to Tip's birthday party," I told the President in the Oval Office. As a congressman Ford could have attended the event without the scrutiny of the press and public. As the President of the United States, he could not.

Well, no one was a more loyal friend than Jerry Ford. He bridled at the thought of bowing out after he had promised O'Neill he would attend. "No, Don," he responded. "Tip is my friend. I'm going."

The President thought that was the end of it, but I felt strongly that he would be making a serious mistake. So I found another occasion to bring up the issue. "Mr. President, about Tip's birthday party, you do know you can't attend," I told him.

"Damn it, Rummy," he said, "it's settled. I am going."

"Well," I replied, "then you're going to have to walk. I'm not going to have the President's armored limousine pull up to a party bought and paid for by a foreign lobbyist who may well be under investigation."

It was one of the few times I saw the genial Jerry Ford get hot.

But in the end, he didn't go. We later laughed about it, and he realized he had let friendship get in the way of his better judgment.

As it turned out, that lobbyist later admitted to bribing a number of members of Congress, some of whom were censured by their colleagues. That was the last birthday party Mr. Park hosted on Capitol Hill.

If in doubt, don't. If still in doubt, do what's right.

If, despite your best efforts, the boss decides to go in a direction other than the one you suggested, it's your responsibility to carry out that decision and support it fully. However, if it is something you feel so deeply about that you cannot in good conscience support it, you have no choice but to resign. There is no middle ground. Not carrying out orders, diverging from guidance from above, or complaining to outsiders undermines the trust and teamwork that are required for an organization to succeed.

Whether you are White House Chief of Staff, a congressional assistant, or an aide to a corporate executive, the ultimate fallout from any decision you make ends up affecting those above you. What you say, what you do, and how you act will reflect well or poorly on those you work for.

I have learned something valuable from every job experience I ever had. Sometimes I learned how to do something better. And sometimes I learned what not to do. Not every job experience is a happy one. Not every boss is reasonable. And of course not every decision an organization makes is wise, beneficial, or fair.

But good work habits can be contagious. If you as an employee at the bottom of an organization perform well, you will be likely to find yourself in a managerial position where you can train and teach those below you to perform well. Eventually, you may well reach a point where you've helped to build an organization that reflects well on its managers and on the top boss. Work hard, do well, and someday that top boss may be you.

CHAPTER TWO

RUNNING A MEETING

Meetings: We all know their pitfalls. The long-winded colleague who enjoys the sound of his own voice . . . the guy whose singular interest seems to be getting in the boss's good graces . . . the fellow who wanders in late with a question that has already been asked and answered . . . or the person tapping loudly on her BlackBerry while others are trying to listen . . . or the joker who forgets to turn off his or her cell phone. Then there is the silent type, careful not to risk offering an opinion until everyone else has. And then invariably the hamburger who is quick to shoot down other people's ideas but without offering his own solution.

At their worst, meetings can be both useless and mind-numbing. It calls to mind an observation made in that endless font of wise management advice, the comic strip *Dilbert*: "There is no specific agenda for this meeting. As usual, we'll just make unrelated emotional statements about things which bother us." Or, as my friend and former colleague Congressman Mo Udall once put it, when referring to a discussion on the floor of the House of

Representatives: "Everything has been said, but not everyone has said it."

It's little wonder that, at least according to one study, the average office worker spends four hours in meetings every week and regards more than half of that time as wasted. A separate survey found "too many meetings" as the number-one reason for unproductive hours in an office setting. No one is immune to these sentiments—not even a Cabinet officer sitting in meetings in the White House and trying to avoid looking at his watch. Time is something you never get back.

Not every meeting has to be a source of dread. If you think about it, a meeting's function is to pool an organization's collective wisdom and knowledge in one room, making it easier for a manager to learn what his team knows that he doesn't, and to provide guidance to all of those involved in one place at one time. Well-managed meetings can be valuable—indeed, indispensable.

The art of listening is indispensable for the right use of the mind.
—*R. Barr, St. John's College*

Over my eight decades I've seen a full range of meeting styles—some more useful and constructive than others. I have been in meetings of all types—with business leaders, kings and queens, presidents and prime ministers, academics, and dictators. I know there are more than a few employees out there who think their boss is a dictator or an authoritarian—and some of them may have even worked for me. But I've actually met with a number of real autocrats over the years. And I've noticed something they tend to have in common. Dictators use meetings to establish a sense of command, even dominance, over their interlocutors.

When I met with Saddam Hussein in 1983—the first high-ranking American official to do so in years—the Iraqi president greeted me in military garb with a pearl-handle pistol at his hip. That left an impression.

I recall Russian President Vladimir Putin sitting at the end of a large table in the Kremlin. With his face revealing not even a flicker of emotion, Putin began to talk in a droning monologue. Thirty minutes passed, then thirty more. No questions or dialogue was permitted to interrupt Putin's speech, which lasted for more than an hour and a half. The Russian ruler was in full "transmit" mode. Everyone else was there to "receive." Only after he'd tested the patience of his visitors was it appropriate for an exchange of ideas of any kind.

Hafez al-Assad—the father of Syria's dictator Bashar al-Assad—added a personal twist to the gamesmanship and theatrics of his official meetings. As Assad similarly held forth at length, his servants plied his guests with numerous cups of tea. When one's cup was half empty, they'd hurry over to fill it up again. That meant Assad's guests had to battle not only tedium, but the call of nature as well. As he went on and on, Assad no doubt enjoyed the sight of ranking diplomats squirming in their seats and then rushing to find the nearest facility at the earliest opportunity.

There are techniques for dealing with people like that in a meeting. For one thing, you don't want them to think that what they're trying to do is succeeding.

To maintain my focus, I would listen carefully to the oration and jot down notes to remind me of what I might say if and when the opportunity arose.

Paying close attention is always time well spent. With folks like Assad and Putin, buried in their mountains of verbiage and cant is almost always something of importance—a useful detail or a subtle but distinct shift in tone that suggests a possible opening.

In one conversation with Putin early in the Bush administration, he held forth at length about the dangers posed by American plans to deploy a missile defense system. But listening closely, and past the rhetoric, I was left with an impression that while Russia would not like it, they would be able to live with our decision to withdraw from the Soviet-era treaty that prevented both parties from building a system to defend against ballistic missiles. That change in tone was of interest back in Washington, D.C.

Similarly my conversations with Hafez al-Assad in the 1980s at the height of a crisis in neighboring Lebanon were correct and civil. But from observing his demeanor and listening for what he left unsaid, it was clear that the so-called Sphinx of Damascus was no friend of the United States, as some American diplomats had hoped or assumed. In fact I deduced that he would do everything in his power to destabilize Lebanon and drive out American and coalition forces. That, it turned out, is exactly what he did.

Another way to handle leaders seeking to intimidate is with a few subtle, but noticeable retorts. For example, I used one meeting with Assad to send a message of our own. I handed him a newly declassified, very detailed satellite image of his country. Back in the 1980s, before Google Maps, our satellite photos were cutting-edge technology, available only to the most advanced nations. I wanted the wily leader to know that if he had his eyes on our forces in Lebanon, America had its eyes on Syria as well.

Prime Minister Margaret Thatcher ran a quite different type of meeting. Words were not things she liked to waste or see wasted by others. One did not need to parse her statements for clues. Instead the long-serving British leader was forthright and, at times, bracingly so.

In one meeting, when I was serving as President Ronald Reagan's Special Envoy for the Law of the Sea Treaty, I spelled out that treaty's serious flaws, which included yielding American sovereignty and potentially hundreds of billions of dollars in royalties to an unelected international body named, with an unintended nod to George Orwell, "The Authority." Her response cut right to the point. "What this treaty proposes is nothing less than the international nationalization of roughly two-thirds of the earth's surface," she said. Referring to her battles in dismantling Britain's state-owned mining and utility companies, she added, "And you know how I feel about nationalization. Tell Ronnie I'm with him."

Neither President Reagan nor I had ever expressed the core argument against the Law of the Sea Treaty quite so crisply. The meeting didn't last longer than twenty-five minutes, and by the end, there wasn't a doubt in my mind where she stood or what she wanted done.

President Lyndon Johnson's meetings highlighted what became known around Washington as "the Johnson treatment"—an unpredictable mixture of charm, insight, guile, southern aphorisms, and brute intimidation. As a junior congressman in the 1960s, I had only occasional contact with LBJ. But the impression I came away with from our limited interactions was that the larger-than-life Texan heard what he wanted to hear and overpowered what he didn't.

In one meeting I attended with a group of congressmen at the White House, called to discuss the situation in Vietnam, Vice President Hubert Humphrey was scheduled to report on his recent trip there, but the President kept interrupting him, leaping up from his chair to make a point or correct something. He was like an overactive volcano, repeatedly erupting. The distinguished members of his Cabinet, most of them held over from the Kennedy administration, were treated in what struck me as a less than respectful manner. It was a wonder to me that they stayed on as long as they did.

President Nixon was not a fan of meetings, but he used them effectively. Perhaps due to his nature, he was careful about venturing his opinions in larger groups, especially with people he did not know well. There was a certain formality and sometimes even awkwardness to those large meetings. In smaller settings with people he liked and trusted, he warmed up and exchanged ideas readily. In those sessions, he enjoyed going around the room, calling on people, hearing what they had to say, and then commenting. He was comfortable with differences of view and had no problem sifting through the opposing ideas of the high-powered intellects he had gathered in his administration.

As President, George W. Bush had a trait often underrated in a good leader. He was an unusually attentive listener. This made meetings useful for him. He caught subtle points and asked precise questions that cut to an issue's core. Because it was clear that he was paying close attention, those in his meetings tended to take special care in the information we presented. It encouraged us to be at the top of our game.

You can learn something from everyone—
from a five-year-old to a head of state.
—Dr. Robert Goldwin

Though President Bush could be jovial and relaxed, he encouraged a disciplined meeting culture. For one thing, he was punctual—almost obsessively so. He didn't waste time, but moved through agenda items in a crisp fashion, giving each participant an opportunity to offer his or her views, and then moved on. The President was not a fan of cell phones or BlackBerrys interrupting discussions. A sharp look from the President tended to deter repeat offenders.

Not all meetings of course involve the fate of nations, but there are certain lessons that can be applied in any gathering with two or more people where the goal is to make or inform a decision. Like most everyone, I have my own approach—unquestionably informed by the example of others. When I bring people together in a meeting, there are a few simple guidelines that I try to keep in mind.

The first consideration for meetings is whether to call one at all.

The default tendency in any bureaucracy, especially in government, is to substitute discussion for decision-making. The act of calling a meeting about a problem can in some cases be confused with actually doing something. People generally don't walk out of such meetings feeling satisfied about what took place.

If as the leader of an organization you call a meeting, make sure you have something to communicate or need to learn in a group setting. Have a goal. It's helpful to circulate an agenda in advance. Begin the discussion by reminding attendees of the agenda and ticking off the things you'd like to cover in the time scheduled.

If the meeting is to be purely informational, without much back-and-forth, that information could probably be as easily relayed in a memo or email. One of the reasons President Nixon preferred to have important proposals put in writing was to ensure that a meeting's outcome would not be unduly affected by whoever had the more assertive voice.

Don't let yourself be driven by your schedule. Meetings do not have to be inevitable, even if they appear on everyone's calendar. For example, when I was the CEO of G. D. Searle, a Fortune 500 pharmaceutical company, a meeting was scheduled on a topic for which I had received the briefing paper only minutes in advance. I could have attended anyway and listened to people talk about something about which I had little understanding. But why do that? I canceled the meeting and set it for a later date when other attendees and I would have had time to prepare.

When you decide to hold a meeting, it is important to avoid meandering sessions. To that end there are occasions when it's helpful to have a meeting where no one sits down. I have a stand-up desk I use for much of the day. I first came across stand-up desks when I noticed some naval officers using them back when I was on active duty. When I moved into my first executive position in government in 1969, I had a stand-up desk. I use it to this day. Aside from the more recently heralded health benefits, standing up while working tends to be an incentive for those who come in for a discussion to say what they need to say, and not linger. I want folks to be comfortable in my office—just not too comfortable.

If you expect people to be in on the landing, include them for the takeoff.

Pay close attention to who is invited, and for goodness sake, avoid making meetings so large that it feels you should have

Standing up while working tends to be an incentive for those who come in for a discussion to say what they need to say, and not linger.

rented an amphitheater. During my last tour as Secretary of Defense, I found it not uncommon to walk into meetings in the White House Situation Room and see more than a dozen people packed in. At least some of those folks did not need to be there. In previous administrations, a single note-taker sufficed. Who knows exactly how many damaging leaks may have resulted from Hollywood-sized entourages sitting in on sensitive high-level sessions?

On occasion, because of security concerns, it was necessary to keep the number of attendees to a minimum. When I met with the government of Saddam Hussein on behalf of the Reagan administration in 1983, I was caught by surprise when I was pulled away from my small group of associates by an armed Iraqi escort. I was hurried down a dark hall and into a room with walls decorated in white leather. Alone in the room was Saddam's deputy prime minister and foreign minister, Tariq Aziz. Large meetings, especially diplomatic ones, often have a stilted quality that can make a Kabuki dance look spontaneous. Clearly, Aziz wanted to have a more personal encounter to get to the bottom of my reasons for traveling to his country—a nation that had made no secret of its hostility to America. His decision was a good one, because we proceeded to have an extended, memorable, and useful exchange.

Stubborn opposition to proposals often has no basis other than the complaining question, "Why wasn't I consulted?"
—PAT MOYNIHAN

There is a balance that needs to be struck in determining who to invite to a meeting. You want those who need to be there to contribute substance to the discussion. But it can also be useful to have people who may not be in a position to directly offer substantive input but will benefit from hearing how and why certain decisions are being reached. For example, at the Pentagon I would try to include a senior public affairs and congressional relations official in some meetings so that any external communications would accurately reflect the decision being made.

Including a range of people can also ensure that a variety of perspectives will be considered and help identify gaps in information and views. Although larger meetings can lead to less candor in substantive exchanges, they can be helpful in that the attendees feel a sense of ownership in whatever is decided—even if the final decision might not go their way.

If you have doubts about whether someone should be included in a meeting, chances are you may have bigger issues with that individual. That is worth considering as well.

Men count up the faults of those who keep them waiting.
—French proverb

Whatever the size or purpose of a meeting, start and end it on time. It's a sign of good organization and also of respect for others. As drill sergeants are fond of saying, "If you're five minutes early, you're on time. If you're on time, you're late. If you're late, you have some explaining to do."

Having meetings start and end on time is not only a basic courtesy, it is efficient. Consider how much time is wasted by starting a meeting fifteen minutes late. If twenty people are in attendance, that means that cumulatively you will have wasted five hours of time that could have been spent on something productive.

As noted, punctuality was a hallmark of the George W. Bush approach. By contrast, in his first weeks in office, President Ford tolerated the tardiness of the Secretary of State to meetings in the Oval Office. I understood that Henry Kissinger was not coming late to these meetings on purpose—he was an extraordinarily busy man, carrying a sizable load for the country. But so, of course, was the President.

Ford didn't like to inconvenience people. He seemed not to mind too much if Henry was repeatedly late, but the late starts inconvenienced everyone else whom the President was scheduled to meet with that morning. Further, it conveyed the misimpression that Kissinger, a dominant figure in the later months of the prior Nixon administration, was as important as the president. That was not helpful to President Ford. And I made a point of saying so. Fortunately, Kissinger understood, and the situation was corrected.

Encourage others to give their views, even if it may ruffle some feathers.

S tay in your lane" is not my favorite phrase. Usually it is deployed by those who don't like other people commenting on their activities. The problem is that few of us, if any, are beyond improvement. An organization with impenetrable silos is not benefiting from the brains and knowledge of its people. In meetings, endeavor to foster a culture in which people can comment on anything as long as their comments are relevant and constructive. When time allows, bring division heads, line officers, and staff together and let them hold forth, not only with respect to their specific areas of responsibility, but on the broader activities of the organization.

When I returned to the Pentagon in 2001 after being in business for about a quarter century, I noticed in my meetings with the military service chiefs that it was a rare occasion when any of the four-star military officers would comment on a matter involving one of the other services. This was despite the fact that each of the services needed to depend heavily on the others to achieve its goals. The Pentagon's term for this cooperation is "jointness." It is a worthy if often elusive objective. What one service does (or does not do)

*Don't allow people to be cut out of a meeting or an opportunity to communicate
because their views may differ.*

can have a direct impact on the ability of another to accomplish its
mission, in peacetime as well as in war. The unspoken code of silence that prevailed made those meetings unproductive. There was
too little of the back-and-forth that can make a meeting useful and
lead to the kind of fresh thinking the Defense Department needed.

I sensed the service chiefs were concerned that if they offered
their professional views on the other services, those services would
feel free to offer similarly frank opinions about theirs. As a result,
I discontinued those meetings. Instead, I decided to fashion a different kind of meeting environment. Rather than the traditional
approach, with the Secretary going down to the conference room
known as "The Tank" to meet with the four service chiefs plus the
Chairman and Vice Chairman of the Joint Chiefs of Staff, I held regular meetings with Chiefs, the senior civilian leaders including the
deputy and undersecretaries of defense, and any four-star combat-

ant commanders who happened to be in town. Each of the senior
military and civilian leaders was expected to attend and to be ready
to discuss broad issues of importance to the Department as a whole
and to do so in front of each other. These meetings were called the
Senior Level Review Group, and became known by the acronym
SLRG (rather unappetizingly pronounced "slurg"). We developed
the agendas carefully and asked those in attendance questions that
were often well outside their direct areas of responsibility, and occasionally outside their comfort zones. I found it sparked discussions
that would not have otherwise occurred. I believe it also helped
create a more "joint" approach—that is to say, it caused us all to
think about the United States armed services as a whole, rather than
from the narrower perspective of one service or specialty.

*Test ideas in the marketplace. You learn from
hearing a range of perspectives.*

I try to pay attention to every attendee in a meeting. I like to
see how they are reacting to what is being said. Sometimes you
can learn as much or more from nonverbal communication as you
can from what is being articulated aloud. If an attendee seemed to
have a practice of being quiet, I would give him or her a heads-up
in advance that I would like them to chime in with their thoughts.
My goal was to try to make them more comfortable speaking
openly, not only about their areas of responsibility, but on matters
of importance to the entire department. The result was an interaction that improved communication and, I believe, increased the
services' ability to work together during a particularly challenging
time for our country.

The purpose of speaking is to be understood.

Most bureaucracies develop their own distinctive jargon and acronyms. I've found that jargon can serve as a cover or excuse for a lack of clear thinking. On one occasion at the Pentagon I became sufficiently concerned about a particularly dense and obtuse presentation that I wondered if English was the briefer's second language. This can be a problem in any large, insular organization accustomed to communicating internally, but not as much with outsiders.

It is a truism that the purpose of talking is to be understood. Good participants present opinions and thoughts with clarity and precision, and with a minimum of jargon or acronyms. Doing so makes it *less* likely that participants will leave with misunderstandings. Importantly, those who write and speak clearly—free of jargon and cant—are most likely to be the ones who think clearly and are therefore indispensable for good decision-making and sound policy.

Nothing betrays imbecility so much as insensitivity to it.
—Thomas Jefferson

When necessary—and it will be necessary—gently cut off the long-winders and folks who seem to dive into the weeds or zero in on obscure details or make diversions that do not contribute to the discussion. You may have to bring a meeting back to the announced agenda items.

I've been accused of giving staff members a so-called wirebrushing during meetings. I confess to being less than patient with folks who bring up irrelevant information or are ill-prepared. I can remember one or two meetings at the Pentagon when I undoubtedly wore my lack of enthusiasm for wasted time on my sleeve. I also tend to lack patience with PowerPoint presentations that convey obvious information or slides with grammatical errors and that lack page numbers.

I am unable to distinguish between the unfortunate and the incompetent, and I can't afford either.
—GENERAL CURTIS LeMAY (USAF)

There were occasions when I abruptly ended a meeting in progress and advised the participants that we would reconvene when everyone had had time to fully prepare. The response was usually surprised looks all around. In my experience some leaders don't end meetings when it's clear they've become a waste of time. Instead they sit there and let the meeting experience a slow, painful death of its own. With a war ongoing and most folks working twelve-plus-hour days, six or seven days a week, I knew they couldn't afford to sit through meetings that simply meandered through the subject matter without adding value. So I encouraged everyone to get up and find something more useful to do.

New ideas often receive a negative reaction at the outset, regardless of their value.

When new ideas are broached in a meeting, there is often an instinctive and immediate opposition. It may be unspoken, but it's there, waiting for its chance. New ideas can be disturbing. There is always the risk that if you offer visible public support for something untested, it will link you to that idea forever. In any organization there can be the kind of person—and I've seen it at the highest levels—who smiles and nods in seeming agreement with a proposal, and then when the idea is adopted and hits a rough patch, goes to others in the organization, or to a friendly reporter, and lets them know that he was against that idea from the beginning. Sometimes new ideas are nutty, and it is understandable that a leader may lack patience with what might be a poor idea. I plead guilty to occasionally being brusque in meetings when impractical or irrelevant concepts are put forward. But no matter how much you believe an individual's idea seems like a dud, a meeting is probably not the place to say so. It is almost always best to offer correction in private. Improvement, not embarrassment, should be the goal. If leaders want new ideas to be surfaced—and what good leaders don't?—they must find ways to welcome and encourage them.

Avoid making a poor decision simply because it is presented by someone who may rub you the wrong way.

A technique I've learned over the years when someone offers an idea I might disagree with is to hear them out, and then move the conversation along to other matters before offering my own view. Then, when the time seems right, resurface the idea by raising a general question about it. That way, it looks less like you are disagreeing directly. Try to make your differences about the substance of a proposal, not about the individual making it.

Ronald Reagan was superb at keeping disagreements from turning into a clash of egos. If someone said something he didn't agree with in a meeting, he'd tell a joke or reach for his jelly bean jar and offer an anecdote to change the subject. That way, the one who made the suggestion would smile along with everyone else, and think, "That President Reagan is such a good man," not feeling for a moment that Reagan had cut the legs out from under him.

Sometimes you may find yourself in a situation where you need to challenge the premises or assertions of others in a meeting. It may take the form of probing questions about a particular slide in a presentation. Doing so can sharpen your thinking, and may lead you to rethink your own views. It also may draw out the ideas of others and lead to a better outcome. Such probing and questioning need not be done in a personal way. This is particularly important in a hierarchical organization; a constructive meeting dynamic is one in which there is a certain leveling effect, by which everyone can and does speak their mind and is not concerned about offending someone higher or lower in the pecking order.

Unfortunately, that's not always how it works out. This was the case a time or two during my years at the Pentagon. I would occasionally read reports that some anonymous military officer supposedly said he was offended by what he saw as abrupt treatment when I questioned his presentation. I found it mildly surprising that a colonel or general charged with leading troops into battle could be so delicate and sensitive. I suspect some might have become so accustomed to the deference they received from their staffs that being asked to explain or defend a position was uncomfortable for them. The fact is some presenters had difficulty departing from PowerPoint slides, thinking on their feet, and responding to a series of probing questions.

In unanimity there may well be either cowardice
or uncritical thinking.
—*Marion J. Levy Jr.*

L arge bureaucracies can be masterful at creating an insular
and self-serving culture in which people reinforce each
other and become captive to what becomes the conventional
wisdom. Meetings are a good place to discover whether an organization might be suffering from groupthink. If everyone in
the room seems convinced of the brilliance of an idea, it may
be a sign that the organization would benefit from more dissent
and debate.

When I served on corporate boards, I developed a reputation
as an engaged director, to put it mildly. If I was going to sit on the
board of a company, I felt it was my duty to the shareholders to
make sure it was running as well as it could. If everything a CEO
and the management team did was perfect and didn't require any
comment, question, or calibration, then what was the point of
having a board of directors?

If you can find something everyone agrees on, it's wrong.
—Representative Mo Udall (D-AZ)

So I asked questions, sometimes a lot of questions. Even when
the board wasn't meeting, I would send memos offering suggestions about things the company was doing, or might consider
doing. That was the role I sought from the boards of directors of

the companies I ran. One CEO once told my wife, Joyce, "Don is a great board member." Then he added, "But you wouldn't want two of him."

The last consideration for a meeting is "What have we missed?"

When ending a meeting, make a practice of summarizing the salient points and takeaways, making sure that all participants know precisely what actions you intend to be taken and by whom. If there are specific tasks to be completed by you or others, the attendees all need to know it.

I've found it can also be helpful to offer a last opportunity for anyone in the room to speak up by my asking, "Is there anything else?" or "What have we missed?" There often is something important that someone was thinking of saying and never found the opportunity for. Also, asking those questions signals to people that the meeting is coming to a close. Hopefully, when a meeting does end, it has been valuable enough that people look forward to the next one. But then again, that's probably too much to ask.

CHAPTER THREE

PICKING PEOPLE

Toward the end of his tragically shortened presidency, John F. Kennedy mused to some friends that there were three people he thought could succeed him in office. The list, according to biographer Robert A. Caro, consisted of Secretary of Defense Robert McNamara, Treasury Secretary Douglas Dillon, and the President's brother Bobby.[1] Notably missing from the list was his Vice President, Lyndon Baines Johnson, who of course did end up succeeding him in November 1963.

Lyndon Johnson, a gruff, larger-than-life Texan, never fit in with the well-heeled, Harvard-educated inner circle of Camelot. And though he was a skilled legislator and Senate leader, Johnson did not excel as an executive.

A few years later, in 1968, Richard Nixon invited me to a late-night gathering in his hotel suite in Miami Beach, Florida, during the Republican National Convention. He had become his party's nominee earlier that evening and was in the process of selecting a running mate. As the group gathered—it included the Reverend

Billy Graham and Republican grandees like Thomas Dewey, Senators Barry Goldwater and Strom Thurmond, several governors, close Nixon aides, and a few members of Congress—a relaxed Nixon put his feet on the coffee table and asked each of us who we thought might be a good fit. Many names were mentioned: New York Governor Nelson Rockefeller, California's Ronald Reagan, and a Michigan congressman named Gerald Ford. But Nixon didn't seem interested in any of them. From the outset, one of the names he focused on was Spiro T. Agnew of Maryland, a new and relatively unknown governor. To my recollection, not a single person in that room, or anyone else for that matter, had volunteered Agnew's name. I had a feeling Nixon was enamored of the idea of "surprising" the press and the country with his choice. I recall no discussion whatsoever as to how well Agnew might govern if that were to become necessary. Ultimately, Vice President Agnew had to resign in disgrace over bribery and tax evasion charges. But even before that, he never demonstrated, at least to my eye, any impressive leadership qualities. At least none that were legal.

People are policy! Without the best people
in place, the best ideas don't matter.
—Dr. Ed Feulner

Neither Johnson nor Agnew was selected for the best of reasons. Both Kennedy and Nixon judged that they would achieve short-term political gain by having them on their tickets, instead of selecting individuals who could step up and be viable successors. And had Nixon been forced to resign before Agnew, the country would have had a felon in the Oval Office. It shouldn't be too much to expect that a presidential nominee select someone who has the ability to be president. Yet time after time, candidates from both political parties have selected running mates who end up being spectacular disasters. In a country of more than 300 million, at any given time there have to be at least a few individuals who can help a candidate politically *and* also potentially be a good president. Lord help us all if that is not the case.

Such failures occur not only on the presidential level. Any number of corporations and organizations have selected senior executives and successors who lacked the ability to lead. Such leaders have forgotten one of the most important elements of leadership. Show me a football coach who leaves the selection of his key players to circumstance or to someone else in the athletic department and I'll show you a team of losers.

The success of an organization will depend on the people you surround yourself with.

The secret to successful leadership and management is not really a secret: It's picking the right people. The well-known phrase "Personnel is policy" is accurate. Leadership depends on the human element more than any other. In fact, I would venture to say there is no more important priority for someone in authority than personally selecting those tasked with carrying out their guidance.

The task for leaders is to seek out individuals who understand and share their strategic objectives, who can help shape those objectives, execute them at every level, and even at times challenge their superior to reach a better outcome. The rules collected in this chapter offer suggestions on how one might go about it.

Don't avoid sharp edges.

In my first executive position as director of the Office of Economic Opportunity (OEO)—a large government agency established in the 1960s as part of Lyndon Johnson's "War on Poverty"— I was put in charge of thousands of individuals and a sizable budget. This was in 1969 and the OEO was highly controversial. The agency had ballooned and become another bloated layer of bureaucracy on top of other bureaucracies in the executive branch. That concern was one of the reasons many Republicans and I had voted against it. Hundreds of millions of dollars were being spent with modest results and too little accountability.

I recognized that the federal government was not going to be able to abolish poverty, but I thought that with the right people, we could refocus the agency's mission and make it more effective. My chief priorities were to end the failing programs, strengthen the successful ones, and then transfer them to the Cabinet departments where they properly belonged.

As a leader joining a new organization, one must often decide whether to leave in place the senior managers inherited from a predecessor or build a fresh team of your own. After a top-to-bottom review, it became clear that the OEO's eight regional directors were the key people driving the current programs. It was they who decided what took place in the field, and that in turn determined how the OEO was perceived in the country and in Congress.

Therefore I faced a difficult decision. I called the regional directors into my office and said, "Look, there has been an election. I have no doubt but that you folks were doing precisely what President Johnson wanted done and have been doing it well. He was the elected President and that was your job. But President Nixon has now been elected. He has a quite different view about the agency, as you know from the presidential campaign. His intention is to change the agency's direction." I described the strategy we were going to implement and observed that, in my view, there was no way any of them could stay in their current posts. I didn't see how they could possibly turn around that fast.

No one wants to hear their new boss tell them they are no longer needed, but in this case it was the truth. Most of them seemed to recognize that as well. In two cases, I found a way to reassign them to other positions in the agency. But I proceeded to recruit individuals for those key jobs who I believed shared the new President's vision. Over the next year and a half, OEO became a laboratory for experimental and innovative programs for improving opportunity in America, not a permanent bureaucracy that managed operations in perpetuity and that angered state and local officials, Republican and Democrats alike.

After Nixon resigned in 1974, Gerald Ford handled his personnel problem in a different fashion. He told the Nixon Cabinet and the existing White House staff that he was going to keep everyone in their current positions. He opted for continuity over change. That was a mistake—and I told him so at the time. I believed Ford needed to establish his own team in order to make clear that this was *his* administration, not a continuation of Nixon's. But he was uncomfortable having to tell people who had served loyally that they would have to leave. Much later he did decide to make some changes. Unfortunately, those late changes left an impression that he wasn't satisfied with the individuals who were departing. That would not have been the case if, at the outset, Ford had simply said that as the new President he wanted to bring in his own team.

Sometimes effective management requires an edge. The always quotable former Texas Governor John Connally used to say, "You can't cut a swath through a henhouse without ruffling a few feathers." My advice upon entering an organization is to build your own team—and do it fast—while recognizing that it won't be the happiest task in your life. Get any reassignments over with as quickly as possible. Tackling that task early will be worth it. You will benefit, and those departing will know they are not leaving because of poor performance, and those who remain in your organization will feel good knowing that they are part of your new team.

Prune businesses, products, activities, and people. Do it annually.

It is human nature to follow patterns, to repeat the same practices simply because that's the way it was done in the past. Don't run on autopilot, especially when it comes to personnel.

When I returned to the Pentagon in 2001, I encountered an impressive young man in uniform standing outside my office door. He was on sentry duty and his assignment apparently was to hold his weapon and provide security for my immediate office. My goodness, I thought, there surely had to be more important things he could be doing than to protect an office in one of the more well-guarded buildings in the world. Our country was in real trouble if the Secretary of Defense was in danger inside the walls of the Pentagon. I asked that he be sent off to more productive work.

In large bureaucracies especially, the tendency is to automatically recruit someone to fill a position as soon as it is about to come open. Of course the more people you have, the greater the cost and the greater the distance between you and your employees and customers. Wise managers stop, take a breath, and consider whether that slot really needs to be filled at all. Put another way, prudent managers prune regularly.

Don't automatically fill vacant jobs. When a dedicated employee retires after fifty years on the job, wait a bit. See what happens. You might find he was doing a job somebody else already at the company could do, or a job that no longer needed doing.

A's hire A's. B's hire C's.

You can tell a good deal about the quality of a manager or leader by the people he brings in as members of his or her team. For whatever reason there seems to be a pattern. Effective leaders—A's—tend to attract other A's, smart and talented people, who in turn create a culture of excellence. By contrast, B's hire C's, and even some duds who could generously be termed D's. One reason for this is that B's are not comfortable hiring people who might outshine them. As a result they tend to recruit and retain people who are nonthreatening to their position. There is an old saying, "Follow the money!" In this case, follow the A's. If you want to find out which managers are A's and which are B's, take a hard look at the teams that surround them.

When it comes time to fill a vacancy, it's not easy to find the A's out there. It's best to conduct an active search. If you wait for the perfect résumé to arrive on your desk, you are already behind the curve. Forward-thinking leaders try to have some names in mind before a key vacancy needs to be filled. The first place to look for talent is right there in your own organization. Promoting from within sends a positive message to current and potential employees that homegrown talent is valued, recognized, and rewarded.

But even if you find several internal candidates who are first-rate, it still makes sense to take a look outside, if for no other reason than to gain an awareness of the talent that is out there and learn what competitive compensation looks like.

Let's say your company is looking for a chief financial officer. Because you make a practice of listening, you may have heard that one of the best CFOs in the business is Sally Smith at Acme Corporation. The first thing I might do is give Sally Smith a call to get a sense of her current situation. Odds are she will not want to leave her position, but there's no harm in checking. But she will almost certainly know others in her field who are well qualified, possibly someone she personally trained, or on whom she has been keeping her eye. If you call up enough CFOs with top reputations and solicit their recommendations, you will be likely to find that one or two names will emerge again and again. Those are the candidates you want to invite in for a meeting. And that's when the real work begins.

Résumés should not require a decoder ring.

I have read hundreds of résumés over the years, so let me suggest a few things that you may not learn from a career counselor. Before drafting a résumé, don't simply follow someone else's template. Instead give a good deal of thought to what you are trying to accomplish. As Samuel Johnson once said, "What is written without effort is in general read without pleasure."

Second, consider a résumé's purpose: Contrary to popular understanding, it is not to get a job. The goal of a résumé is to get you to the next step. It is to make you stand out so that a recruiter or employer will decide it is worth their taking the time for a face-to-face interview.

Picking People

There are some folks—career counselors, outplacement experts, sometimes even parents—well-meaning as they may be, who fail to emphasize the importance of being absolutely 100 percent accurate in every word in a job application or résumé. Recently, a well-credentialed man showed me his résumé. He had served with distinction in the U.S. military, but his résumé read as if he had been Chairman of the Joint Chiefs of Staff. It said he had "run" this and "created" that. A seasoned employer sniffs out puffing in a nanosecond, and tends not to like it.

When I was twenty-nine years old and running for Congress, I met with the editor of the *Chicago Sun-Times* in the hope of getting that newspaper's endorsement. He asked me a series of questions. I had to respond fast and explain my situation to him in considerable detail: Who was I? Who had I talked to? Who was for me? Who was against me? What was my strategy? What were my strengths? What were my weaknesses? Then that crusty old newspaper editor proceeded to check out everything I had told him immediately after I left his office.

During that same congressional campaign, I was introduced by Arthur C. Nielsen Jr., a prominent Chicago business leader, at a fund-raising event. He told the audience I had been a fighter pilot in the U.S. Navy. Though I had been a naval aviator, I had not been a fighter pilot. As I rose to speak, I was torn. I could avoid an awkward moment by not contradicting and possibly embarrassing my friend and supporter over a relatively minor factual error. On the other hand, I didn't want to leave anyone with an inaccurate view of my background. So I bit the bullet and politely clarified his comment by saying, with a smile, that I sure wished I had been a fighter pilot, but I was in fact a flight instructor. If you let something like that go, it can damage a career, whether in politics or any other vocation.

When it comes to drafting a résumé, I prefer to read about a person's background on a single page. More pages may be attached as necessary, but the first page needs to stand out. I also look for a date showing when it was last revised, an indication that thought had been given to keeping it accurate and up to date.

If applicants want to keep potential employers from discarding their résumés at first glance, avoid jargon. People who have served in the Department of Defense are notorious for the use of acronyms. At the Pentagon, I routinely came across résumés that, unless you had lived in that person's shoes, you would have absolutely no idea what they were about from such things as JCS, PA&E/ATL, CFLCC, P-DASD, DARPA, JIEDDO, BNONA. I was Secretary of Defense twice—and in two different centuries—and I still don't know what some of those acronyms mean.

A manager can only know how someone might work out by meeting them, engaging them in conversation, asking them questions, and listening carefully to their answers and to the questions they ask you. An interview is your opportunity to size up a candidate, kick their tires, so to speak, and see if you're going to want to spend eight to ten hours of your day with them, week after week. Sometimes even the most talented person, one who has a résumé longer than your arm, might not be the best fit in an organization. It's important for both the employer and the candidate to know that sooner rather than later.

Dick Cheney likes to joke about his first interview with me. It was back in 1968, when I was in my fourth term in Congress and he was in graduate school seeking an intern position on Capitol Hill. I don't remember our meeting as well as he contends he does, but it does give me pause when he recalls it as "the worst interview" of his life. At the time I was looking for someone with a legal background, and he was a budding academic. He wasn't the best fit for me and I let him know that, probably with my usual skill and delicacy. As it happened, I resigned from Congress a few months later to go into the executive branch and one of the first things I did was ask Cheney to come work with me, which began many decades of friendship.

I often start interviews, logically enough, by asking applicants about items on their résumés. I look for something unique that stands out. I ask about things their résumés may not reveal. What do they like to do when they are not working? What do they read? I ask about their family. The answers to these types of questions can signal how well someone might fit with your organization and gets beyond what's written on their résumé. One thing I look at is what an applicant does when he or she is not on the job. I lean toward people who have lives outside of work—an interesting hobby, perhaps, or fluency in a foreign language, for example.

My first civilian job interview was with Congressman David Dennison. It didn't exactly hurt that he, like me, had been a wrestler, or that his brother had, as I had, been not only a naval aviator but also an instructor of flight instructors. Employers will have their own preferences and yes, even their own biases. Mine veer toward individuals who have been Eagle Scouts, or have served in the military, or who enjoy sports or reading. Military experience, in particular, says something about a person. It tells me that the individual has volunteered to serve and very likely has been given and taken on significant responsibility much earlier than many of his or her peers in the private sector.

I also prefer individuals who are positive and show enthusiasm about something. I have seen some candidates come into the office who looked like their cat just died. Who wants to be with someone day in and day out who brings down the atmosphere of the whole room? My counsel for those going into an interview is to hear a voice in your head saying: Smile! Show some energy! Be alive!

During a conversation around our dinner table a great many years ago, our daughter Marcy became concerned that one of us was in a less than sunny mood. It was a minor matter—I can't even remember what it was about—but for Marcy it cast a pall. Seven years old at the time, she said, "It takes everyone to make a happy day." Maybe it is because it came from one of our youngsters, but I have always found what she said to be rather profound. If one person is out of sync with everyone else, everyone feels the effect. If there are two otherwise equally qualified people, but one has a sense of humor, some energy, and optimism, that is the one for me. I'd bet most managers feel the same way.

Personal challenges or hardships can tell you a good deal about an individual. I've found that those who have had to struggle and work their way up to a position of responsibility often develop the grit that leads them to work a bit harder and be more willing to address tough issues than those who have had an easier ride.

The other assistant I hired at the Office of Economic Opportunity besides Dick Cheney was a young man named Ron James. James was from Iowa but grew up with his grandmother in Evanston, Illinois. He joined the Army, became a paratrooper, and after his military service found his way to my congressional office in Washington, D.C., looking for a job. I saw in him the drive and determination to succeed that later brought him to the height of government service as an assistant secretary of the Army.

I confess to favoring people who ask thoughtful questions. I have less patience for those who ask something that could have been learned simply by visiting an organization's website. One of

the better questions a candidate can ask should also be a pretty obvious one: What are you looking for in a job applicant? The answer
can help an individual better understand how he or she might or
might not fit in that organization.

Many people have the ability to review something and make it better. Few are able to identify what is missing.

There's a rare trait I seek out in a potential colleague: the ability to identify what's missing. It's easy to be critical and wield
the red pencil—to find ways to correct something. Considerably
more difficult is to raise ideas that hadn't even been considered or
otherwise help change the way one looks at a problem and questions the status quo.

In the computer industry, a number of companies sold cell
phones. But it took a certain mind to decide that cell phones might
also be useful as minicomputers, with Internet and email as key
components. In government, it took a different kind of President
with the right advisors to decide to make an overture to China or
to change U.S. policy toward the Soviet Union.

When I chaired the U.S. Ballistic Missile Threat Commis-
sion in 1999, a profound thought emerged from our discussions.
I can't even be sure who among the members was the owner of
the thought—it might never have even come up had we not had
a group around the table with different ways of thinking. It was
the notion of "unknown unknowns." In the intelligence community, as well as almost anywhere else for that matter, there are
always things that will surprise you. We knew, for example, that
we lacked certain knowledge about how rapidly the Chinese were

deploying advanced ballistic missiles. But what can bite you even more are the things that you don't know you don't know. The idea of surprise—surprise of all kinds—deeply influenced my thinking when I returned to office as Secretary of Defense. It helped prepare me at least on some level for the September 11 attacks and their consequences. That wouldn't have happened had I not surrounded myself with people who looked at things from different perspectives—who could add to what was missing.

Those who think that they know, but are mistaken, and act upon their mistakes, are the most dangerous people to have in charge.
—*Margaret Thatcher*

When I left the Department of Defense in 1977, some shareholders in G. D. Searle questioned whether I was the right choice to lead the company. Their concerns were understandable, insofar as I had no business management experience and absolutely no experience in the pharmaceutical industry. However, I did recognize those important facts and understood that I would have to rely on a team of top-notch biochemists, technical experts, and a strong leader in the research and development division.

Because I didn't have a law degree, I also knew that I would need a strong general counsel who could ensure that our decisions and activities were on the right side of the numerous laws and regulations in the dozens of countries where Searle operated. As the incoming CEO, I knew I needed to put in place a team that could help me move the company ahead and could bring to the table the skills I lacked. If I hadn't made certain at the outset that we had top-notch people in the key posts, the company would have faced real difficulties. Fortunately, one of the first things I did was bring in John Robson, a seasoned attorney, and Jim Denny, an experienced business and financial expert. The three of us proceeded to put together a first-rate group of managers to the benefit of the company and the shareholders.

I observed an example of the lack of trust displayed by a national leader when I met with Georgia Governor Jimmy Carter in 1976, several weeks after he had won the presidential election. I was departing as Secretary of Defense and President-elect Carter wanted to have a discussion about the Defense Department. He had a number of questions. One surprised me. He wanted to know how a president gets a ship to move from one place to another.

I found it an unusual question coming from a U.S. Naval Academy graduate, but I proceeded to explain the procedure: The commander in chief would issue an order to the Secretary of Defense, who would pass it down the chain of command. But Carter kept pressing. "How do you know it actually moved?" Even though he had served in the Navy, he seemed to lack trust in the system.

I remember saying to him, "Governor, the Department of Defense is one bureaucracy where you won't need to worry whether your orders will be followed." There may be other departments in the executive branch that will not respond promptly to a direction from a President, but not so in the Pentagon. "The risk with DoD," I added, "is that you might direct the Department to do something and later regret it."

A leader has to be able to rely on the expertise, judgment, and responsiveness of his team. That requires trust.

Talent hits a target no one else can hit. Genius hits a target no one else can see.
—Arthur Schopenhauer

The term *diversity* has accumulated a good deal of unfortunate baggage in recent decades. Too often, it can simply mean tokenism—diversity for diversity's sake. But true diversity can be an important strength in an organization if it brings together a range of perspectives, experiences, skills, approaches, and backgrounds. With the exception of an Einstein or Mozart, who could go off alone and create works of genius, most of us can accomplish major goals only by working with others. Even Einstein recognized that many of his breakthroughs depended on the work of those who came before him. As a reminder of that, he kept a picture of Isaac Newton on the wall of his study.

Some of the best ideas can come from the sparks and thoughts generated during lively discussions around a conference table or lunch conversation among people who have opposing views. A leader will often draw inspiration from such discussions—ideas he would not have discovered on his own.

I mentioned earlier President Nixon's unfortunate decision in selecting a vice president. That was an exception for him. Generally, Nixon made excellent hiring decisions. He recruited an impressive and broad talent pool, including people with widely different personalities, management styles, backgrounds, and viewpoints. You might walk into the Oval Office and find the brilliant academic Henry Kissinger discussing foreign policy or the witty Pat Moynihan discussing the labor market. Or you might see the hard-charging populist and former Democrat John Connally, whom

Generally, Nixon made excellent hiring decisions. He recruited an impressive and broad talent pool, including people with widely different personalities, management styles, backgrounds, and viewpoints.

the President greatly admired, debating the state of the economy with the cerebral, policy-minded George Shultz or the courtly Arthur Burns. Nixon was comfortable with—and benefited greatly from—the energy that came from the brightest minds and their competing ideas. As a result, he put forward some of the more interesting, and in some cases, controversial policy initiatives of any modern-day administration—from the establishment of the Environmental Protection Agency (EPA) to the end of the military draft, to wage and price controls to federal block grants for states and even experiments with vouchers for the public schools.

It also helps to have people around you who are unbounded by an organization chart or bureaucratic silos, individuals who have the ability to think and offer opinions on a broad array of topics, and who can elevate an otherwise pedestrian conversation.

I drew a valuable lesson in this regard from President Nixon when he asked me to go to Brussels as U.S. Ambassador to NATO. I was able to bring only two people with me. One was my longtime assistant, Leona Goodell. The other was Dr. Robert Goldwin, the dean of St. John's College in Annapolis, also known as "the great books school." Goldwin had no background in government, much less diplomacy. But he had one of the most thoughtful and wide-ranging intellects I have been privileged to work with. A conversation with Bob left you with a fresh perspective and knowledge you hadn't previously considered. When I returned to the White House with President Ford, I again called Bob to service, and he became the President's one-man think tank and intellectual compass. In the White House solarium, he conducted seminars for the President with some of the finest minds in America. The discussions he arranged covered everything from education to crime and hunger. If you can find your own Bob Goldwin, you'll be well served.

As someone who has spent several decades in public service, I've always found it refreshing and helpful to be around people who didn't always agree with me. Among my friends when I served in Congress was the leftist antiwar activist Al Lowenstein, who would later serve a term in Congress himself. Al had a delightful sense of humor, and while we didn't agree on a good many issues, we enjoyed spending time together. Joyce and I also used to spend Sunday afternoons playing tennis with Ethel Kennedy and her friends. I count as a good friend the distinguished historian Jean Edward Smith, who was kind enough to read and edit early drafts of my memoir. Sometimes he'd scribble things in the margin, indicating his good-natured disagreement with some of my political views.

Never hire anyone you can't fire.

No matter how stellar their qualifications, a potential employee should not have to be coaxed or begged into accepting a position. A leader does not want to be or perceived to be beholden to a subordinate. It is not healthy for the employer, the employee, or the organization.

I've seen instances where a manager felt he had to make all sorts of promises or rearrange things to accommodate someone he was trying to hire or appoint. Sometimes it almost seemed that the two had changed roles—the person doing the hiring was the one selling himself and his organization to the one who was seeking the job. Those sorts of relationships seldom work out. It can result in a situation where so much is promised that it is hard to alter the arrangement in the event circumstances change, as they often can.

The cemeteries of the world are full of indispensable men.
—CHARLES DE GAULLE

It is understandable for a sought-after subordinate to request special terms or ask for extra time to make a decision. But if a leader finds himself having to bend over backward to accommodate the desires of a potential employee, he would probably be better off finding somebody else. In the long run, he'll likely be glad he did.

Don't begin to think you are indispensable or infallible, and don't let others think you are.

No matter how capable he may be, every leader needs to know that he is not indispensable. Any of us could get hit by a truck, and if real leadership capability resides in only one or two people, the top person has failed as a leader. Preparing for an orderly succession in key posts is an important responsibility for the head of any organization. Having a capable deputy and a strong senior leadership team in place not only ensures that those at the top can maintain a healthy balance between work and life; it also ensures that there will be people on hand who can continue leading after you leave. Steve Jobs spent considerable time at Apple building a team that could take over for him when the need arose. When Jobs died, some analysts feared the stock of the company would crater. But because he had a capable leadership team and a solid plan of succession, the transition was orderly and the company's stock price rose 60 percent in the six months following his death. If, however, leaders behave as though they are not concerned with what happens to the organization when they are no longer around, it may be time for the board to start making those plans for them.

Mistakes in hiring are the employer's error, not the employee's.

Like many in positions of responsibility, I have learned from my own experience that bad personnel decisions can have exceedingly harmful results. When that occurs, as it undoubtedly will, your task, unpleasant as it may be, is to face up to your mistake and take steps to correct it—and fast. Do not wait. Errors, especially personnel errors, do not get better with time.

One of my biggest mistakes as Secretary of Defense was leaving the U.S. Army with less than satisfactory leadership for too long a period of time. The Secretary of the Army proved to be a problem. Tom White, a former Army brigadier general, seemed to see his job as representing the views of the Army to me, instead of being the President's (and my) representative to the Army. In short, he seemed to have it backward. He gave little support to the commander in chief's agenda to transform the U.S. armed forces into a more capable and rapidly deployable force. When the President and I decided to cancel an $11 billion, forty-ton, 155-millimeter howitzer (inaptly called the Crusader), which required two large cargo aircraft to transport, Secretary White and the Army campaigned against our decision. With that, I had had enough. I called the Secretary in to my office in April 2003. The meeting was chilly, and brief. I asked for his letter of resignation and in short order he was gone.

In retrospect, I made a serious mistake by recommending someone to the President who had been a career officer in the Army as the civilian candidate to lead it. When you are trying to change an entrenched organization it doesn't make a heck of a lot of sense to put someone from that same organization into the top leadership role. They may have been part of that culture for so long and have such a vested interest in its patterns that it can be difficult to have the perspective required to recalibrate it. I realized my mistake and corrected it.

People get fired for a variety of reasons. There are some who, even though they may be quite capable, drag down the entire team. Then there are others who may have contributed at one point, but are no longer doing so due to changed personal or company circumstances. Sometimes these are individuals who simply should not have been put in their positions in the first place.

It may be small comfort to an individual losing his job, but the fact is, letting a person go is a difficult thing for a boss to do. Some leaders can't do it at all. Even presidents sometimes delegate that unpleasant task to subordinates. A good leader needs to have the stuff to sit down with a subordinate, eye to eye, and explain why a change may be needed. It is also a mark of respect.

Losing a job is almost always a shock for an employee and their family. But it is not an unfamiliar event in our highly mobile and competitive society. Sometimes by letting someone go who may not be a good fit, you are actually doing them a favor. With the change, that individual can reevaluate their skills and find a niche where they can be more productive, however daunting that task may seem at the time.

Some of the most successful people in the world have known that kind of disappointment. Henry Ford faced bankruptcy on five separate occasions before he eventually founded the automotive company that bore his name. Walt Disney was let go from a newspaper because he "lacked imagination." Albert Einstein was expelled from school. Abraham Lincoln failed as a businessman and several times as a political candidate before attaining the presidency. People with grit, perseverance, and determination learn to pull up their socks and go about the task of remaking and improving their lives.

CHAPTER FOUR

THINKING STRATEGICALLY

Strategy may be one of the most overused words in the English language. It also may be one of the most misused. We have all been in meetings where someone says, "We need a strategy on this," or "Let's put a strategy paper together." Just as often, people around the table nod in affirmation, even though there may not be a common understanding of what exactly the word means.

During election years, we are treated to the spectacle of politicians of all stripes talking about their strategies for this or that. What often happens is that candidates confuse a laudable goal—for example, "giving our children a world-class education"—with a strategy for achieving it. In the Pentagon I often heard buzzwords such as "strategic communications," when what was actually being discussed had little to do with strategy, or even communication for that matter. There were offices with the word *strategy* written outside the door. I was never quite clear what went on in some of those rooms, and I'm not sure the people inside them did, either. "Strategy" requires a good deal more than simply announcing that you have one.

If you're coasting, you're going downhill.
—Joyce's father, L. W. Pierson

S trategy is a general plan of action fashioned to achieve a major goal. It is the process by which goals are prioritized and resources marshaled to achieve those goals. Tactics are then used to implement the strategy. Strategy doesn't begin at one point and end at another. It involves planning and evaluation, requiring trade-offs and decisions along the way. It takes work, thought, and time.

Some managers don't like investing time in strategic planning. Organizations tend to put it off in favor of the demands of the moment. And with good reason. The urgent often takes precedence over the important. Leaders have many other things they can be doing. People spend countless hours of precious time responding to *other* people's priorities. They spend precious little advancing their own.

Think back on the last few weeks. How much time did you spend responding to the emails that appeared in your inbox, or participating in meetings initiated by others? How much time did you spend answering incoming calls discussing somebody else's priorities?

Without the discipline and time invested in strategic planning, one of two things is likely to happen. Your organization will be buffeted by outside events and forced to be reactive. Or it will stay on autopilot, propelled by the inertia of policies and plans that were decided months or years before.

*Give your staff guidance against which to test their
decisions. Otherwise their actions may be random.*

Without clear objectives and agreed priorities, each element or
individual within an organization is free to pursue their own. As a
result, parts of the organization will inevitably be working at cross-
purposes with others. Large, mature organizations are generally
resistant to strategic guidance from the top, which makes clear priorities and strategic goals from the leadership all the more essential.

If you are working from your inbox, you are working on other people's priorities.

With emails and phone calls coming in over the transom
every hour of the day, it's easy to get lost in inbox items,
forgetting what your main objectives are or spending too little
time on them. The task of a leader is to have an organization work
out of his or her outbox. In every management position I held, I
generated dozens of queries and requests to the staff each day, so
that our team was working on our agreed priorities. In the Pentagon, these memos became known as "snowflakes" because the
white pieces of paper fell with abandon on various offices in the
building. To this day, I still send out dozens of memos and letters
each week. I also keep a "tickle" file of my notes to remind me
when I should hear back from the addressees or if I need to remind
them to get back to me—gently, of course.

Having others work off your outbox also has an added advantage. Sending memos throughout the organization enables folks down the line to understand what the principal is thinking and what problems he or she is puzzling over. The employees can then self-organize to be more useful than they otherwise would be. In large organizations, it is important that folks at all levels have a clear idea about the thinking of those on top.

If you don't know where you're going any road will get you there.
—Paraphrase of Lewis Carroll

If you don't have a strategy, you don't have a road map. As a result, you don't have a way for those in your organization to know what they need to do to reach the agreed goal. You also don't have a way to measure and track your progress. In short, without a strategy you're probably heading for failure.

Strategy, as I see it, has four steps:

Step One Set the Goals

Setting the right objectives and priorities is the crucial first step in the development of any strategy, for the military, for government, for a business, or for a nonprofit. I have no doubt that George Marshall had a full appreciation for the capabilities of the countless lieutenants who served under his command, but his was a wider point: When you invest the time and thought to identify the right objectives, the rest of the plan follows logically.

---

*If you get the objectives right, a lieutenant
can write the strategy.*
—GENERAL GEORGE C. MARSHALL

Determining and establishing priorities for an organization is
the most challenging part of strategic planning because it involves
deciding among competing interests. As British Prime Minister
Tony Blair once put it, "The art of leadership is saying no, not yes."
Or as Steve Jobs once said, "People think focus means saying yes
to the thing you've got to focus on. But that's not what it means
at all. It means saying no to the hundred other good ideas that
there are." You cannot be everything to everyone. Setting goals
also means that you have decided what you will *not* do, which is
every bit as important as deciding what you will do.

If you don't know what your top three priorities are, you don't have priorities.

In a good many meetings, I would ask senior officials what their
top priorities were. This can be an unsettling question, especially the first time it's asked. If there was hesitation on their part,
it was telling. And if they rattled off a list of six or eight "top priorities," that was telling as well.

He who defends everywhere, defends nowhere.
—SUN TZU

The task is to condense your top goals to three or four. If you have more than that, you have little chance of achieving them.

After a while, my question became so routine that sometimes as I walked the corridors, someone would smile and volunteer their top priorities without my asking.

Your best question is often "Why?"

If you've spent time around youngsters, chances are you've heard them ask an adult a string of questions, one after the other, with just one word: "Why?" As exhausting as it can be for someone answering "why" questions over and over again, it can be a useful technique for leaders when setting goals at the strategic level.

At Searle, I made the decision to freeze the company's dividend to shareholders. Why? My reason was to be able to divert more money from dividends to pharmaceutical research and development. Why? Only by increasing R&D could we have a chance of developing new pharmaceutical products and make our firm more of a long-term growth company with strong stock appreciation for the shareholders. Why? Because shareholders would benefit from capital gains as the stock price went up (and capital gains are taxed at a lower rate than dividends).

The strategic goal at Searle was to become a more successful research-and-development based pharmaceutical company. (It worked. During the eight years I served as CEO, Searle's stock price increased by more than 500 percent and annual profits by more than 450 percent.)

To rank as *strategic*, a goal must have far-reaching consequences—the kind that will fundamentally affect the direction of an organization. Objectives or tasks of a lesser scale and consequence can be important and are useful in advancing toward a broader goal, but they are not likely to be truly strategic.

In business a strategic goal might be to double market share in four years. In a pharmaceutical company, a strategic goal might be to develop, gain FDA approval for, and market three major new products over the course of eight years.

For a member of the Cabinet in the U.S. government, a strategic goal might be to cut the time it takes for the Department of Veterans Affairs to respond to claims filed by our veterans to thirty days. (It currently averages an inexcusable 375 days for the VA to respond to claims in some parts of the country.)

Open-ended goals are necessary in some cases, but whenever possible, set specific target dates. Inevitably some dates will slide to the right, but due dates and short- to mid-term deadlines focus the mind and cause folks to manage their time accordingly.

Goals also need to be realistic. It can be easy to set goals that don't provide any real guidance, such as "Defeat the enemy" or "Win the war" or "Maximize revenues while minimizing costs." They may be desirable outcomes, but they are so vague that they do little to suggest how one might proceed to reach them.

One likely apocryphal anecdote from World War I involves an Allied military officer asking his staff how to deal with German U-boats sinking merchant ships. The response from one officer was immediate. "Sir, one solution is to boil the ocean," he supposedly said. "That will force all the submarines to the surface." When pressed on just how that would be done, the officer reportedly replied, "I came up with the idea. I leave the details and implementation to you."

It is easier to get into something than it is to get out of it.

As the United States planned for military operations against al-Qaeda terrorists in Afghanistan in the days after 9/11, those of us in the administration agreed on the desired strategic outcome. At least at the outset, that goal was to protect the American people by attacking the radical Islamist terrorist organization that had killed nearly three thousand Americans and removing the Taliban regime that had hosted many of the al-Qaeda terrorists.

In those early days I recall no intent—expressed publicly or privately—to engage in a large, open-ended occupation in that poor, war-torn, and landlocked country, nor to try to establish an American-style democracy there. Nation-building wasn't something the U.S. military was organized, trained, or equipped to do. While a worthy goal, such an undertaking would tie down our military and run the risk of the Afghan people becoming dependent on American support or, eventually, bridling under what they might see as an occupation.

Over time, the administration arrived at a different conclusion. I do not recall the National Security Council having a definitive meeting to consider the consequences and costs of a long-term and large-scale military presence or to make a final decision to do so. In retrospect the goals seemed to have migrated gradually, over the years—the classic definition of "mission creep." Now, more than a decade later, there remains a sizable U.S. and NATO military presence in Afghanistan.

Whether it applies to a country or an organization, leaders must be mindful that once you engage in an ambitious and complex endeavor, the pressures and incentives to expand and perfect that effort grow. But there are limits to what any organization can do. The failure to recognize those limits can complicate and even undo the original goals that were set.

Don't be afraid to see what you see.
—RONALD REAGAN

Shortly after he took office as the nation's fortieth president, Ronald Reagan astonished some of the diplomatic talent around him when he turned to his national security advisor, Richard V. Allen, and declared, "My idea of American policy toward the Soviet Union is simple, and some would say simplistic. It is this: We win and they lose." At first blush, that might have sounded like bravado, or a clever line from an accomplished actor. But in fact it was a truly new, big, bold, and ambitious strategic goal—a goal fundamentally counter to the prevalent thinking in most Western diplomatic circles.

Some in the foreign policy establishment—a number of whom had spent many years trying to reach accommodation with the Soviet empire—shook their heads in embarrassment. Many on the left, particularly during the Carter administration, had resigned themselves to U.S. parity, or coexistence, with the Soviet Union. Until Reagan, in fact, no U.S. president had expressed the conviction that a day could come when the Soviets would find themselves, as he memorably put it, "on the ash heap of history."

Most everything done in President Reagan's administration with respect to his Cold War policy was measured against his single, unambiguous goal. In the first years of his presidency, he delayed negotiations with the Soviets so that he could first rebuild the capabilities of our country's armed forces. When it came time to negotiate with Soviet leader Mikhail Gorbachev, he was determined to do so from a position of strength. He took steps to support resistance movements in communist nations. He devised, announced, and pursued a missile defense system that the Soviets came to believe could render their nuclear arsenal less effective.

He attacked the Soviet Union not with weapons but by articulating bold, eloquent truths, statements that were derided by some critics as "needlessly provocative" and "dangerous." Despite arguments to the contrary, his decision to label the Soviet Union "an evil empire" was calculated to advance his broad central goal. It sent a clear signal to the Soviet leadership that in his administration it would not be "business as usual." Over time, his words and actions contributed to a crisis of confidence within the Soviet system and gave encouragement to opponents of the Soviet empire.

Then from a position of strength Reagan pursued initiatives that led to a fundamentally altered U.S. relationship with the Soviet Union. He encouraged their moves to greater openness and economic reform. And he watched as that inherently untenable system finally collapsed from its internal contradictions. Ronald Reagan, the widely ridiculed former actor, was one of the twentieth century's most formidable strategists.

Step Two Identify Your Key Assumptions

When cannon fire opened up on the beleaguered Union garrison at Fort Sumter in April 1861, few thought their country would be dragged into a multiyear civil war—much less one that would take the lives of more than 600,000 soldiers of the

North and South combined. President Abraham Lincoln and his war Cabinet knew the Confederacy was massing its armies but assumed that after one or two decisive victories, public support for secession in the South would wane and the rebellion would crumble. The hope, and expectation, was that a negotiated peace would bring an early end to the Civil War.

Lincoln tasked one of his lesser-known generals, Ulysses S. Grant, to penetrate as deep as he could into Confederate territory on a mission to demoralize the South. But as Grant marched south, he came to realize that President Lincoln's assumption of an early erosion of southern support for the Confederacy was off the mark. "Up to the Battle of Shiloh, I, as well as thousands of other citizens, believed that the rebellion against the Government would collapse suddenly and soon, if a decisive victory could be gained over any of its armies," Grant wrote in his impressive memoir. After the bloody encounter at Shiloh, Grant wrote, "I gave up all idea of saving the union except by complete conquest."

As Lincoln and his generals learned, assumptions are not facts; they are merely reasonable suppositions about the future. It's understandable, indeed it should be expected, that some assumptions will prove to be wrong. The very reason for labeling them assumptions is to stress that they are not facts.

If a key assumption turns out to be wrong, it will require a major change in strategy. If you are in an irregular military conflict, but you follow the logic of conventional conflict to set your goals, you are likely to be ineffective. If you are in an electoral contest requiring base mobilization, but you think you are fighting over the few remaining undecided voters, you might lose the election. Accordingly, it is crucially important to think through your assumptions before you begin to develop or execute your plan.

It is possible to proceed perfectly logically from an inaccurate premise to an inaccurate and unfortunate conclusion.

The assumptions stage of strategic planning tends to be one of the most neglected. Assumptions are often left unstated, it being taken for granted that everyone around a table knows what they are, when frequently that is not the case. The assumptions that are hidden or held subconsciously are the ones that often get you into trouble.

The importance of assumptions was underscored for me in 2001, during my early months in the Bush administration. I began reviewing the nation's top-secret plans for major military operations and contingencies around the world. These scenarios ranged from Iran launching an attack on a neighboring country to an emergency evacuation of U.S. citizens due to a civil uprising in a foreign country. I asked to meet with the Defense Department's top military planners and began a review of the plans on the shelf to become familiar with them, to ensure they were current, well thought through, and in a form appropriate for briefing the new President.

The first plan I was briefed on involved a military response to assist the Republic of Korea in the event of a North Korean invasion. South Korea, of course, was a key American ally. The thousands of American troops stationed there since the 1950s were likely to be targets of any attack. As implausible as a North Korean attack seemed for a regime dedicated to its own self-preservation, that country's leadership hadn't earned high marks for rational thinking.

The objective of the plan was straightforward enough: to defend South Korean sovereignty and defeat the North Korean threat. What I found troubling, however, was that there was no discussion of the key assumptions in which the plan was rooted. How, I wondered aloud, could we have a plan in place for a possible conflict on the Korean peninsula if we first hadn't carefully considered, discussed, and agreed on the most likely conditions our military might face?

What design would I be forming if I were the enemy?
—FREDERICK THE GREAT

The planners had jumped right into briefing their Korean plan in midcourse, instead of starting at the beginning. There was, for example, the small matter of how we assumed the enemy might act. Of course there was no way to know for sure, but we had to make educated assumptions based on history and the best current intelligence. For example, the briefing had not specified whether North Korea should be assumed to have nuclear weapons, and if so, how many, and whether the regime might use them against us and our coalition allies. Needless to say, the possibility of a nuclear engagement with North Korea would significantly affect any plan of ours.

There were other assumptions that would be vital to the planning, but which had not been discussed: For example, would the North Korean leadership, as they had in the early 1950s, call on China for support? Would the Chinese remain neutral? Would the Japanese government allow U.S. air and naval forces based in their country to be used as part of our Korean campaign, or would they object?

Hoping that the briefing on the Korean plan was an anomaly, I sat through another on a contingency elsewhere in the world. It was much the same. The planners and expert logisticians had figured out many of the important details—numbers of troops, logistical support, potential targets, types of weapons that could be used. All of this was important, and I had no doubt their estimates were accurate. My concern was that the plan had not addressed up front the important variables that could fundamentally affect it. When I began to pose questions and probe as to why the planners had chosen one course of action over another, it was clear that they weren't prepared to discuss the key assumptions.

I ended the meeting and asked that we convene again the coming Saturday. However, this time we would approach it differently. The military planners would be asked to present and discuss the assumptions on which their plans were based—and the assumptions only. That Saturday we met for hours and never discussed any of the plans, only the assumptions.

From then on, briefings on DoD contingency plans began with a careful discussion of the underlying assumptions. Only after there was a broad agreement that we had identified the key assumptions would the briefing proceed. If there was any grumbling, it soon ended. Establishing assumptions at the outset became a formal part of the planning process. The briefings improved considerably and the briefers faced a less prickly Secretary of Defense.

Identifying key assumptions continued to be an important part of the planning process as we prepared for a possible conflict with Saddam Hussein. For months in advance of the conflict in March 2003, the U.S. Central Command, the Joint Chiefs of Staff, and the senior civilian leadership tested assumptions. To no one's great surprise, a number of them later proved to be wrong. Some of the more difficult ones involved trying to anticipate the political decisions of others. One assumption, for example, was that Turkey, a NATO ally, would permit U.S. forces to transit their territory and to enter the northern border of Iraq. That proved incorrect, although by a margin of only a few votes in their parliament.

Assumptions can also reflect bias, overgeneralization, or poor intelligence. For example, we were told by several of Iraq's neighbors that once an invasion started, we should move fast or protests in the "Arab street" would cause difficulties for their governments. That too proved incorrect. Other assumptions reflected a view that the Iraqi government and military would be likely to act as it had in the past. We were concerned, for example, that Saddam's forces might blow up bridges, burn oil fields, or use chemical weapons if Baghdad was in danger of falling (as during the Iran-Iraq War when Saddam unleashed chemical weapons against Iranian forces). When assuming and preparing for the worst, it can be a blessing that some assumptions ultimately prove to be wrong.

Assumptions are equally important in the private sector, where suppositions about future market conditions, such as what projected demand for a product might be or how the competition will react, are essential to a business plan. A key assumption might be that consumer demand for a product will increase by 10 percent over the planning period, or that no competitor will be able to develop and market a product as effective as yours within a five-year period. These could be reasonable assumptions when your plan is being developed, but could prove to be wrong, sometimes even in a relatively short period. But unless you take the time and effort to state your key assumptions first, you're not likely to know when circumstances change and that your business plan will need to be substantially revised.

Step Three Determine the Best Course of Action

The third step of strategic planning is to evaluate a range of possible courses of action that will allow you to achieve your goals and that are consistent with your key assumptions. Often the choices are among less than attractive options.

June 1940 had been a trying month for Britain and the nation's new wartime prime minister. Many believed the United Kingdom was on the verge of surrender. The British Army had to evacuate from Dunkirk. America had little interest in being dragged into another European war. Nazi forces occupied France and French leaders had signed an armistice with Hitler. At the forefront of Prime Minister Winston Churchill's worries was what would happen to the formidable French fleet, at the time the fourth-largest navy in the world. The French ships were dispersed, but the bulk of them were in the Mediterranean, off the coast of Algeria at Mers-el-Kébir. Churchill knew that if the fleet became part of Germany's naval forces, Hitler would be likely to dominate the high seas and Great Britain would be in still greater danger.

Churchill had to make one of the more excruciating decisions of the war. He could do nothing and let the French fleet fall into Nazi hands. He could try to negotiate a diplomatic accord with the new Vichy government to ensure that the fleet remained neutral. He could demand the French navy surrender their ships to Britain and if they refused, he could order the Royal Navy to sink the French ships, thereby attacking the country that only weeks earlier had been Britain's closest ally. Churchill and his war Cabinet agonized over a course of action.

By June 27, after weeks of futile negotiations, he resolved on a bold stroke—one that would dispel any rumors that Britain was about to throw in the towel and ensure that Nazi Germany could never use the French fleet to isolate and invade Britain. Churchill gave the French admirals four options:

- have their fleet become part of the Royal Navy;

- travel to British ports with smaller crews;

- sail to the French West Indies or to the United States to be decommissioned; or

- at their refusal to accept any of those options, prepare to be sunk by the Royal Navy.

If the French did not give their answer within three hours, their ships and crews would promptly be attacked and sent to the bottom of the Mediterranean.

At 5:30 p.m. on July 3, 1940, the deadline passed and the British navy opened fire. Seven French ships were sunk or permanently damaged, and 1,297 French sailors were killed. As Churchill drily noted at the time, "The French were fighting with all their vigor for the first time since the war broke out." The course of action Churchill had decided on was agonizing, but it was a decisive moment for Britain, which until that point had been seen as rudderless and losing.

At the top there are no easy choices. All are between evils,
the consequences of which are hard to judge.
—DEAN ACHESON

At the level of grand strategy—involving truly large-scale decisions—almost every possible course of action comes with negative consequences. Few issues that reach the President's desk are risk-free or without potentially unpleasant outcomes. The same goes for a business leader. If they were easy decisions, they would have been made at a lower level. It's always the toughest decisions that find their way to the top. Further, CEOs, presidents, and prime ministers often are asked to decide on matters on which their most senior advisors are not in agreement.

Many look back on the Cold War and think America's strategy, which preserved freedom in Europe and East Asia, came with relative ease. They glide past the point that winning the five-decade-long "twilight struggle" was possible only through the expenditure of many trillions of dollars, the risk of nuclear war, two regional wars in East Asia that took tens of thousands of American lives, and the perseverance of leaders of both political parties. Nothing big—certainly nothing big in historical terms—comes easy. Too often leaders search for the risk- and cost-free answers to hard problems. They rarely exist, and often the clever ideas are self-defeating illusions.

When faced with a key decision, I've found it helpful to create an option paper. I watched President Nixon do that to his benefit. His national security advisor, Henry Kissinger, was adept at providing papers that set out the possible options on a particular issue, along with the pros and cons of each possible course of action and an indication of which option each of his advisors favored and why.

Leave all options on the table. Taking them off demystifies the situation for the competition.

Another way to think through a range of options is to borrow a technique I learned from Dr. Herman Kahn, the brilliant strategist who founded the Hudson Institute and was said to be an inspiration for the title character in the film *Dr. Strangelove.* The number of scenarios he could dream up was stunningly wide-ranging.

Kahn had a clever way of sorting through ideas. I called it the "above the line and below the line" approach. He would start by drawing a horizontal line across a piece of paper. He then considered the entire universe of ideas, potential courses of action, or options that he was mulling. He placed those that seemed more favorable above the line, and those less appealing "below" it. That way, no idea was discarded. By returning to his list and working on it, Kahn could draw new ideas by considering the entire range of options—eventually reducing the number above the line to the point where he would zero in on an optimal choice. This inclusive approach provides time to reflect, rather than make a quick decision. It also allows you to reconsider those you have put below the line, which can help develop options you might not have thought of otherwise.

Be precise. A lack of precision can be dangerous when the margin of error is small.

B efore executing your strategy, it is useful to try to state each of its key elements—your objectives, your assumptions, and your proposed courses of action—in no more than a few minutes and preferably without notes. If you're having difficulty distilling and communicating these key elements succinctly, it may be a sign that you need to keep refining them. If others can't understand your plan, it's probable that it has not been well enough thought through. So stay at it.

If a plan cannot be well understood, it probably hasn't been well enough thought through.

There is a time and place for a calculated ambiguity, particularly in diplomacy. But strategic planning isn't one of them. If the plan can be interpreted differently by those in your organization, it is likely your people will not all be working toward your goal in a well-coordinated effort. In business, ambiguities can cost money. In the military, ambiguities can cost lives.

Step Four Monitor Progress Through Metrics

I t's not enough simply to select your preferred course of action and assume the planning process is over. Good strategists periodically reevaluate how well their plan is working and whether it needs to be adjusted. This involves reviewing your goals to see if they are still achievable, reexamining your assumptions to see if they are still valid, and testing your course of action to assure that it is still the preferred one.

What you measure improves.

I am a believer in "metrics"—key numeric indicators of how well something is working. The reason is simple: What you measure improves.

Measurement is a powerful tool. Self-monitoring focuses the mind and motivates. If I want to lose some weight, I get on a scale every day to see how I'm doing. If I am concerned about a budget, I itemize expenditures and track them on a regular basis to see where I am spending too much. Through frequent inspections, the military does the same thing. If a drill sergeant conducts a series of inspections on how well a cadet makes his bed, you can be darn sure that after the first or second inspection, he'll able to bounce a quarter off the sheets. By measuring or inspecting, you instinctively act and make decisions in ways that make you more likely to achieve the desired result.

Too often, especially in government, people focus on efforts instead of results, on inputs instead of outputs. Politicians and government officials are generally not held to rigorous standards of performance as their counterparts in business are. Soaring rhetoric and empty promises from a CEO work for only so long before he or she is shown the door. Measuring is the key to knowing whether you are making progress toward your goals.

You get what you inspect, not what you expect.

At Searle I did something unusual. I announced a list of indices that we would measure regularly and publish in our Annual Report. These key metrics included sales, research and development spending, earnings-per-share margins, and the like, but also metrics not generally made public. By doing this, we announced to our shareholders and employees precisely what we would be measuring and what we expected to improve. We held our own feet to the fire, knowing that if everyone was going to see our progress, or lack thereof, we had to do everything possible to improve.

All of this is not to say that metrics are foolproof and can always be trusted. One old Soviet story has it that Stalin demanded that shoe factories produce an impossibly large number of shoes. The factories met their quotas, but the shoes were each one inch in size. The lesson is: Don't simply develop metrics; develop the *right* metrics.

To see which direction things are moving in, apply the "gate test."

My friend Bill Bennett, who served as Secretary of Education in the Reagan administration, introduced me to a simple but reliable metric that he called the "gate test." He said the way to see which of two alternatives is preferred is to lift a gate between them and watch which way things move. People vote with their feet. People and money move from a place that is less desirable to a place that is more hospitable.

If you removed price differences on similar consumer products, would more consumers choose your products or those of your competitor? Are Afghans moving back to their country (as they did in the months after U.S. forces toppled the Taliban) or are they moving to other countries? Measuring which direction things are moving can be telling.

If, for example, a customer would select a rival's product over yours, all things being equal, you need to ask what you can do to change that outcome. If your organization or your community is seeing an outflow of people instead of an inflow, what qualities do you lack that others offer? What might be done to change that calculus? Only by learning the answers will you have a better chance of fashioning a more successful strategy.

If you can't measure it, you can't manage it.
—PETER DRUCKER

In the weeks and months after the 9/11 attacks, I tried to find metrics that our government could track to indicate whether we were making progress in the so-called global war on terror. After a meeting in October 2003 with the combatant commanders—the four-star generals and admirals in charge of conducting military operations—I drafted a memo expressing concern that we lacked the metrics to know whether we were actually reducing the threat posed by radical Islamist terrorists. My first question was "Are we winning or losing the global war on terror?" I came to the conclusion that "Today, we lack metrics to know if we are winning or losing the global war on terror. Are we capturing, killing, or deterring and dissuading more terrorists every day than the madrassas and the radical clerics are recruiting, training, and deploying against us?"

In other words, was the strategy in the administration's War on Terror achieving the results we needed? Was it working? Yes, we all wanted to defeat al-Qaeda. Yes, we all wanted to win the hearts and minds of Muslims around the world. The more difficult question was how to develop a plan as to how we could do that, bringing to bear every element of our national power, and what metrics could tell us how well we were doing. That is the challenge the West faced then and, I would submit, it faces to this very day.

My memo reflected a truth about strategy. The central paradox of planning is that no plan will be executed as originally conceived. There is always the challenge of the unexpected.

CHAPTER FIVE

PLANNING FOR UNCERTAINTY

In April 2001, the Defense Department began an exhaustive review of the nation's defense strategy—"The Quadrennial Defense Review" was the study's elaborate statutory name. The conclusions would guide how we would shift resources for the twenty-first century and how the U.S. military would prepare for future conflicts.

I forwarded to President Bush a memo that captured my view that we were badly mistaken if we thought we could say with any accuracy what the future would hold. The original memo written by Lin Wells, a Pentagon policy official, succinctly summarized the unpredictable nature of great power relations:

- If you had been a security policy-maker in the world's greatest power in 1900, you would have been a Brit, looking warily at your age-old enemy, France.

- By 1910, you would be allied with France and your enemy would be Germany.

- By 1920, World War I would have been fought and won, and you'd be engaged in a naval arms race with your erstwhile allies, the U.S. and Japan.

- By 1930, naval arms limitation treaties were in effect, the Great Depression was under way, and the defense planning standard said "no war for ten years."

- Nine years later World War II had begun.

- By 1950, Britain no longer was the world's greatest power, the Atomic Age had dawned, and a "police action" was under way in Korea.

- Ten years later the political focus was on the "missile gap," the strategic paradigm was shifting from massive retaliation to flexible response, and few people had heard of Vietnam.

- By 1970, the peak of our involvement in Vietnam had come and gone, we were beginning détente with the Soviets, and we were anointing the Shah as our protégé in the Gulf region.

- By 1980, the Soviets were in Afghanistan, Iran was in the throes of revolution, there was talk of our "hollow forces" and a "window of vulnerability," and the U.S. was the greatest creditor nation the world had ever seen.

- By 1990, the Soviet Union was within a year of dissolution, American forces in the desert were on the verge of showing they were anything but hollow, the U.S. had become the greatest debtor nation the world had ever known, and almost no one had heard of the Internet.

- Ten years later, Warsaw was the capital of a NATO nation, asymmetric threats transcended geography, and the parallel revolutions of information, biotechnology, robotics, nano-technology, and high-density energy sources foreshadowed changes almost beyond forecasting.

- All of which is to say that I'm not sure what 2010 will look like, but I'm sure that it will be very little like we expect, so we should plan accordingly.[2]

It stands to reason that leaders skilled at identifying and forecasting significant trends have a distinct advantage over their competitors. If you can find a smart person with a knack for successfully predicting the future, hold on to them for dear life. Most of us don't have that ability. An equally valuable but less obvious skill is the wisdom and humility to recognize the limits of our predictive abilities.

That does not mean planning is unnecessary. Although blueprints are rarely followed as drafted, the process of drawing them up forces you to think through various contingencies, so that when they arise you are prepared to adjust. Planning done well allows for improvisation. It allows for an openness to being wrong. This applies as much in a corporate boardroom as in a military headquarters.

The previous chapter discussed the key elements of formulating a strategy for an organization or business. This chapter focuses on ways to adapt your strategy for the inevitable uncertainties that can force your plan to go in a markedly different direction.

Plans are nothing; planning is everything.—Dwight D. Eisenhower

No plan survives first contact with the enemy.
–Helmuth von Moltke the Elder

Because a successful strategy requires time to achieve its stated goals, there are occasions when it takes tenacity and determination to stick with your chosen direction, even when it suffers setbacks or becomes unpopular. At the same time, good leaders understand the importance of not staying wedded to a course of action after new circumstances require a change.

The reality is that for every given offense, there is a defense, and for every given defense there is an offense. Moreover, your competitors have brains. They will watch what you do and adjust their actions accordingly. Because of this truth, goals that were reasonable at the outset, assumptions that were once valid, and courses of action that were preferred yesterday can prove not to be so tomorrow.

When asked on the eve of the Battle of Waterloo about his plan to achieve victory over Napoleon's forces, the Duke of Wellington replied, "If you want to know my plan, you must first tell me what Bonaparte is going to do." This should not be taken as an argument against planning. Rather, it's an argument against thinking one can choreograph something as complex as war. Wellington knew that the enemy would have its own plan. He also knew that while he could not master fortune, he could bend it in his direction by being prepared for the unexpected. Over the next several days, Napoleon's forces were routed at Waterloo, and the French emperor surrendered and was exiled.

> *This strategy represents our policy for all time.*
> *Until it's changed.*
> —MARLIN FITZWATER

Knowing when to change a plan is not easy. The signs that you may need to adapt can be subtle or ambiguous. Alert leaders are able to adjust course because they identify the important indicators early and see emerging trends before others see them. Strategic leaders are good observers, but they do not mire themselves in minutiae and micromanagement.

"Free of the obsession with detail by which mediocre leaders think they are mastering events, only to be engulfed by them," is how Henry Kissinger described Anwar Sadat. The President of Egypt was one of the most impressive leaders I've met. We first crossed paths in Cairo in 1970 at the funeral of his predecessor, General Gamal Abdel Nasser. The U.S. intelligence analysts assessed him to be a second-rate leader, and not likely to last the transition to become Egypt's next president. That proved to be far off the mark.

Sadat radically changed the landscape of the Middle East with a trip to Jerusalem in 1977 and an enduring peace accord with Israel several months later. There were hints that he was pondering some bold strokes seven years earlier when he told our delegation that he "had no problem with America, except for your support of Israel." He said this even though Egypt had been firmly in the Soviet camp for more than a decade. Sadat shifted Egypt's strategy from being a Soviet ally and an opponent of Israel to being a U.S. ally and an anchor of stability in that troubled region.

He who cannot change the very fabric of his thought will never be able to change reality.
—ANWAR SADAT

Soon after the terrorist attacks of September 11, 2001, the Bush administration undertook a total reevaluation of our nation's counterterrorism strategy. If we needed any reminder that it had been a failure to that point, I had only to walk a few hundred yards from my office to the part of the Pentagon where 184 Americans perished when American Airlines Flight 77 hit the building. Previous administrations had treated acts of terrorism as law enforcement matters, as crimes to be dealt with after the fact, if and when the perpetrators could be arrested. Grand juries were convened. Indictments in absentia were issued. And, for the most part, the terrorists remained at large, planning and executing further attacks. This approach, in place for years, had not protected the American people. More than three thousand were killed at the World Trade Center, at the Pentagon, and in a quiet field near Shanksville, Pennsylvania.

Moreover, in an era when terrorists could obtain increasingly lethal weapons capable of killing hundreds of thousands of our citizens, our new circumstances required a new approach. America could no longer afford simply to wait to be struck as in the past, and only after the fact attempt to find, capture, and try the terrorists in civilian courts. President Bush changed the strategy to one of preemption and sought to stop radical Islamist attacks from occurring in the first place. To do that, America needed to take the offensive, to go after terrorists where they were, disrupting their networks, capturing or killing their leaders, putting pressure on their state sponsors, drying up their flow of money, and working to combat the radical ideology that fuels their recruitment and funding. Agencies of our government would need to be oriented to the new, unambiguous goal of prevention. In hindsight that new strategy seems logical. But at the time the President made his decisions, they were a significant departure from the policies of the previous four presidential administrations.

When you know a thing, to hold that you know it; and when you do not know a thing, to allow that you do not know it; this is knowledge.
—*Confucius*

As Secretary of Defense in 2001, I knew we faced a difficult task. The Cold War had ended. The Soviet Union was firmly on the ash heap of history. There was no immediately identifiable military threat to our security. We had, in effect, to defend against the unknown, the uncertain, the unseen, and the unexpected. To do that, we had to put aside comfortable ways of thinking and develop capabilities to deter, dissuade, and defeat adversaries that had not yet fully emerged. We had to transform our armed forces in ways that encouraged intelligent risk-taking and a more entrepreneurial approach. We needed a Defense Department that not only tolerated but promoted people who were proactive, not reactive, and who behaved less like bureaucrats and more like innovators and venture capitalists.

Part of that mind-set involved not waiting for threats to emerge but striving to anticipate them before they appeared. One major shift in that direction was to move from the "threat-based" approach that had dominated planning for the past fifty years. In the Cold War, that made sense. We knew the threat came largely from the Soviet Union, and we could reasonably determine where they might attack—the plains of Central Europe. In the twenty-first century that was no longer the case. So we adopted a "capabilities-based" approach—one that focused less on who might threaten us or where and more on *how* we might be threatened and what capabilities we could develop to deter and dissuade potential enemies.

I likened it to dealing with burglars. You can't know who might break into your house, or when. What you can know is how they might get in. They might try to break a window, so you install an alarm system with sensors on the windows. They might try to pick a lock, so you put a dead bolt on the door. They might try to scope out the neighborhood, so it helps to have regular security patrols to keep the bad guys off your street. Having a German shepherd around doesn't hurt, either.

With experience, leaders can find a level of comfort even with the likelihood of uncertain and imperfect information. It also means coming to terms with the reality that there will inevitably be things you won't know, and outcomes you will not have fully anticipated.

Learn to say "I don't know." If used when appropriate, it will be often.

There is often a great deal more certainty expressed in the public debate than there are information and data to support that certainty. Although my television set is generally tuned to the news or a sporting event, every so often I come across an opinion show or financial channel where people pop up to tell millions of viewers what's going to happen, with absolute conviction. As my friend Dr. William Schneider likes to say about folks like that, "That fellow has had one year's worth of experience fifty times." The talking heads say this person is going to win an election, or that company's stock is going to go up, or the economy is doomed or on the brink of boom times. This thing will "never" happen, while that one "always" will.

Over the years I've come to be wary of using the words *always* and *never*. They are two of the more dangerous words in the English language. I admit to being a bit of a stickler about precision, but there are very few situations in which you can say with 100 percent certainty that something will never happen or that something else always will. By using those words, you are setting yourself up to be proved wrong. Pundits by and large can get away with being wrong. Leaders never do—or, I should say, *almost* never do.

Those who know, don't talk. Those who talk, don't know.
—Lao Tzu

At the Pentagon, I was repeatedly asked by reporters to predict how long the wars in Afghanistan and Iraq might last. Or how much a war would cost. Or how many casualties there would be. Each time I fought the temptation to answer the question. I didn't always succeed. And whenever I fell into that trap, I later regretted it. There's nothing wrong with saying the words "I don't know."

At the time, because of recent U.S. military successes in places like Grenada in the 1980s, there was a belief that America's military could overpower any country quickly and skillfully with relatively little loss of life. Some advocates of an invasion of Iraq said foolish things—that it would be a "cakewalk," for example. As someone who had a close friend die in the last days of the Korean War, and as a member of Congress during the Vietnam era, I know that it is only from a pinnacle of near-perfect ignorance that anyone could suggest that an armed conflict would be "easy," that the outcome could be certain, or that its length or cost could be predicted. Any military conflict is fraught with uncertainty. "Every war is going to astonish you in the way it has occurred and in the way it is carried out," Dwight D. Eisenhower once said.

The unexpected is the prince of the battlefield.
—*Carl von Clausewitz*

In the run-up to the invasion of Iraq, I worked with senior military and civilian officials in the Pentagon to develop a list of things that could conceivably go wrong. The list later became known as "Rumsfeld's Parade of Horribles," because it included a series of ugly possibilities, such as an outbreak of civil war between the Sunni and Shia religious groups, U.S. forces getting bogged down for "8 to 10 years," Iran or Syria entering the war, and even the possibility of a failure to find stockpiles of weapons of mass destruction.[3] I developed the list so that those of us in the Department of Defense and National Security Council would think through in advance the possible adverse consequences that might result if President Bush did eventually make a decision to go to war.

I didn't write the memo to try to predict the future. I knew I couldn't do that. Nor did I write it in an attempt to anticipate everything that could conceivably go wrong. Indeed, my reason for writing the memo was to make the opposite point: that we *couldn't* anticipate what might happen.

In a business setting, that point is equally valid. A company's senior officials might have every expectation that a new product has all the signs of being a big success. They might have given careful thought to a marketing strategy, tested various assumptions, and set reasonable, achievable goals. Then out of nowhere another company introduces a competing product. Or there is an unanticipated legal challenge. Or the economy experiences a sharp downturn, reducing consumer spending. These are events that even the best experts have trouble predicting. In fact, the "experts" can be more wrong than anybody else.

To be absolutely certain about something, one must know everything or nothing about it.
—Olin Miller

An American psychologist, Philip Tetlock, conducted a study of hundreds of people who earned their livings from consulting or commenting on political, business, economic, or other trends. All of his test subjects had specific fields of expertise and areas of specialization in which they were widely considered "the best."

Over a two-decade period, Tetlock asked them to make more than eighty thousand predictions. Most of the questions were divided into three alternative scenarios. Each of the subjects was asked to select the most likely outcome. These experts forecast such things as a sizable win for Al Gore in the presidential race against George W. Bush and Quebec's secession from Canada. Interestingly, nearly two times out of three, the events predicted by the "experts" proved to be wrong. In fact, the study revealed that those who were best known—the most specialized and highly regarded experts—had not the best but the *worst* predictive ability. One could have done better by simply flipping a coin.

Nothing ages so quickly as yesterday's vision of the future.
—Richard Corliss

On literally hundreds of occasions I have been in a room where I was presented with a series of sharp-looking charts that projected three to five years into the future: a company's earnings, a nation's GDP growth, real estate values, interest rates, stock prices, or election outcomes. Just as often, in the federal government I sat through briefings where analysts made predictions about everything from the size of the Soviet economy to the staying power of the insurgency in Vietnam to Saddam Hussein's chemical weapons stockpiles. Often when I observed the confident faces of the folks presenting their cases, a thought came to mind: Maybe not! During an NSC briefing by a top CIA official about Saddam's WMD programs, for example, I wrote a note I still have saved to this day. It reads: "caution—strong case, but . . . could be wrong."

Tell them what you know. Tell them what you don't know. And only then, tell them what you think. And be sure you distinguish among them.

— *General Colin Powell*

In November 1999, Rafid Ahmed Alwan al-Janabi arrived in Germany on a tourist visa. Fleeing his native Iraq, he told German intelligence authorities he was seeking political asylum. Al-Janabi said he had worked as a chemical engineer in a mobile biological weapons lab in Iraq, and that he had been a part of Saddam Hussein's weapons of mass destruction program. That information was passed on to U.S. intelligence officials, who assigned al-Janabi the code name "Curveball."

A decade after he provided this information, Curveball changed his story and contended that the details about Saddam's WMD programs were not accurate. But some of his information had made it into a CIA National Intelligence Estimate as well as into Secretary of State Colin Powell's supposedly definitive presentation on Iraq's WMD programs given at the United Nations in January 2003.

Many intelligence reports in war are contradictory; even more are false, and most are uncertain.
—CARL VON CLAUSEWITZ

In his address, Powell presented Curveball's later recanted information as fact, without caveats acknowledging that Curveball was an uncorroborated single source, or that he may have had a motive to lie (it was later learned that he wanted to stay in Germany), and that some of the information he supplied was contradictory. As the information was passed up through the intelligence community, level by level, to the President's National Security Council, questions about Curveball's information had not been examined sufficiently.

If it were a fact, it wouldn't be intelligence.
—FORMER CIA DIRECTOR GENERAL MICHAEL HAYDEN

The name "Curveball" still evokes a certain passion from critics of the Iraq War. He is seen as one who lied about Iraqi WMD programs and led the United States to war. But the fact is that the information from Curveball represented but a small fraction of the intelligence data gathered on Iraqi WMD over many years, by many nations. The overall case on Saddam's weapons programs rested on satellite images, UN reporting, and Saddam's own record of developing and using WMDs against both Iran and his own people. Still, the case of Curveball is instructive.

May the words I utter today be tender and sweet, for tomorrow I may have to eat them.

—*Congressman Mo Udall (D-AZ)*

On those occasions when I've forgotten my own rules about uncertainty, I have not unfairly paid a price. This was certainly the case with regard to WMD in Iraq. I was roasted for a response I made during a TV appearance when I said we "knew" where some of Saddam's WMD stockpiles were located. I had previously been quite careful not to make such an unqualified assertion. I could and should have made the same point to the press by saying that we knew where the "CIA's designated *suspect* WMD sites" were located. But what I meant was not what I said and that's another rule about life: You can rarely take anything back. It didn't matter what I intended to say, what I had meant, or what I'd said in other places on different occasions; the fact that I made that one insufficiently qualified statement followed me all the way through my time at the Defense Department. As the old joke goes, "I stand by what I meant to say."

Certainty without power can be interesting, even amusing. Certainty with power can be dangerous.

In 1953, Isaiah Berlin wrote an essay called "The Hedgehog and the Fox." The essay described two distinct ways that people tend to look at the world, which in turn governs how they make decisions. The metaphor was borrowed from an ancient Greek poem: "The fox knows many things, but the hedgehog knows one big thing." This theory played out in the wild. When confronted by a predator, the fox resorted to a number of different strategies. The fox knew various maneuvers that generally ensured its survival. The hedgehog, by contrast, generally had one response— one that was both simple and effective. It would curl up into a ball and transform its sharp quills into formidable spikes.

Berlin argued that human beings generally fall into one of those two categories. There are hedgehogs, who tend to develop a strong conviction in one or two big ideas. And there are foxes, who like to try out all sorts of strategies and techniques when confronted with an issue. Hedgehogs tend to be ideologues; foxes tend to be pragmatists. Each has its strengths and weaknesses.

President Richard Nixon was a leader who tended toward the mold of the fox. He was a voracious consumer of information, ideologically flexible, and one who diligently invested his time in a range of issues, from school desegregation in the South to the all-volunteer military to his most enduring legacy in foreign policy, the opening of China. He was comfortable discussing a wide range of subjects. He also was a man of contradictions, willing to make sharp shifts in strategy to accomplish his goals. A man generally considered one of the nation's fiercest anticommunists developed a strategy of détente based on a relaxation of tension with the Soviet Union. A politician who was later accused of hostility to minorities was also willing to establish affirmative action programs within the federal government.

President Ronald Reagan, by contrast, struck me as more of a hedgehog. He tended to have a strong point of view and approached issues from a largely unshakable perspective. His main idea was a belief in the power of freedom, which governed his support for free trade, free markets, more freedom for individuals to make their own decisions, and a determination to confront the Soviet Union in the belief that the Soviet people desired and deserved freedom.

In business terms, foxes tend to be generalists with knowledge and interests in a broad range of subjects and an ability to adapt to changed circumstances. Hedgehogs tend to focus on a few big ideas, develop deep conviction, and then set about to make things fit into their way of seeing a problem.

Both approaches have vulnerabilities. A fox can sometimes be too clever—too willing to change and compromise at the expense of a coherent strategy. As one playwright put it, "You can persuade a man to believe almost anything provided he is clever enough." In President Nixon's case, it could be argued that his wide and diverse field of interests allowed him to reach great heights—such as the overture to China—and shocking lows, such as a willingness to cover up an unlawful act.

Hedgehogs, by contrast, can fall victim to their own certainty and conviction. They can be slow or unwilling to adapt. Generalists are good at challenging premises that specialists long ago stopped questioning. When it comes to dealing with uncertainty, then, the fox can have an advantage over the hedgehog.

As a leader, you might consider which of these approaches you tend to take, as well as the approaches favored by those around you. Sometimes the hardest thing to do is to appraise yourself. I've found that to be the case in my own career—particularly when someone would say something about my leadership style that didn't track with how I saw it.

Whether you are more like the hedgehog or the fox, there are some techniques that anyone might use to ensure you are looking at the world and your choices in an optimal way. Leaders generally want to seek some balance in their approach between the two.

One way is to draw information from a variety of sources, as many and as wide-ranging and diverse as possible. Don't rely completely on the specialists. They may be too close to see that something fundamental might have changed. Seek advice also from generalists, who will be likely to have a better grasp of broader trends.

> *What should they know of England who only England know?*
> —RUDYARD KIPLING

Try to get information from outside your immediate circle. While Secretary of Defense, I was a voracious reader. I wanted as much information as I could get my hands on, including information from outside the Defense Department. Organizations tend to develop their own biases. Insularity can breed "groupthink" and lead to unfounded conclusions and certainty.

In government, I found that officials frequently relied on classified material, thinking that because someone put a SECRET or TOP SECRET stamp on it, it must have greater weight. Sometimes war correspondents writing in the newspapers have just as valuable an assessment of what is happening on the ground, if not better, than official reports do. Open-source material from media and public data can be helpful in developing a more accurate picture.

Be open-minded. Suspend initial judgment while seeking additional information. If data or facts contradict an initial conclusion, it could be an anomaly—or it could be a sign that your thinking is outdated. Try not to let your expectations influence how you receive and process information. Be cautious of data or facts that track perfectly with your personal preferences or opinions.

The absence of evidence is not necessarily evidence of absence; nor is it evidence of presence.

The mere fact that you cannot see something when you look does not mean it isn't there. Avoid dismissing a hypothesis as an impossibility simply because there isn't immediate evidence to support it. If you don't know whether something exists, that doesn't mean it cannot or does not exist. It could simply be outside your current awareness. Continue searching and remain open-minded.

When your working assumptions or forecasts prove incorrect, go back and try to discover why they turned out to be wrong. Finding out what you missed and why you missed it can help improve your predictive skills.

I titled my 2011 memoir *Known and Unknown* because the phrase highlighted the fundamental and critical concept of uncertainty. Responding to a question at a press conference on February 12, 2002, I had summarized categories of knowledge as follows: There are known knowns: the things you know you know. There are known unknowns: the things you know you don't know. But there are also unknown unknowns: the things you don't know you don't know.

My comment did not win immediate admirers from the Pentagon press corps. Late-night comics and English professors ridiculed the concept. Then a curious thing happened. What I had said began to strike a chord with a considerably broader and more enlightened audience. Scientists referenced the concept favorably. A bestselling book examined "unknown unknowns" and called them "black swans"—events that are rare, that are "predicted" only retrospectively, and that have a large impact. The concept began showing up in news articles and op-eds. I am told one rap group even named their album after it, though I can't say I have listened to it yet.

What I was trying to do was gird reporters—and the public— for the reality that in government, as in business, some things will not be known and that we are likely to be surprised by them.

CHAPTER SIX

THE UNKNOWN UNKNOWNS

One mark of a good leader is the ability to deal with surprises as they come. Indeed, how an individual copes with surprise in his or her personal life, in business, or in government can make the difference between success and failure. Surprises come in many forms. They are rarely pleasant. In the business setting, Eastman Kodak and Polaroid were sent to the bankruptcy courts after the rapid rise of digital photography. The collapse of the housing market in 2008 threatened to bring down a number of major financial institutions in the United States. Government service, as I would learn, offers a good number of surprises as well.

I was in my office in the Nixon White House on a Monday morning in June 1972 when I glanced at a headline in the *Washington Post*: GOP SECURITY AIDE AMONG FIVE ARRESTED IN BUGGING AFFAIR. The first sentence of the story, written by two young reporters named Carl Bernstein and Bob Woodward, was enough to pique my interest: "One of the five men arrested early Saturday in the attempt to bug the Democratic National Committee headquarters is the salaried security coordinator for President Nixon's reelection committee." That certainly didn't sound good.

That morning, at the White House senior staff meeting in the Roosevelt Room, the story quickly became a subject of discussion. Some officials did not take it seriously, laughing at the story and dismissing it as an election-year distraction. I suspect some even thought it may have been planted by Nixon's political opponents to make his reelection campaign more difficult.

My mood was neither lighthearted nor paranoid. In a book later written about the scandal, the author who was in the meeting quoted me as saying at that meeting, "If any jackass across the street [meaning at Nixon campaign headquarters] or here had anything to do with this, he should be hung up by his thumbs today. We'd better not have anything to do with this. It will kill us." I don't recall if that's precisely what I said but it certainly was how I felt.[4]

The Watergate scandal, as it would soon become known, was a shock to me and most other people in the White House who served in the Nixon administration. After Nixon's triumph that November, five months after the break-in, winning every state except Massachusetts and the District of Columbia, a steady drumbeat of new revelations in the press followed, each one more sensational and shocking than the last.

I had no idea who was behind the Watergate break-in or what the motive might have been. Nor did I imagine that it could involve the President himself or any of his senior aides, or that it would eventually consume the administration for most of the next two years. Still less did it cross my mind that a sitting president might have to resign in disgrace—something that had never happened in two hundred years of the American experiment. For most of us in the administration it was the very definition of an Unknown Unknown. We didn't know what we didn't know.

The inevitable never happens. It is the unexpected always.

—*John Maynard Keynes*

Over my time in the military, in public service, and in business, I have been witness to literally dozens of these sorts of unforeseen transformational events: the serendipitous discovery of NutraSweet, which improved the fortunes of Searle's shareholders; the bombing of the U.S. Marine barracks in Beirut in 1983, which led me to be appointed President Reagan's Special Envoy for the Middle East; and, to be sure, the terrorist attacks of September 11, 2001.

When surprise occurs on a large scale, it alters human behavior. It changes what until that moment was the "regular" or "normal" order of things. In some cases, surprise can lead to the bankruptcy of a successful business (such as Bear Stearns), and in others, to the fall of great civilizations (such as Troy). The element of surprise, often aided by stealth and speed, can be the key to success in warfare. It can be a great equalizer, advantaging the militarily weak over the militarily superior.

What you see is what you get. What you don't see gets you.

Surprise bedevils leaders of all political persuasions. On the last day of 1977, Jimmy Carter had been president of the United States for just under a year. For the Shah of Iran, it was his thirty-seventh year as his country's supreme ruler. The atmosphere in Tehran's Niavaran Palace was celebratory, as President Carter and his wife, Rosalynn, made their first state visit to a stalwart American ally.

Carter raised his glass of champagne and offered a New Year's Eve toast. "Under the Shah's brilliant leadership, Iran is an island of stability in one of the most troublesome regions of the world," the President said. The Shah, Carter went on to observe, enjoyed "his people's total confidence."

A little more than a year later, the Shah was on a plane fleeing to exile in Egypt. Tens of thousands of Iranians had taken to the streets. The Shah's government, far more fragile than President Carter and the U.S. government had understood, quickly crumbled. In its place emerged the radical Islamist regime of Ayatollah Khomeini. Over the next three decades no country in the world would sponsor more terrorist attacks than Iran.

Warning time not used is wasted time. It's like runway behind a pilot.
—GENERAL LEE BUTLER

Many mention the failure to find WMD in Iraq as if intelligence failures of that magnitude had never happened before. In fact, practically no one in the intelligence community had seen Iran's fall coming. Months before the revolution, any CIA analyst reading an Iranian newspaper or asking questions of the thousands demonstrating against the Shah or listening to audiotapes of Ayatollah Khomeini (then still in exile in France) could have had at least an inkling that all was not well for the American government's close ally.[5] But the CIA had been gathering much of its intelligence from the Shah's secret police force, the SAVAK, and had a skewed view of the signs of the pending revolution in Iran. Six months before those dramatic events, the CIA concluded that Iran "is not in a revolutionary or even a pre-revolutionary situation." The Carter administration, and much of the world, had been taken by surprise.

No one ever sees successful camouflage.

From Pearl Harbor to 9/11, there has been a tendency to think of surprises as blunders, or the result of incompetence. And while both of those attacks were examples of colossal failures of intelligence, they were much more than that. They were "failures of imagination." Dr. Thomas Schelling explained how and why surprise attacks occur in his forward to Roberta Wohlstetter's study of the Pearl Harbor attack. His short essay is the single most brilliant piece of prose I have read on that subject.

As Schelling points out, more often than not surprises are the result of bureaucracies coping with too much information, rather than too little. There were warning signs and indications in both cases that were either missed or not given proper weighting: decoded radio intercepts of Admiral Yamamoto's order to attack Hawaii and observations of aircraft practice launching torpedoes in a Japanese port, eerily similar to the real targets; Osama bin Laden's fatwa against the United States as well as Khalid Sheikh Mohammed's foiled "Operation Bojinka," his late 1990s plot to blow up a dozen airliners carrying four thousand people over the Pacific. Those indications were ignored or at least minimized amid the "noise"—the many thousands of other pieces of equally troubling intelligence about various threats to the United States and our interests.

Penetrating so many secrets, we cease to believe in the unknowable. But there it sits nevertheless, calmly licking its chops.
—H. L. MENCKEN

No one was sleeping at the switch in either case. Hundreds of seasoned intelligence professionals and policy-makers were concerned about the threats posed by Imperial Japan, and later by al-Qaeda. They expected that each would be likely to try to attack us at some point. However, as it turned out, they expected wrong. In the case of 9/11, intelligence professionals anticipated al-Qaeda would strike U.S. embassies abroad as they had in 1998 or attack our ships in port as they had in 2000. The idea of terrorists wielding box cutters to turn American airliners into guided missiles was not all that improbable; it was simply "unfamiliar," to use Schelling's word describing the attack on Pearl Harbor. "The contingency we have not considered seriously looks strange; what looks strange is thought improbable; what is improbable need not be considered seriously," he wrote.[6]

When surprise occurs, such as when the economy enters an unexpected recession or a conflict begins seemingly out the blue, the natural reaction is to immediately ask *who* made the "obvious" mistake. It is much easier to believe that our leaders are incompetent than to accept the less pleasant reality that ours is a world where uncertainty and surprise are the norm, not the exception. Unfortunately, not even the wisest among us is able to anticipate and head off every conceivable unpleasant surprise. Not even the best-funded and best-trained intelligence services can anticipate every unknown unknown. After all, as Dean Rusk, Presidents Kennedy's and Johnson's Secretary of State, put it, "Only one-third of the world is asleep at any given time and the other two-thirds is up to something."

The only thing that should be surprising is that we continue to be surprised.

One way of dealing with the likelihood of unknown unknowns is to bring a wide variety of people together and brainstorm the range of possibilities. Given the reality of surprise time and again, it's worth considering what we may be missing at any given decision point. It is a useful mental exercise to carefully think through the what-ifs.

What might we wake up to tomorrow that we had not anticipated? What are the dangers that we are focused on, but which may seem likely only because they are familiar? How might we expand our imaginations to break through the "poverty of expectations" that enabled surprise attacks like Pearl Harbor and 9/11 to be so stunningly successful? How can we better anticipate or at least think through some of the "unknown unknowns"?

Having considered the possibilities, even if they seem remote, can make a difference in your immediate reaction if that possibility were to occur. And that initial reaction—what you do, how well you do it, and how long it takes—can save lives in war or a great deal of shareholder value in business.

The U.S. government spends billions of dollars each year trying to minimize surprises. According to one report, all in all, there are 271 separate government organizations and 1,931 private companies—with some 854,000 people holding security clearances—working in some intelligence capacity.[7] For starters there are the CIA, the Defense Intelligence Agency, the DNI, the FBI, INR, NSA, and a number of other agencies and branches with still more acronyms.

Corporations also spend millions of dollars to hedge against the risk of surprise, investing in oil futures against a spike in prices or in foreign currencies to offset a sudden drop in a country's economy, for example. This is the stuff of leadership—breaking from the mold of a conditioned, bureaucratic way of thinking. To be sure, bureaucracies require doctrine, techniques, and procedures. These are essential to efficient operation and management in large organizations. At the same time, trying to reduce every decision to a prescribed formula or an iron law can lead to focusing on the familiar, all but ensuring surprise—and if not, certainly contributing to an ineffective response once surprises occur.

This war isn't like the last war, and it isn't like the next war. This war is like this war.
—*Admiral Vern Clark, Chief of Naval Operations*

Complacency with an existing plan or road map can have unexpected and unpleasant consequences. Doctrines and rules can become outdated. The Maginot Line was billed by French generals and engineers as an impenetrable series of defenses. With underground railroads, dining halls, and even air-conditioning, it had the hallmarks of a leap forward in military innovation. Advocates believed it would ensure that the Germans could not again invade France, as they had in World War I. They were convinced that the static, defensive combat of the last war would continue to be the way wars would be fought in the future.

What the French failed to consider was that German planners had no intention of fighting through the Maginot defenses. In 1940, when the tanks of the Wehrmacht roared westward, they first occupied Belgium and the Netherlands and then pushed south into France, outflanking most of the Maginot defenses, while German aircraft flew over them altogether. Hitler's blitzkrieg rendered the Maginot Line obsolete. The French had, disastrously, prepared to fight the last war.

Never assume the other guy will never do something you would never do.

Surprise often arrives when one side assumes that the enemy or the competition thinks like it does and will do what it would be likely to do in a similar situation. In the intelligence community, that kind of thinking is called "mirror imaging." There are circumstances where rationality, self-interest, and self-preservation do not apply to other actors. If they did, suicide bombers would not exist. Iranian leaders, if expected to act as we might, would not threaten to annihilate Israel, thereby risking the lives of hundreds of thousands of Iranians who could perish in an Israeli retaliatory strike.

The perfect battle is the one that does not have to be fought.
—*Sun Tzu*

The use of surprise as a technique in war is at least as old as Sun Tzu's legendary book, *Art of War*, written two and a half millennia ago. In 2005, China's senior diplomatic minister, Dai Bingguo, presented me with a copy of the book in English and also the original Chinese. The book was housed in a wooden box, equipped with a pair of gloves to handle the delicate silk pages. At the heart of Sun Tzu's book is a philosophy of competition that centers on winning without bloodshed by taking advantage of secrecy and surprise so that the enemy is unable to fight back. To this day I wonder if the gift from the Chinese leader was a warning or an offer of advice—or both.

Surprise can be easier for a smaller and weaker force. In the U.S. experience against guerrilla insurgencies and terrorist networks, whether in Vietnam or Iraq, we have seen that the enemy tends not to be limited by parliaments or delayed by large bureaucracies or a free press, where issues are vetted many times before finally being adopted. They are able to achieve surprise with relative ease, whether it be a roadside ambush or a mass casualty attack on the scale of 9/11.

After an assassination attempt on Prime Minister Margaret Thatcher in 1984, the Irish Republican Army (IRA) issued a chilling statement. "We only have to be lucky once, you will have to be lucky always." Terrorists have the advantage of surprise, and often use it with devastating effectiveness.

Aside from our Revolutionary War, where militias and minutemen became guerrilla fighters able to blend into the background, the United States has not been known for its use of surprise as a military technique. That was not the case, however, during the fight against al-Qaeda. In Afghanistan, Taliban forces were surprised by an American offensive that blended Afghan Northern Alliance forces with embedded U.S. Special Forces, CIA officers, and precision airpower. One of the more memorable moments was a cavalry charge on horseback. Small groups of special operators fought like the enemies they were facing, employing guerrilla tactics to create outsize effects.

In the run-up to the war in Iraq, because of lengthy diplomatic efforts to avert the need for an invasion, there was no opportunity for strategic surprise—that is, surprise on a large enough scale to keep Saddam in the dark about our plans. President Bush's public diplomacy and the parallel decision to engage in a gradual buildup of forces were designed to be visible to Saddam in the hope they would persuade him to allow the United Nations inspectors access to his weapons facilities. Nonetheless, CENTCOM Commander General Tommy Franks was able to achieve tactical surprise by keeping Saddam's generals guessing as to precisely when, where, and how the invasion might be launched. The U.S. kept an Army division off the coast of Turkey, which undoubtedly led the Iraqis to believe that coalition forces would come from north and south simultaneously. Tactical surprise was also gained by commencing the ground advance slightly before the air attack. Saddam and his generals believed that the war, like 1991's Persian Gulf War before it, would begin with weeks of a bombing campaign before any ground forces would enter Iraq. The lightning advance of U.S. ground troops to Baghdad demoralized Iraqi forces and led to the fall of Saddam's government within three weeks of the start of major combat operations.

During the long fight against the Iraqi insurgency, General Stanley McChrystal and the Joint Special Operations Command (JSOC) also made effective use of surprise. His goal was to make JSOC more nimble and agile—much like the al-Qaeda enemies they were hunting. JSOC was organizationally flat, reducing red tape and layers of bureaucracy that had been previously needed to approve missions. Instead of a strict hierarchy where information flowed up and down the chain of command, he established a network where information was shared across agencies and military units. Knowing that the intelligence needed to track down the insurgents was highly perishable, they brought in CIA and NSA analysts to work alongside JSOC analysts in a single "fusion" cell. Bureaucratic turf fights and stovepipes that hindered agencies from sharing information were unacceptable impediments to success. By 2006, there were no forces more feared in Iraq than the men of JSOC who descended in the cover of night to capture or kill al-Qaeda operatives.

Under McChrystal's command, these concepts were perfected into a high art for special operations forces, combining the latest technologies with the best trained and equipped military on the face of the earth. Using stealth, speed, and surprise, JSOC, which included Army Rangers and Green Berets, Air Force combat controllers and Navy SEALs, became home to the most effective military units in the world. In Iraq, they killed al-Qaeda's chief, Abu Musab al-Zarqawi, and dozens of other senior lieutenants, until by 2008 al-Qaeda had been largely routed from the country.

At night, JSOC units would converge on a terrorist hideout, take suspects into custody, subdue those who resisted, and sweep up evidence found at the scene—notepads, cell phones, computers. These would be analyzed in near real-time by language experts. Patterns would be established—who was communicating with whom about what, where their safe houses were, what websites they visited, the email addresses they used, and the like. Within a few hours, JSOC would be able to make another raid with the intelligence gleaned from the first. Because JSOC became so

skilled at turning missions around rapidly, the enemy had difficulty reacting in time. This might happen two more times before
dawn. As a result, al-Qaeda in Iraq was largely dismantled.

In business as well, surprise provides an advantage by reducing
the competition's reaction time. Southwest Airlines, for example,
was known to keep its plans for new routes secret until days before
it launched them. Surprise can also be helpful in marketing. Major
marketing campaigns usually begin with a big launch, instead of
dribbling out information over time, so that the product or service
is available in the marketplace before the competition can blunt
its value.

The probability of leaks escalates exponentially each time a classified document is exposed to another person.
—Former CIA Director Richard Helms

On a national level, particularly in a democracy, surprise is
considerably more difficult to achieve. Surprise depends
on secrets and secrets are hard to keep in an age of cyberattacks,
WikiLeaks, and a free press that decides on its own what should or
should not be made public.

One of the more famous cases of a political leader successfully
using surprise and secrecy to advantage was President Nixon. In
1970, shortly before I was to embark on a trip to Europe to con-
sult with our allies on the trafficking of illegal drugs, the President
asked to speak with me privately. He told me that, if an opportunity arose, he wanted me to pass on a message to the Romanian
Prime Minister that the President of the United States wanted to

initiate contact with senior Chinese officials. He asked that the contact be made through the U.S. military attaché in Paris, Major General Vernon "Dick" Walters.

As a result, while I was not involved in the secret negotiations, I did have an early hint of what was to come. Curiously, one of the people who were not brought into the President's plan was then—Secretary of State Bill Rogers. This must have been a dilemma for the President. Nixon was concerned that diplomats at the State Department would bristle at the idea of a presidential initiative that did not directly involve them and thought they might throw up roadblocks. The President apparently believed that they would not be able to restrain themselves from leaking the China plan to the press, thus allowing opposition on Nixon's right to rally, as well as giving the Soviets an opportunity to interfere.

Although Nixon liked and respected Bill Rogers, who had served with him in the Eisenhower administration as attorney general, he apparently concluded that if the State Department learned Rogers had kept this crucial information from them, Rogers's ability to manage the department could be weakened. The effect was the opposite. Having been left out of the loop on the Nixon administration's most important diplomatic initiative, the nation's most senior diplomat came to be seen as not having the confidence of the President. Rogers departed soon thereafter. Despite these difficult trade-offs, Mr. Nixon had delivered a historic surprise that outfoxed the Soviets and impressed the world and even some of his critics in the media. The historic opening to China in 1972 was accomplished before any domestic or international opposition could crystallize.

When you're in a bind, create a diversion.
—Alf Landon

A s Gerald Ford's White House Chief of Staff, I was in my office one day in the West Wing when my secretary buzzed me and said there was man on the phone named Alf Landon who wanted to speak to me.

"Is this *the* Alf Landon?" I asked.

My secretary was in her mid-twenties, so it was no surprise when she asked, "Who is Alf Landon?"

I explained that he had been the governor of Kansas and ran for president against Franklin D. Roosevelt back in 1936. Landon, a Republican, had once been a major figure in American politics.

I picked up the phone and greeted him. "Governor, this is Don Rumsfeld. Do you want to talk to President Ford?"

"No," he replied. "I want to talk to you."

We were approaching a heated Republican primary in which President Ford would face a major challenge from California Governor Ronald Reagan. Landon apparently had been following the nomination fight. "Jerry is getting pounded on the Panama Canal issue," he said. Landon was referencing Governor Reagan's attacks on President Ford for agreeing to sign a treaty ceding control of the canal to the Panamanian government. Reagan had a famous line expressing his opposition to the plan: "We built it! We paid for it! It's ours and we're going to keep it!"

Then Landon said to me, "You know what Teddy Roosevelt used to say?"

"Well, I know some things he said," I answered. "But what do you have in mind?"

Landon replied, "Teddy used to say, 'When you are in a bind, create a diversion.' That's what Jerry needs to do. You tell Jerry he's in a bind and he needs to create a diversion. He should go after Fidel Castro in Cuba."

I gathered that he wanted Ford to denounce Castro and make the communist regime's crimes against its people front and center in his primary campaign. Governor Landon's advice was not followed in this case, but he was expressing an important concept. Sometimes surprise can be deployed to one's advantage in order to shift the conversation and create a diversion. Voters didn't expect the mild-mannered Ford, whose administration was pursuing a policy of détente with the Soviet Union, to launch a rhetorical assault on Fidel Castro. In other words, rather than simply waiting to be thrown off by the actions of others, it can be useful to take action to shake them up yourself.

CHAPTER SEVEN

CONFRONTING CRISIS

A t forty-seven, Charles Percy was a self-made millionaire. From poor beginnings, he became a successful business and community leader through a combination of hard work and savvy. He had a deep, almost perfect, politician's voice. Former President Eisenhower urged him to run for public office and predicted that one day Percy could be elected president.

In 1966, Percy challenged the longtime Democratic incumbent, Paul Douglas, for a U.S. Senate seat in Illinois. Percy had once been a student of Douglas's at the University of Chicago. The race between professor and student was hard-fought. The polls were tight. Then, six weeks before Election Day, something horrific occurred.

In the early morning hours of September 18, 1966, Percy's daughter, Valerie Jeanne, was stabbed to death in her bedroom by an unknown assailant. Her stepmother, Lorraine Percy, came across the intruder in the home after hearing some noise. She was the first to discover Valerie's body. The young girl was twenty-one years old. To this day her murder remains unsolved.

I was at home with my family outside Chicago when the murder occurred. Early that morning my mom and dad arrived at our home, and woke us up to tell us the horrible news. By then, the story was being broadcast on television and radio across the country.

I was the Percys' congressman, and as CEO of the Bell & Howell Corporation, Chuck Percy had been one of the prominent businessmen to endorse and assist me in my initial race for Congress four years earlier, and I valued his friendship. We didn't have many similarities. He had run a successful business, and at that point I had not had a leadership role in the business world. He was wealthy; I wasn't. But since he was running for the Senate, and I was running for reelection to the House, we campaigned together and hoped we'd soon be working together in the Congress.

The news of his daughter's murder was devastating. We felt it also because our oldest daughter, then ten, was also named Valerie Jeanne. We couldn't begin to imagine the horror parents would feel at the loss of a child, and in such a savage way. My immediate instinct was to get dressed and drive to the Percy house on Lake Michigan to see if I could be helpful.

I found myself in the middle of a frantic situation. The Percy family was deeply shaken, trying to handle the terrible event as best they could. A devout Christian Scientist, Chuck was in a room upstairs with a spiritual counselor. The house was already teeming with investigators and police from multiple jurisdictions, including the FBI. A crowd of reporters had gathered outside the Percy residence. The phone was ringing constantly. I stepped in and spent the next few days at the Percy home, assisting the various investigators in their efforts, dealing with press queries, and trying to provide a buffer between a grieving family and the outside world.

Percy promptly suspended his campaign and with his family left Illinois to grieve out of the media spotlight. When Chuck returned to Illinois, he announced that he would continue his Senate race, a campaign his daughter Valerie had helped as a volunteer. Percy won his contest that November and went on to serve in the United States Senate for eighteen years.

Valerie Percy's murder had all the elements of what we think of when we use the word *crisis*. It was unexpected. It was sudden. It was terrible. And it completely changed the environment. Chuck Percy had the delicate task of balancing his desire to serve with the terrible grief for his lost child, as well as the pressing needs of his heartbroken family.

His political opponent, Senator Douglas, had to consider how to react to the devastating tragedy while still trying to discreetly draw contrasts with the man seeking to replace him. The Percy campaign had to deal with a pressing media corps and an international spotlight while seeking the support of the people of Illinois. Local, county, state, and federal investigators had to keep from tripping over each other while operating under intense scrutiny and with a growing awareness that they couldn't solve a murder that gripped the nation. Reporters had to sort fact from fiction and decide how to inform the public without catering to sensationalism.

My role in all of this was peripheral, but memorable. There was no guidebook or road map telling any of us what to do or how to do it. We were all finding our way, trying to manage an unexpected, chaotic, and tragic situation as best we were able.

Over the course of many decades, I have witnessed different leaders respond to a variety of crises with varying degrees of success. In October 1962, the Cuban Missile Crisis and the possibility of nuclear war loomed large for our nation, and for me, running in my first campaign for Congress against a local Democrat who happened to also be named John Kennedy.

In 1974, as U.S. ambassador to NATO, I had to deal with an intense mediation between two members of our alliance, Greece and Turkey, which were poised to go to war with each other over the island of Cyprus. The following year, I was with President Ford in the Oval Office when Saigon fell on the final day of the war in Vietnam. And as George W. Bush's Secretary of Defense, I was involved in numerous crises, from recovering a downed American EP-3 aircraft and crew held captive by the Chinese military to the Abu Ghraib scandal to the 9/11 attacks, when I felt the building shake from the massive explosion on the other side of the Pentagon.

The road you don't travel is always smoother.
—Representative Duncan Hunter Sr. (R-CA)

Just as no war is identical to another, no two crises are likely to be identical, either. Revelations about sexual abuse involving a Penn State football staff member are quite different from, say, the BP oil spill, which in turn is notably different from a financial scandal at a local church. In each case human beings need to respond to a rapidly emerging, unexpected event. Leadership comes from recognizing that reality and using your God-given talents to make decisions, some of which, however well intentioned, may prove to be imperfect, even wrong.

In 1962, before he was elected president, Richard Nixon published a book called *Six Crises*. In it he discussed how he had handled six complex and different situations, from his investigation of American Soviet spy Alger Hiss to the accusations of financial impropriety that led to his nationally televised "Checkers" speech. The book gave readers insights into how he had coped with these crises and portrayed him as a problem solver who could tackle tough challenges effectively. In many instances, that was exactly who Nixon was. Yet his handling of the Watergate scandal some years later would be in a textbook on crisis management only as an example of what *not* to do.

So what knowledge can one impart on the critical issue of crisis management? Not enough, I'm afraid. What might make sense in handling one event might not be the best approach in another. Few crises have an obvious solution, and no decision that results from a crisis is likely to escape criticism or second-guessing. Nonetheless, there are a few guidelines that experience suggests are worth considering.

Trust your instincts. Success depends, at least in part, on the ability to "carry it off."

Perhaps the biggest mistake one can make is to fall into the trap of thinking that somewhere out there is a perfect response to every crisis. When Gerald Ford assumed the presidency after Richard Nixon's unprecedented resignation, there were only a few who might have advised him to turn around almost immediately and pardon his disgraced predecessor. But Ford understood better than most that Nixon had suffered terribly over Watergate and so had the country. He was convinced that our nation did not need a long-drawn-out "trial of the century" with the former President in the dock. Even Ford's harshest critics now concede that he made the right decision.

At the moment, years later, when Flight 77 hit the Pentagon, did I instantly fashion a perfect long-term crisis response plan? Hardly—life doesn't work that way. In the minutes after the building shook I didn't sit down and prepare a flowchart detailing precisely what steps needed to be taken. Instead, by instinct, I started moving, first in search of an explanation as to what happened . . . then looking to see if there were people injured who needed help . . . and only then beginning to think through the tasks we would have to undertake to prevent further attacks.

There was a need to advise the President and pass on what little information was available, gather the latest intelligence reporting, and meet with military leaders to decide on the next steps. None of us had much time to think things through. We had to trust our instincts.

Of course, sometimes letting your instincts take over can lead to unfortunate results. When Richard Nixon lost his bid for governor of California in 1962, two years after narrowly losing the presidency to John F. Kennedy, he conceded defeat in bitter and ungracious remarks in which he uttered the famous line to the assembled reporters: "You won't have Nixon to kick around anymore, because gentlemen, this is my last press conference." It was a personal crisis for Nixon, who believed he was finished in politics. Understandably, he felt down and apparently victimized by a hostile press; but his remarks came across as petulant and angry. It was no way to launch a political comeback, and his comment would haunt him and damage his relations with the press for years.

Following the fall of Saddam Hussein in 2003 after looting occurred in Baghdad, I uttered the phrase: "Stuff happens." I was intending to remind the press that some looting and disorder usually occur during every major upheaval—on occasion, even in our country. But my comment was taken as a sign of indifference to what was happening in Baghdad. It left an inaccurate and regrettable impression that stuck to me for some time to come.

Don't "overcontrol" like a novice pilot. Stay loose enough from the flow that you can observe and calibrate.

I n recent years, the famous British maxim from World War II— "Keep Calm and Carry On"—has seeped back into the popular culture. So much so that it has become almost a cliché. But there is wisdom there. Everything that is done in a crisis is observed by someone—whether members of your family, colleagues at work, or a larger group such as the employees and shareholders of a corporation, the American people, or even people across the globe. As such, a leader's words and actions need to be well calibrated.

When something completely out of the norm occurs, the last thing a leader should do is panic or, perhaps more to the point, give the appearance of panic. Besides being unhelpful to decision-making, it reduces confidence in those looking to you for reassurance and a sense that there will be a path forward.

Shortly after the shooting of Ronald Reagan in March 1981, Secretary of State Al Haig said to the White House press corps and the country, "I am in control here." Haig was trying to reassure the nation that even though the President was incapacitated, the country was in capable hands. Unfortunately, his comment left the opposite impression. Since he was not the Vice President, but remembered by many as a retired general, Haig's comment had an ominous dimension.

Thinking back on 9/11, I cannot recall feeling panic—or seeing it in others. When the Pentagon trembled with the force of a massive explosion, a different kind of instinct kicked in—a sense of focus. A sense that there was a job to do, and that there were a great many people—the President of the United States foremost among them—who would be looking to us for guidance in the wake of a horrific tragedy. Many in the Pentagon that morning ran toward the problem, instead of away. They ran into the burning part of the building to rescue the wounded. The President too demonstrated remarkable composure. Just a few hours after the attack, the President said, "Don, we'll be coming to you soon."

> *The reason I don't worry about society is nineteen*
> *people knocked down two buildings and killed thousands.*
> *Hundreds of people ran into those buildings to save them.*
> *I'll take those odds every [expletive deleted] day.*
> —JON STEWART

When I arrived at the Pentagon's national command center to be briefed and weigh our options, smoke was seeping into the room through the ventilation system. After a few hours, it became difficult for us to operate. I was urged to fly to an off-site command center. We had already evacuated nonessential Pentagon employees, but I felt it was important to stay in order to demonstrate that the headquarters of the world's most powerful military was still in operation and that we would not be shut down by a handful of terrorists.

During Hurricane Katrina, still another crisis, the Bush administration underestimated the scrutiny that would follow the President's actions in the aftermath of the 2005 storm. He first was criticized for not returning to Washington from his ranch in Texas until two days after the storm came ashore. Worse, his decision to fly low over New Orleans en route to Washington, D.C., without landing in the vicinity gave an impression of detachment. The President and his staff were rightly aware that, were he to land in Louisiana, his presence on the ground would distract resources away from the still urgent relief efforts. But the image of the President in comfort and safety looking out the window of Air Force One at the devastation below became an unfortunate symbol, of which his critics made ample and effective use.

It is difficulties that show what men are.
—*Epictetus*

Whatever the crisis may be, it is important to make sure there are people down the chain of command who are aware of what is happening, and are ready to step in should something else unexpected take place.

During the 1980s and '90s when I was in business, I was active in what were called "continuity of government" exercises. The exercises were designed to ensure the survival of an effective U.S. government in the event of a major catastrophe—such as a nuclear war. Every year or so, I would get a call asking me to report to a secret site. Those involved would be out of communication with the outside world for a period of days, as we rehearsed a range of possible crisis scenarios.

Exercises and an actual event are of course notably different. It's one thing to participate in a simulation of an attack against America. It was quite another to be experiencing events in real time, with the conflicting information, the anxiety in people's voices, and the reality that colleagues may be dead or dying.

On the morning of 9/11, for the first time in U.S. history, the continuity-of-government plans were activated. The President was whisked aboard Air Force One and taken to the security of a U.S. Air Force base. Vice President Cheney was moved deep below the White House to a hardened complex. Though I decided not to go, the Defense Department plan called for me to board a helicopter and fly to a secure remote site. Instead, I had the Deputy Secretary of Defense, Paul Wolfowitz, go to ensure an uninterrupted command. He was not enthusiastic, but he understood his duty.

Of course, not every business deals with the need for continuity on this scale. Nonetheless it is still worth thinking through who will step in to take on responsibility in an organization if the leader is unavailable. That chief executive may become incapacitated or key members of the executive team might leave the company unexpectedly. There could be a scandal that implicates a senior financial officer. For this reason, if no other, it is wise to have deputies in place in key areas—individuals to step forward and take on the job of the principal.

First reports are often wrong.

In a crisis, conflicting reports are the norm. Leaders must therefore learn to accept incoming raw information with caution. Sometimes with a great deal of caution. It takes time for the truth to emerge, while the temptation to rush to judgment is great.

During the evacuation of Saigon in 1975, Secretary of State Henry Kissinger publicly announced that all Americans had been evacuated from Vietnam. On hearing the report, Secretary of Defense Jim Schlesinger quickly informed the White House that while everyone else had gotten out, the Marines who had been defending the embassy compound were still on the ground. Kissinger was not happy that what he had told the press turned out to be not accurate. Those of us in the Oval Office with President Ford discussed what to do. We could let the inaccurate information stand, in anticipation and hope that before long the Marines would safely make it out. Or we could add to an already difficult and confusing day by issuing a correction.

With most problems, one learns 80 percent of what can be known relatively rapidly, but the remaining 20 percent can take forever.

As White House Chief of Staff I argued that we needed to correct the error. "This war has been marked by so many lies and evasions," I said to President Ford, "that it is not right to have the war end with one last lie."[8] Ford agreed and sent his press secretary, Ron Nessen, down to the press to issue the correction.

In the early hours after the September 11, 2001, attacks, members of the National Security Council and other civilian and military advisors had to cope with a number of inaccurate early reports. There was, for example, information circulating that the U.S. military had shot down an airliner. There were reports that the State Department had been bombed. There were reports that a plane en route to the United States from Korea had been hijacked. Various news broadcasters speculated on the air about a connection between the attacks and Saddam Hussein. All of these reports turned out to be false. Nonetheless, President Bush and his team had to keep taking steps to try to defend the nation without parsing every new bulletin for its accuracy. If you're waiting to get a fuller, more perfect picture, you may end up responding too late.

Proper preparation prevents poor performance.

Hurricane Katrina, which wreaked havoc some ten months into President Bush's second term, set the tone for his next three years. The federal, state, and local government responses, as reported by the press, fed a narrative of incompetence, bureaucratic bungling, hapless leadership, and indifference to the plight of minorities. The reality was that the President and his administration had mobilized more resources more rapidly than in any response to a catastrophic event in American history—46,000 National Guard soldiers and 22,000 active duty troops and more than $85 billion in humanitarian and reconstruction aid. But these facts couldn't make up for the scope of the devastation and the gross incompetence at the local and state levels in Louisiana.

Another reality of the Katrina response was that the agency tasked with being in charge of a major catastrophic disaster—the new Department of Homeland Security (DHS), of which the Federal Emergency Management Agency is a part—was not prepared to deal with a disaster of that magnitude. DHS had been created in haste in the weeks after 9/11, under pressure from the Congress to come up with a quick legislative fix. Katrina became DHS's first test of its readiness and capabilities. Both were found lacking. With its only real power being the ability to grant contracts and dispense money, the fledgling department was no match for the scope and severity of that crisis.

> *Luck is what happens when*
> *preparation meets opportunity.*
> —Seneca

The best way to deal with a crisis, of course, is to be prepared before it occurs. Shortly after the 9/11 attack, I sought approval from Congress to establish the office of an Assistant Secretary of Defense for Homeland Defense, a position that had never existed. It turned out to be a fortunate decision. It allowed the Department of Defense to have in place a capability to respond rapidly to any major crises within our borders—not only terrorist attacks, but major earthquakes, hurricanes, or other catastrophic events where military assets might need to be rapidly deployed.

Preparing for events that have not happened and may never happen can be costly, but it is important for business leaders and senior managers to spend time thinking about potential problems that could confront them and how they might respond.

Finally, there is perhaps nothing more valuable than experience. During the American invasion of Grenada in 1983, the United States military suffered a humbling experience. Though the initiative there was successful, the branches of the U.S. armed forces were unable to communicate with each other as they moved to gain control over the island. Each of the services had purchased their own equipment with insufficient thought beforehand as to whether they could communicate with the others. The Navy had their own communication devices, the Air Force had something different, and the Army had something else entirely. As a result, members of the most powerful military in the world had to resort to using public pay phones. In the years following, major efforts were undertaken to promote interoperability and jointness among the Army, Navy, Air Force, and Marines.

That lesson is equally applicable to the private sector. It can be helpful to study the experiences of competitors to see how they have handled, or failed to handle, various crises. One would have thought, for example, that the officials at BP would have studied the mistakes made during the *Exxon Valdez* oil spill in order to handle a similar situation more skillfully. Airline companies prepare themselves for how to deal with their responsibilities in the event of a fatal plane crash. Mistakes will always be made, but the least we can do is try to make original mistakes, rather than repeating old ones.

Speed kills. It creates opportunities, denies the enemy options, and can hasten his collapse.

A cting quickly in a crisis can instill confidence in those still reeling from events. It can also give one an advantage over an enemy or competitor. One of the more impressive examples of a company acting swiftly and skillfully in a crisis occurred in the autumn of 1982, after seven people in Chicago died from poisoned Tylenol capsules.

How Tylenol's parent company, Johnson & Johnson, responded is considered a textbook example of excellent crisis management even thirty years later. The company quickly issued a nationwide recall of Tylenol products, costing them millions of dollars. It halted production of Tylenol capsules, canceled all advertisements, and offered to replace capsules that already had been purchased with newly tested, safe tablets. It then developed what has since become standard for over-the-counter medications: tamper-proof containers.

In the case of the Tylenol scare, speed proved essential. The corporate leaders took control of events before a mind-set developed that all J&J products could be dangerous and before a perception formed that the company was unwilling or unable to deal with the problem responsibly. Because of their efforts, Johnson & Johnson's stock rebounded within a year. Today, consumers purchasing Tylenol capsules give little if any thought to an incident that could have permanently damaged, if not destroyed, that brand.

At the same time, speed can be a risk in a crisis. Acting too quickly can lead to poor decisions, especially if actions are taken before you have the key information and the necessary planning in place. In the aftermath of the 9/11 attacks, there was considerable pressure on the Bush administration to *do something— anything*—in response to the deaths of more than three thousand people. Understandably, President Bush shared that sentiment and was anxious to waste no time in crafting a response that was more than simply "pounding sand," as he put it. But he understood the danger of hasty action. Responding rashly, without a solid strategy in mind, might assuage the impatient, but it would not be a recipe for longer-term public support. It took time to fashion a plan, select the right targets, and move the necessary forces and capabilities into place. We needed cooperation from other countries, including Afghanistan's neighbors, some of which were skittish about supporting the U.S.-led operation. In a crisis, then, a leader's skills will be tested in managing the tempo as well as the nature of a particular response. The danger of acting too swiftly or not swiftly enough can be a challenge either way.

A crisis can result in people spreading inaccurate information, as well as information that while not inaccurate, lacks context, which can contribute to a sense of panic. If there is a public interest at stake, share the nonsensitive and unclassified information you have with the media and the outside world. Tell them what you know—and, just as important, tell them what you don't know.

Providing information to the public has its perils, of course, especially if it later turns out to be incorrect. Even in a crisis, the media and public have little patience or sympathy for those who, even with the best of intentions, say things that later prove to be wrong.

But getting information out quickly can be of help in accomplishing your goals. President Kennedy won overwhelming support for his actions during the Cuban Missile Crisis in large part because his ambassador to the United Nations, Adlai Stevenson, made an impressive case to the Security Council about the buildup of Soviet missiles on the island. A year earlier, when Kennedy oversaw the failed Bay of Pigs invasion, which sought to remove Castro, the President again earned support by quickly acknowledging what had gone wrong and accepting responsibility.

One of the more famous examples of this happened during the Revolutionary War when a group of Continental soldiers considered a mutiny over Congress's refusal to pay their salaries. As the commander of those forces, George Washington had pressed Congress repeatedly for more aid to his men and had failed. Warned of the crisis within the Army, Washington held himself accountable in a dramatic fashion. Appearing before a group of the conspirators, the revered general took personal responsibility for the condition of the Army and pledged to do all he could to right the situation. Then he held out a letter he had received from a member of the Congress. Before reading the letter, Washington paused. There was quiet in the room for an uncomfortably long period. As the crowd became curious about the general's hesitation, Washington looked up at them. With perfect timing, he said, "Gentlemen, you will permit me to put on my spectacles, for I have not only grown gray but almost blind in the service of my country." The emotional statement brought some in the crowd to tears. If Washington could sacrifice so much to lead their army, how, the soldiers wondered, could they now turn against his leadership?

Leaders often win plaudits for successful actions, even if the credit properly belongs to a much larger group or others. But if they accept the accolades, they had best also be prepared to accept responsibility and be accountable. If you are not prepared to live with the fact that your actions may lead to failure, then you probably ought not to be in leadership.

You never want a serious crisis go to waste.
—*Rahm Emanuel*

President Obama's first White House Chief of Staff, and later mayor of Chicago, Rahm Emanuel, received some grief for his comment "You never want a serious crisis go to waste." While to some his remark sounded sinister, it points to a fundamental truth. A crisis offers a leader a chance to act boldly to improve things in ways he might otherwise not be able to do. The shock of a sudden and unexpected event can help leaders dislodge the status quo. The urgency of a crisis allows for greater latitude in decision-making and more opportunity to develop a consensus for change.

After the Soviet Union launched the world's first satellite into orbit, the perception developed that America was "losing" the space race. It created a crisis, at least a psychological one, in the minds of Americans. I served as a member of the House Committee on Science and Astronautics some months after President Kennedy proposed that the United States land an American on the moon and return him safely by the end of the decade. It was an audacious goal, and one that certainly would not have won widespread public support had it not been for the Soviet Union's highly visible, indeed spectacular success and the critical challenge it posed to global U.S. leadership.

President Lyndon Johnson also took advantage of a crisis atmosphere for a quite different end: to win support of his prosecution of the Vietnam War. After the Gulf of Tonkin attack on U.S. naval vessels in August 1964, the President persuaded 416 members of the U.S. House of Representatives to support a resolution giving him more authority in Southeast Asia. The resolution passed without a single dissenting vote.

Many of us who voted in favor of the President's request, as I recorded in my notes at the time, did so with misgivings.[9] I for one wondered whether the authorization might be interpreted too broadly. Over the next four years, LBJ carried a dog-eared copy of that resolution in his pocket almost everywhere he went. He didn't hesitate to cite it when it served his purposes.

When I returned to the Pentagon in January 2001, President Bush had given me the mandate to work to transform the Defense Department, making the military quicker and more flexible for the new century. He wanted a military ready for the Information Age, not the Industrial Age. It was a tough assignment, considering that some of the changes the President sought ran directly against Washington's fixed interests in the Congress, the defense contractor community, and the permanent bureaucracy in the

Department of Defense, each of which advocated for particular weapons systems and fiercely defended its interests. The 9/11 attacks provided an impetus to achieve many of the changes that were needed to meet the threats of the twenty-first century. Most of the previously intractable opposition yielded in the face of the new and uncertain threats to our national security.

In almost every crisis—whether in a small organization or as part of a dispute between nations—there is one consistent thread: Leaders must have the ability to communicate effectively with those affected. More often than not, that is done through the media. And reporters bring an entirely new dimension to unfolding events.

CHAPTER EIGHT

MEETING THE PRESS

In 1962, I conducted my first press conference. I was beginning my first run for election to the U.S. House of Representatives. I was twenty-nine years old and probably looked even younger. To most people in Illinois's 13th Congressional District, I was a complete unknown. Facing reporters and cameras and talking in effect to hundreds, if not thousands, of people whose votes I was seeking was a totally new experience for me. It did not come naturally.

Fear of public speaking is often cited as one of the more common fears that people have. My view of how to handle it is straightforward and parallels my attitude about a lot of difficult tasks: Just do it!

After a few weeks on the campaign trail, my wife, Joyce, and my friend and campaign manager Ned Jannotta took me aside and told me the brutal truth: I was not a good public speaker. I put my hands in my pockets, they said. I looked at my notes more than at the audience. I spoke too closely to the microphone.

Very few of us are good at something when we first start out. We

There are only three responses to questions from the press: "I know and will tell you"; "I know and I can't tell you"; and "I don't know."—Dan Rather

get better with practice. Joyce and Ned decided I needed to practice in an empty auditorium while they offered blistering words of criticism, which as you might imagine was not the most pleasant experience. I practiced my stump speech and they shouted things like "Stand up straight. Stop popping the microphone. Keep your hands out of your pockets." It was like training an ape. Do it right, you get a banana. Do it wrong, you get popped with a club. Eventually I started to improve.

Let your words be as few as will express the sense you wish to convey and above all let what you say be true.

—Stonewall Jackson

The best advice I can offer about public speaking, whether to an audience of a thousand people or a single reporter, is to always talk about something you know. Seems obvious, yet on a number of occasions I've seen folks give remarks on subjects about which they have only a passing familiarity—and stumble in front of a crowd at the first question. It can be awkward for everyone.

Just as important, make a speech your own. Few communication tools are more valuable to leaders than their public remarks. Yet there are some who get a talented speechwriter to craft a fine speech, then spend too little time on the speech themselves. As a result, the presentation can fall flat, because it doesn't fit with the speaker. The remarks don't sound like the individual delivering them.

If in writing it takes over thirty minutes to write the first two paragraphs, select another subject.

—Raymond Aron

Anybody who wants a speech to work needs to invest time on it, work it, edit it, re-edit it, and change it around until it is truly yours. I edit a speech so many times that it occasionally has exasperated those assisting me. In one instance, a writer came back to me with my latest round of edits. He said, "Mr. Secretary, you can edit what I wrote all you like. But you changed a quote by Pericles. You can't edit Pericles."

I took the speech back, looked over that passage, scribbled something on the page, and handed it back. The writer was not any happier. I had written, "As Pericles *should have said*."

You're either a target or a source.
—Robert Novak

In almost every organization occasions arise when senior management will need to deal with the media. In business those interactions are certainly not as frequent or well publicized as they are for a president, a Cabinet secretary, or a member of Congress. Nonetheless, for any leader they can be important opportunities to communicate the purpose of an endeavor, gain publicity for a product or a policy, or explain something that has not gone well. Because government officials have a responsibility to inform the people they serve, their interactions with reporters are frequent. This has both advantages and disadvantages—depending on whether you are a "source" or a "target," or both.

It may be an unusual comment to hear from a once-public figure who weathered his share of public controversies, but I actually like the folks who work in the media. Well, most of them. Journalists as a rule perform a valuable public service. They can expose corruption and wrongdoing. They identify areas of mismanagement. They travel around the world to cover stories of war and upheaval. Journalists are important in keeping the public informed, which is essential for the health of our democracy. Reporters have contributed throughout history—sometimes losing their lives in the process. Ernie Pyle reported from the front lines during World War II and died on the battlefield. More recently, *At-*

lantic editor Michael Kelly was killed while reporting on the war in Iraq. Many others could be mentioned.

The attacks of September 11 and the military response President Bush ordered in the weeks and months thereafter put a heavy responsibility on the Department of Defense to keep the public informed. As a result, almost every week or two I stepped in front of the cameras, whether in the Pentagon or at a military base or in a foreign country. I believed it was important to communicate on the activities of the Department, to learn what questions were on the minds of the reporters, and, on occasion, to correct things that were flat-out inaccurate. My primary objective was to communicate the information we wanted to convey. Before a press conference, it's important to know what the "news of the day" is so you have a sense of what reporters will be likely to ask, but my focus tended to be on conveying what needed to be said. That's why we would typically begin news conferences with a brief prepared statement before going to the reporters' questions. Their questions, of course, were designed to advance the reporters' story lines, not ours.

As a result of those experiences, it became my practice to think of the press as one of the many groups that leaders in our interconnected world needed to engage. Over the years I have developed a few basic rules for dealing with the media.

I find journalists generally to be well-informed, interested, willing to learn, and, on a personal basis, outgoing and friendly. But it can be a mistake to place too much faith in their affability. Most are perfectly willing to have a friendly cup of coffee with you one afternoon and then slam you with a two-by-four on the front page the next morning. Correspondents are not looking for friendships; they're looking for sources and scoops. They are, in short, doing their jobs.

As easy as it can be to bash the press—and there is on occasion ample justification to do so—indulging in or expressing negative feelings toward this important and influential collection of individuals is not particularly useful. I observed that attitude up close in Presidents Johnson and Nixon during their toughest days. Their hostility toward the media did not serve either of them well, nor did it help them get their messages across. "If one morning I walked on top of the water across the Potomac River," Lyndon Johnson reportedly fumed, "the headline that afternoon would read: 'The President Can't Swim.'" LBJ seethed at the coverage he received over the Vietnam War and as a result was accused of committing the cardinal sin for a politician: misleading the press. As for Nixon, the difference between him and his political rival John F. Kennedy, the legendary *Washington Post* editor Ben Bradlee once observed, "is simply this: Jack Kennedy really liked newspaper people and he really enjoyed sparring with journalists."

From what I observed, JFK did like the reporters who covered him, and that was one of the reasons he was so effective in cultivating positive coverage. By contrast, Nixon's discomfort and hostility came through to his detriment. His preoccupation with "enemies" including in the press may well have contributed to some of his more unfortunate decisions.

I have known more than a few leaders in business and government who were not comfortable talking to reporters and who harbored an intense dislike of the media after being burned once or twice. They talked only to those they liked and trusted—a group that diminished in size over time. Those who adopt that approach usually come to regret their unwillingness to engage.

People respond in direct proportion to the extent you reach out to them.

—Vice President Nelson Rockefeller

I learned something about the importance of outreach from Nelson Rockefeller, the former governor of New York, then serving as Vice President. He offered an insight into human nature that is useful to keep in mind when dealing with everyone, including the press.

As we rode together in a presidential motorcade, there were sizable crowds, five or six people deep on both sides of the street, hoping to catch a glimpse of President Ford, who was in a limousine ahead of us. Our car, an open-top convertible, followed the Secret Service cars. The Vice President turned to me, his thick-rimmed glasses perched on his nose. "Watch this," he said. He put one hand out the open window and gave a slight wave to the crowd. He caught several people's eyes, and they waved back in a similarly muted manner.

"Now watch this." Rocky waved in a somewhat more extravagant way, his arm sweeping a small arc beyond the open window. Sure enough, people along the route saw him and responded with exactly the same waves. Then he said, "Watch this." He turned his body toward the side and raised both of his arms, waving them from side to side. Once again, the people along the route repeated his motion, waving their arms back at him.

Then to my surprise Rockefeller stood up in the back of the car, extending his body above the retracted convertible roof. He waved vigorously with a beaming, ear-to-ear grin. His exuberance was promptly matched by the crowd's response. The American flags some were holding were practically blurred, they were being waved so fast. The crowd became fully energized.

As Rocky sat down, he turned to me with a satisfied smile. "Don, there's a lesson there," he said. "People respond in direct proportion to the extent you reach out to them." In private interactions, Rockefeller could be an intimidating bully, as I had observed firsthand a number of times in White House meetings. Yet I could see why he had been such a successful politician for so many years. He knew that if you reach out to people, generally they'll reciprocate.

In 2011, when I was preparing for a book tour to talk about my memoir, *Known and Unknown*, I knew I would be asked to relive some of the more controversial moments in my career. I was cautioned by friends to decline invitations from some of the media commentators most likely to be difficult. Better to avoid tough, unpleasant questions altogether, they advised. When an opportunity arose to appear on Jon Stewart's *Daily Show*, some suggested I skip it. I understood that Stewart was not by anyone's definition a Bush administration enthusiast. But I had seen a couple of video clips of his interviews and, while hard-hitting, he was without question an intelligent, serious person. So I decided to follow the Rockefeller Rule.

I hope I'm not hurting Stewart's career by saying this, but my appearance on *The Daily Show* turned out to be one of the more interesting and enjoyable exchanges I had with a TV commentator. I had by then done more than a dozen interviews, and noted that a number of the interviewers obviously hadn't read my book—including some of the bigger names in journalism. Stewart was not like that. He listened. His questions were informed and thoughtful, albeit with a healthy dose of humor and a few profanities laced throughout. Most important, by going on his show I was able to reach a much different audience—a more diverse and dare I say younger crowd than that which tunes in to the nightly network news.

There are always going to be some characters in the media who have it out for you or your point of view. They probably aren't worth your time. But those are the exceptions. I hope more conservatives and Republicans will take a chance on appearing on less friendly networks to get their views out to a broader audience. Similarly, some liberals and Democrats boycott places like Fox News. That is as unhelpful to them as it is to those networks' viewers. We all benefit from healthy exchanges with those who don't share our views, as do the audiences.

A few decades ago—even a few years ago—nobody would have imagined that a thoughtful political exchange could take place on a network called Comedy Central. Yet today there are a large and still-growing number of outlets through which Americans can talk with one another. The sources of information today are almost infinite and nearly instant—from digital cameras to YouTube to talk radio to Skype to blogs to literally hundreds of 24/7 television and radio channels. This is all new, and a welcome change from the days when all news was filtered through gatekeepers at the three major television networks and a handful of newspapers.

Not all negative press is unearned. If you're getting it, see if there's a reason.

Those in the business world tend to have a distinctly different experience with the media than those in government.

Rarely does a CEO face a public grilling from a reporter on a TV show. With few exceptions—such as during the 2010 BP oil spill in the Gulf of Mexico—a corporate leader can go through an entire career without having to hold a nationally televised press conference. To the extent that a company executive can stay out of the headlines, that's probably not a bad thing.

Senior executives do, however, have to engage with a group of professionals who are not unlike journalists—namely, the securities analysts who closely track industries and companies and publish their findings for interested investors. These analysts often speak with the financial press as experts on a given industry or company.

In 1977, some months before I arrived at Searle, a company spokesman made a presentation to a large gathering of securities analysts. Because his prediction didn't pan out, some analysts assumed the worst—that they had been misled. As a result, they soured on the company, published critical reports, and the stock price suffered.

The temptation after such an experience might have been to put distance between the company's leadership and the industry securities analysts to avoid still more critical reports. I did the opposite. Not long after I arrived, I invited some of those same analysts to the corporate headquarters in Skokie, Illinois, just north of Chicago. However, rather than meeting them in a group, I invited them to come in one at a time so that our senior managers and I could address their specific questions and concerns directly.

Along with our chief operating officer, John Robson, and chief financial officer, Jim Denny, I met with each analyst individually for coffee the morning of their visit. We explained Searle's strategy and answered any questions they had. We then offered direct access to the company's division presidents, and encouraged the analysts to ask anything they liked. After that, they were free to walk around and talk to anyone—no matter their position. I did impose one condition. At the end of the day, I wanted them to come back, have another cup of coffee with us, and give us their insights about the company's strengths and weaknesses. These were, in effect, investigative reporters and keen observers. I wanted to know what they had learned that we might not have known. I also hoped to have an opportunity to correct any false impressions they might have come away with, and put things in proper context.

In an organization of significant size, it's of course not possible to talk to everyone. Outsiders, especially those with a trained eye for emerging problems, can often find out things senior managers have not yet discovered.

I adopted a similar attitude at the Pentagon. The Department of Defense is an enormous institution—so vast that no Secretary of Defense can possibly know a fraction of what is happening at any given time. Pentagon reporters have a network of sources and are able to discover troubling issues long before they are likely to make their way up to the Secretary of Defense. By identifying problem areas, the press often performs a valuable service both for the Defense Department and for the American people.

That was one of the reasons I found it useful each morning to peruse the "Early Bird"—a summary of news items about the Department. Sometimes I would jot notes in the margin of articles and pass them along to officials or the public affairs office to try to find out more. When someone was quoted saying something about the Department I found interesting or of concern, I didn't hesitate to pick up the phone and ask about it. And if I found a story that was not factual, the reporter might expect to hear a thought or two the next time I saw them.

Reporters were one of the main reasons the actual circumstances surrounding the death of former NFL star Pat Tillman became known. When I heard that Corporal Tillman had been killed in Afghanistan in April 2004, the first report I saw was that he had died in combat with Taliban forces. In fact, the U.S. Army awarded him a medal for heroism. Later it turned out that those early reports were not accurate. He had been killed by friendly fire from soldiers in his own unit. That fact was unacceptably slow in coming out, even though some in his unit and in the Army command must have known what had happened. His family—and the American people—deserved to know the truth, and the media played a useful role in making sure the truth got out.

Don't accept an inaccurate premise in a question. Rephrase it if necessary.

The natural human inclination is to agree with a premise or argument contained in a question, instead of challenging it. And, unsurprisingly, reporters prefer to have you answer their question the way they ask it. But their question may contain a hidden argument, sometimes even one that is favorable to you. But if you accept it, it can boomerang back later on.

Good reporters can be provocateurs. They know in advance what questions they need to ask to get a lively quote. Some reporters fashion their questions in a way that can put the interviewee on the defensive.

*Arguments of convenience can lack integrity and
often come back to trip you up.*

What I do in such circumstances is to rephrase the question so it
is based on a premise that I consider more accurate or germane. By
doing so, you can then give a response that is based on the actual
facts.

I remember being in New York City in 1965 and tuning in to
a local news report on the conservative columnist and author
William F. Buckley's quixotic campaign for mayor. A brilliant
speaker—lively, intelligent, humorous, and with, as he might
have said, a sesquipedalian vocabulary—he was running for office
to make the case for conservatism in a city not known for anything slightly resembling it. (Asked by a reporter what he'd do if
he won, he famously retorted, "Demand a recount.") The local
reporter told Buckley that he had been interviewing one of the
candidate's supporters. This pro-Buckley voter allegedly said he
was supporting Buckley because he would run black New Yorkers
out of the city.

Buckley, in a calm and measured manner, responded something to this effect: "Well, let's say you did interview a supporter
of mine this morning. And let's assume you asked the question
the way you have indicated and the person actually answered
your question the way you have said. And your question to me is:
'What's my reaction?'" Pausing, Buckley then shifted tone and an-
grily shouted, "My answer is: You can take your swamp fever vote!
I don't want it, and I don't need it!"

Persuasion is a two-edged sword—
reason and emotion, plunge it deep.
—Dr. Lew Sarett

Buckley's response has stuck in my head for decades. It had drama, substance, and emotion. Before answering the question he had raised doubt about the accuracy of the reporter's assertion, suggesting it was a fabrication designed to embarrass the candidate.

Buckley's answer reminded me of an observation by professor, poet, and author Dr. Lew Sarett, who was married to my mother's sister and had a voice that was mesmerizing for a young boy. He once said, "Persuasion is a two-edged sword—reason and emotion, plunge it deep." Emotion is what gets people interested and energized. But it is reason that sustains it. When making an argument, keep both in mind.

Record interviews to ensure accuracy.

When I had one-on-one interviews with reporters I made a practice of taping the conversation. I often asked reporters to make tapes of their own, so they could refer back to the recordings for accuracy. When I was in the Pentagon the second time, our practice was to post the transcript of an interview on the DoD website when the article was published. Reporters understood this in advance, which may have encouraged them to be especially careful in their use of quotes attributed to me. The value of this approach was never more obvious than in my dealings with Bob

Woodward, whose third book on the George W. Bush administration put words in my mouth I had not uttered. Originally, when I was asked by the folks in the White House to cooperate with Woodward, I declined. I agreed reluctantly only when I was told that it was a request by the President.

When Woodward's book was published, we simultaneously released the complete transcript of his interview with me, which I had told him we would do. One blogger took the time to compare what Woodward wrote about our interview with the actual transcript and concluded, "Rather than practicing history, Mr. Woodward was writing a story in which the material he gathered as a journalist is routinely compromised in the service of his narrative."[10]

Nothing proves more persuasive than a clearly stated fact.

Ours is a world awash in opinion, punditry, and prognostication. Clearly stated facts tend to crowd out conjecture, particularly as a story develops over time. Harold Geneen, the former CEO of ITT, once wrote, "There is no word in the English language that more strongly confers the intent of incontrovertibility than the word 'fact.'" He went on to note that few words are more misused. In many news stories and in everyday conversation we see phrases like "apparent facts," "assumed facts," or "the facts as we know them." But experience shows that those "facts" often turn out to be wrong.

In press conferences, I was a stickler for correcting reporters' questions when they were stated as opinions or as "the general consensus." Usually what was actually happening in a given situation was more complex.

Trust leaves on horseback but returns on foot.

Any leader may on occasion face a dilemma when informa-tion is printed about a company or organization that isn't fully accurate, even when it may be positive or helpful to that endeavor. Sometimes this is attributable to leaks from within the organization. Other times a reporter is simply wrong. Regardless of whose responsibility it is, it is a mistake to let inaccurate infor-mation stand. Providing information to the press that proves to be inaccurate will erode your credibility. If an error is made, correct it quickly—preferably within the hour.

When I was in the Pentagon, if other officials or staff members in the room observed that I had misstated a fact, they knew they ought to intervene and correct it, or slip me a note so I could do so right away. Some might find this embarrassing, but it can be far more em-barrassing for an error to find its way into print or television.

Credibility takes years to build, and one second to lose. The best way to avoid being accused of misleading the press is to be comfortable responding to questions by saying, "I don't know." For those who engage the press, it is best to get used to using that phrase. It's liberating. You are far better off being seen as not fully informed than as untruthful or evasive.

There are occasions when it's simply not possible to tell report-ers all you know about a matter. "I'm working my way over to figuring out how I won't answer," was how I phrased my response to a question about a sensitive CIA operation in Yemen during one Pentagon press conference. Likewise, when asked about the possibility of a war with Iraq, I responded, "Anyone who knows anything isn't talking and anyone with any sense isn't talking.

Avoid infatuation with or resentment of the press.
They have their job to do and you have yours. —*Joyce Rumsfeld*

Therefore the people that are talking to the media, by definition,
are people who don't know anything and people who don't have a
hell of a lot of sense."

If a reporter asks whether a military operation is under way in
a certain country, and the truth is that there was, is, or might be
such an operation, sometimes a response from the Rather rule, "I
know but I can't tell you," can be dangerous because it's taken as
a confirmation. The best thing to do is avoid that trap in the first
place. It was my practice to tell reporters in advance that I do not
respond to questions as to whether or not a sensitive operation is
under way. As Secretary of Defense, I had an obligation to say or
do nothing that in any way could endanger the men and women
in uniform or make their jobs more difficult.

Regrettably, not everyone sees it that way. There are individuals in the Pentagon and across the government who are privy to sensitive information and yet for whatever reason consider it acceptable or advantageous to them to pass secrets to journalists. Those who do so are committing crimes. They have lost their moorings and are willing to put the lives of men and women serving our nation at risk. We tried to see to it that anyone who leaked classified information was stopped and punished, but we were rarely successful.

Don't do or say things you would not want to see on the evening news.

It is best to assume that everything you or your organization has done, is doing, or does in the future will eventually become public knowledge. This is true whether you are serving in government or in the private sector. It is rare that a month goes by without some knuckleheads being embarrassed, reprimanded, or fired for something they posted on Twitter or Facebook. If you would not be comfortable having a comment shared with millions of people on the nightly news, then for goodness' sake don't say it, Tweet it, Skype it, or YouTube it—and, if you can, don't even think it in the first place.

With the press there is no "off the record."

Occasionally I would have an "off the record" session with a small group of the Pentagon press corps, usually when we traveled. These more casual discussions were designed to provide background information. Their intent was to engage the members of the press on a range of topics, quite apart from any particular deadline or news cycle, and have a more open discussion than is possible in a large group with cameras going and tape recorders whirring.

I recall only one time when anything from those sessions was written about, which says a good deal about the professionalism of the Pentagon press corps. Yet even in off-the-record sessions where the ground rules were clear, I understood that reporters were taking mental notes, and remembering things that could later find their way into their articles as background information, even if not attributed to me. So my advice to anyone thinking they might be able to keep something "off the record" is that it's probably futile. As I joked at one press conference, which was very much on the record, "Anything I say that I shouldn't have is off the record." With the media in the Information Age, "off the record" doesn't exist.

It would be a strategic error to assume that everyone in the press is seeking the truth.

—General Pete Schoomaker

Observers of a certain age may remember that in the immediate aftermath of the assassination of John F. Kennedy in 1963, various reporters and pundits immediately rushed to link the assassin, Lee Harvey Oswald, to "right-wing" extremists. It turned out, of course, that Oswald had lived in the Soviet Union, was married to a Soviet, and spent time in communist Cuba. There was far more evidence pointing to his being a Soviet sympathizer and a leftist than a right-winger.

You can wreck any story if you check the facts.
—ANONYMOUS CHICAGO REPORTER

As serious as that misrepresentation was, it was considerably easier to correct misleading information in those days when there were only a handful of major national newspapers and three or four evening news channels. Today, inaccurate and misleading information lingers forever on the Internet and in the minds of people who never see or hear a correction.

Today the media has reporters devoted to what they call "fact-checking." They critique what public figures say and chronicle any misstatement they may make. That's fair. Those of us who have been in the public eye expect it. But what happens when reporters or bloggers get much bigger things wrong? Who fact-checks the fact-checkers? What happens when false information circulates for years and adversely affects people's lives?

As for what is not true, you will always find abundance in the newspapers.
—THOMAS JEFFERSON

When I was at the Defense Department, *Newsweek* magazine published an article by an award-winning reporter claiming that members of the U.S. military at the Guantanamo Bay detention facility had flushed a Koran down a toilet. This led to a furious reaction among Muslims around the world, including riots in which innocent people were killed. *Newsweek* later admitted that their information was false and expressed regret over the story. But that provided precious little comfort to the victims or to their families. Meanwhile, those who reported and printed that false story went right on with their careers.

A lie travels halfway around the world before the truth gets its shoes on.
—*Mark Twain*

The problem of misleading or inaccurate reporting, or of a rush to judgment, is exacerbated in time of war. Major media outlets reach multiple audiences near instantaneously— the American people, members of the military, foreign officials, as well as the enemy. During the George W. Bush administration, America engaged in the first war of the twenty-first century. The United States government has proved to be painfully slow to adapt to the new challenges of the Information Age.

As a young boy during World War II, I remember following in the newspaper, weeks later, the advance of U.S. forces with pins on a map. The only news we received was from radio, newspapers, and short bulletins shown before the feature film at the local theater. The horrors of one of the worst wars in human history were often out of sight. There was no television back in those days. Photographs, news reports, and mail from servicemen and -women were censored to conceal military movements and protect the troops.

What we are experiencing today is vastly different. Thousands of photographs and millions of words get exchanged over the Internet from war zones all over the world. A single photo taken with a digital camera can have consequences that affect the morale of troops, build reactionary support for the enemy, undermine the mission back home, and even influence the outcome of a war. Videos of the enemy attacking U.S. forces can be uploaded onto YouTube from a smartphone and made available to an audience of millions in near real-time.

If the American revolutionaries had had reporters embedded with their units, it's next to impossible to imagine the United States winning the war for independence, given the repeated military failures and demoralizing hardships the colonial forces suffered. And if video cameras had been beaming back live images of U.S. forces fighting on the beaches of Normandy and among the hedgerows in France in 1944, the Allied advance would have come under withering public criticism—and conceivably been halted as a result.

The growing glut of unfiltered, raw information and images can be overwhelming. During the conflicts in Afghanistan and Iraq, the massive and unprecedented flow of information available to the public from all sorts of sources could be disorienting. It was as if our carburetors were being flooded. Some of the information was accurate and reported by legitimate news sources. Some was misleading and out of context. In other cases, news outlets such as Al Jazeera blatantly carried the lies our enemies fed them without any calibration whatsoever.

To this day our government lacks the ability to handle this new challenge skillfully. Official media operations still function much as they did decades ago: on a five-day-week, eight-hour-day media cycle, while world events are a 24/7 phenomenon. During the Bush administration, we took care that the information we put out was accurate—and we were rightly hammered if an official said anything that proved to be mistaken. Meanwhile terrorists put together media committees designed to disseminate false information about the United States and members of the military, and were considerably more successful than we were with our long-delayed rebuttals as we attempted to find out the facts.

"I am bound to say that I am reasonably satisfied with the traditional arrangement under which we politicians leave you journalists to get on with your job while you journalists tell us how to do ours," British Prime Minister Margaret Thatcher once said. "It is an arrangement which, for all its exasperations, is essential to the functioning of parliamentary democracy." That remains true today. But, it should be said, this requires accountability on both sides.

The desire of reporters, editors, and publishers to attract readers, viewers, or listeners is understandable. But in their haste to be first with a story, journalists today can take too little time to check facts or find a supporting source.

Sometimes biases can exacerbate the problem, such as the inaccurate story in 2012 by ABC's Brian Ross asserting that the shooting of innocents at a movie theater in Aurora, Colorado, was "connected with the Tea Party." There are certainly people who continue to believe that false report, just as there are those who still write that the United States orchestrated the attacks of September 11 or repeat the allegation that President Barack Obama is not an American citizen.

The desire for speed over accuracy is one of the more serious challenges facing the media today. Many of the incentives that drive the media—ratings, readership, awards, salaries, fame, profits, bonuses—produce pressure to be first with a sensational story. But if it is not the media's responsibility to get their facts right, then one has to ask, whose it is? And if the media fails in its responsibility, shouldn't there be a penalty, other than an occasional correction buried in the back pages days after the offense was committed?

In fact, there is a penalty. Every false story, every rush to judgment, every one-sided news report, leaves a bad mark on the journalism profession. As their credibility suffers, eventually people lose trust in certain media organizations and their audiences decline.

I know that most reporters did not enter their profession to report false information or mislead the public. Most entered because they aspired to inform their fellow citizens, uncover wrongdoing, and do work they could be proud of. I may have had my issues with a few journalists, but never with the notion of a free and unfettered press. When dictators take over a country, one of the first things they do is shut down the independent media. They know what all of us need to remember: A functioning and balanced press is a fundamental strength of democratic governance, and, at its best, journalism remains a noble calling.

CHAPTER NINE

WHAT WRESTLING CAN TEACH

John Wooden, the legendary coach of the UCLA Bruins basketball team, is widely regarded as one of the best coaches of all time. Asked what he thought was the key to winning ten national championships over twelve years—and an unprecedented seven championships in a row—Wooden's answer was obvious and insightful. He said he put a premium on discipline.

Discipline yourself and others won't need to.
—JOHN WOODEN

Wooden's teams probably practiced harder and longer than any other team in the NCAA. If you missed a layup, for example, you were running sprints after practice. As a result, Wooden's players, who included future NBA superstars like Kareem Abdul-Jabbar, were consistently in top physical condition. Those players learned an important lesson that is as applicable in life as it is on the basketball court: the direct relationship between effort and results. In other words, if you work hard enough at something, you will get better at it.

There are limitations, of course. I could have practiced basketball every day of my life and not come close to being a Kareem Abdul-Jabbar. In fact, when I was in high school, I tried out for the basketball team and quickly realized I wasn't tall enough, fast enough, or just plain good enough to make the team. But each of us can find the hobby, sport, or vocation that best suits our interests and talents. For me, that sport was wrestling.

Over the years, people attempting to sum up my approach to government and business have given considerable if occasionally amusing attention to my years as a high school, college, and Navy wrestler. Reporters went looking for wrestlers with whom I competed and quoted their critiques of my wrestling style, as though it were the key to how I operated. "Rumsfeld had earned a reputation for quick takedowns," one reporter wrote in the *New Yorker*. The image of some tough guy bouncing opponents around or pinning someone to the mat was irresistible. It also had very little to do with my life.

I did not try out for wrestling when I was fourteen years old because I was searching for a metaphor to guide the next six or seven decades of my career. Nor was I looking for a sport that would offer grand lessons about the world, though I guess, as with many things, wrestling does offer some.

I became a wrestler for more practical and mundane reasons. Because there is a range of weight classes in wrestling, I realized that it might be ideal for my less-than-imposing physique. Unlike in other sports, I could compete against opponents my size. So on a lark I entered my high school intramural tournament as a

Whatever you are, be a good one.—*Abraham Lincoln, county champion wrestler*

freshman, having not a lick of training or experience on the wrestling mat.

I don't know of another sport that is quite as physically grueling for the relatively short time that a wrestler is engaged in a match. It was not uncommon to finish practice with a puffed-up ear, mat burns, or assorted bruises. It turned out that I was reasonably good at wrestling, and I enjoyed it. If there's a lesson from that, it's this: Try to excel at something that best matches your abilities. Abraham Lincoln was six foot four. That made it unlikely he'd ever have a successful career as a jockey. Instead he also chose wrestling, a sport that made more sense given his famously long reach.

Working at something that best matches your abilities may seem a pretty obvious lesson, but some folks can toil away at tasks and vocations for which they simply are not well suited. How many frustrated artists or actors are there who spend their time trying to be something they weren't meant to be? There are people who don't have any interest in details yet decide to become lawyers, or who don't have a head for numbers but try to be accountants and end up disappointed.

Once you've wrestled, everything else in life is easy.
—DAN GABLE

Though physically suited for wrestling, I was new to the sport and didn't have the technical knowledge or experience to truly excel. I knew that to compete successfully, I had to practice and train even harder, enter more tournaments, and compete with better wrestlers in order to learn what I could from them. What I lacked in experience and natural talent I had to make up for in perseverance.

A fellow wrestler once called me a "plugger." He was suggesting that I wasn't the most polished or technically proficient, but I was scrappy. I kept plugging away, observing, trying different moves, and steadily getting better. After a long and exhausting wrestling practice, and with no shortage of studying to do, it was tempting to hit the showers. But instead, after most workouts I would run two miles to get in top shape. I knew that if I didn't discipline myself to make that extra effort, I wouldn't be as competitive.

Wrestling taught me what every young person needs to learn at some point: discipline. In college I competed in the 157-pound weight class. Before a weigh-in, I had to watch what I ate. I sometimes spent time in a rubber suit running around in the heat of the school's boiler room. There were many moments when I'd be ready to toss it in and go off with friends to have a milkshake at the diner. But I kept at it for more than ten years.

If it doesn't go easy, force it.

—My dad's assessment of my basic operating principle at age ten

Others recognized that there wasn't much that deterred a young Don Rumsfeld—even if it sometimes met with less than stellar results. When I was ten years old, we were driving along in the old family car, a green 1937 Oldsmobile, when one of the rear retread tires went flat. My dad pulled over near a gas station, opened the trunk, and got out the jack and the spare. He then went into the station. While he was gone I took the jack and put it under the car. I started pumping, assuming the car would elevate off the ground. I kept at it for some time, but the car didn't go up. My father returned to find me pumping the jack. He got down on the ground, looked under the car, and explained to me that the jack needed to be placed under the car's frame—not under the gas tank, which had collapsed to about half its previous capacity. My dad summarized to my mom what he called "Don's basic operating principle": "If it doesn't go easy, force it."

There was something to be said about that principle when it came to wrestling. I kept trying to find and perfect new holds that suited me. One day I watched a friend on the team, a state champion named Lenny Vyskocil, execute a takedown called the fireman's carry. I was impressed by the move and decided to try to master it. At just the right moment, the attacker takes the opponent's right arm and his right leg, drops to one knee, throws him over the shoulder, and lifts him up, much as a fireman would do when carrying someone from a burning building. The fireman's carry, when executed well, can end the match, with the opponent pinned to the mat right off the takedown. It was a particularly effective move against opponents who were stronger and had muscles in places where I didn't even have places. With the fireman's carry, I managed a few takedowns and quick pins in matches where the odds were against me.

There is also an intellectual component to wrestling that folks who have not participated in the sport might miss. It is a bit like a chess match, where you need to analyze your opponent's moves and plan your own. Of course the goal is clear—to pin your opponent to the mat before he can pin you or to win on points. But there are a great many combinations and techniques one can use to achieve that goal.

A match can be won or lost at any moment. The first time you are less than totally focused, you can find yourself on your back looking up at the ceiling.

Put yourself in the other person's shoes.

It may have been from wrestling that I learned one of life's more important lessons: Always try to put yourself in the other person's shoes. Pay attention to what your opponent might be thinking or about to do.

Trying to understand someone else's perspective can help not only in business negotiations or diplomacy, but also with more mundane matters, such as bargaining over the purchase of a car or house or even resolving a problem with a neighbor or a youngster. Taking time to consider what the person across from you is thinking, what they want to achieve, what their goals are, what their concerns are, and what issues they face can put you in a considerably better position to achieve your own objectives. I suppose you could say that in any number of contexts, even negotiating with a foreign leader, it can be useful to think of it as a mental wrestling match.

For example, I developed a close working relationship with Russian Defense Minister Sergei Ivanov. It helped that he was a highly intelligent and thoroughly enjoyable person to work with, but part of what made the relationship work may have been the fact that we both took the time to try to understand each other and our respective countries' interests and motivations. In my case, I tried to put myself in his shoes.

After the Cold War, Russia had gone from being a world superpower to a nation that was undergoing a difficult transformation. Russia still expected to be seen as deserving of international respect, and given its size and formidable nuclear arsenal, that desire was not unwarranted. We knew, for example, that it did not please them when their American counterparts talked endlessly about the West's "victory" in the Cold War. We had reason to be proud of that historic accomplishment, but we didn't need to rub it in a decade later. How would we as Americans feel if the situation were reversed?

We also knew that Russia was facing problems. Theirs was the first society in history in which male life expectancy was *declining*. Russia was losing its technological edge with an out-migration of scientists and skilled workers. Entering the Pentagon in 2001, I dictated some thoughts on how we might approach this sensitive and important relationship. "Discussions with Russia ought not to be stovepiped into segments," I suggested. "What they want is in the political and economic areas—dignity, respect, standing and foreign investment to help their economy." I shared my thoughts with the President and others on the National Security Council.[11] I noted that it was certainly possible that Russia would decide to ally itself with what I dubbed "the world's walking wounded"— North Korea, Cuba, Iran, Syria, and Iraq. But with the right incentives and a constructive approach by us, they might opt instead for closer ties with the West. A degree of humility on our side, I contended, might go a long way. They didn't need lectures from us on what their interests were. As a result, my relations with Ivanov were consistently friendly and constructive. I tried to look at the world, and our two countries, from his perspective, while always keeping in mind America's interests as well. I think it helped for a time to improve U.S.-Russian relations.

Similarly, during the buildup to the invasion of Afghanistan, I worked to develop relations with that troubled nation's neighbors. With most of those countries—the "stans" as they are called—we had practically no relationship. They were used to being bullied by their stronger neighbors China and Russia. So I tried to think through what Turkmenistan, Kyrgyzstan, Kazakhstan, Tajikistan, Pakistan, and Uzbekistan might want from the United States, the tone we might take, and where we might find areas of common interest and cooperation—cooperation America needed if we were to be successful in supporting our forces in Afghanistan. The result was unprecedented support from those countries in terms of basing rights, overflight rights, and the like.

A similar approach is helpful when considering hiring someone. I try to look at their résumé and background and ask: Where might they want their career to be heading, and how might that coincide with our needs? What kinds of incentives would encourage them to do their best? I try to consider their interests, concerns, and perspectives just as I consider ours. Taking a few moments to think about the hopes and aspirations of others—trying to put yourself in their shoes—is well worth the time and effort.

In sports as in life, keep something in the tank.

Something else I learned from wrestling is to try to keep something in reserve. Sometimes a match comes down to how much fuel you have left in your tank in the closing minutes. If you go hard at something from the outset with everything you have, you may exhaust yourself before accomplishing your goal. In wrestling, it helps to let an opponent reveal his moves before you go at him 100 percent.

When negotiating, never feel that you are the one who must fill every silence.

A similar notion is applicable to the business world as well as in diplomacy. In a negotiation, for example, it's generally not good practice to come out immediately with every argument and counterargument you may have in your arsenal. The wiser course may be to offer some of your points, and then see how the other side reacts. It often helps to leave some things unsaid. Never feel it is you who must fill every silence, even though it may seem awkward. Wait it out. Let others talk and fill the silence. You probably will learn a great deal.

You always have two choices: your commitment versus your fear.
—*Sammy Davis Jr.*

O ne of the more unexpected people whose paths I came across was the entertainer Sammy Davis Jr. He had a good relationship with President Nixon, and I came to know him because of his interests in the problem of poverty and minority outreach. He volunteered his assistance when I was serving as the director of the Office of Economic Opportunity.

An African American often described as "the world's greatest entertainer," Sammy was a pioneer who made his way into popular movies and TV shows before largely white audiences. He was one of Frank Sinatra's famous "Rat Pack" in the 1960s. But by the early 1970s, around the time I met him, Sammy's career had peaked a few years earlier. In 1971, he recorded a song called "The Candy Man." Sammy mentioned to me that he didn't like the song, thought it silly, and was almost embarrassed when he performed it. Wouldn't you know it? It became a number one hit and helped relaunch his career.

Sammy knew that life offers endless opportunities. When you suffer disappointments, pick yourself up, pull up your socks, and move on.

I too learned that lesson about managing disappointment, and more than anything else, it was wrestling that taught it to me. After high school I continued wrestling in college, and later while serving in the Navy, I was encouraged to compete for the worldwide All-Navy title, which I won in 1956, qualifying me to enter the tryouts for the U.S. Olympic Team.

What Wrestling Can Teach

The man I faced in the finals of the eastern U.S. Olympic trials was a top wrestler from Maryland named Ernie Fisher. He was a younger, stronger wrestler, and there was no reason in the world I should have beaten him. But once on the mat and after we had moved around a bit, I attempted a fireman's carry. I happened to catch him at exactly the right moment and pinned him, as I recall, in the first round, winning the tryout and qualifying for the finals. My hope was to try to make it onto the U.S. team, albeit as a long shot, and to travel to the opening ceremonies in Melbourne, Australia. It wasn't to be. During a practice session with a heavier wrestler, I heard a pop: My shoulder had separated, and my Olympic hopes, as modest as they were, were over.

By then I had devoted close to ten years to the sport. But life can work that way. Of course, the alternative is to avoid disappointment by not even trying.

When you pass the age of eighty, the number of wrestling matches you engage in tends to be small. For one thing, once you go down on a mat, you can't be confident you'll be able to get back up without some help. Still, the larger lessons of the sport stay with me to this day—the correlation between effort and results, the importance of sizing up opponents, thinking about things from the other guy's perspective, the benefit of surprise, and being willing to tackle big challenges. If you try, you may lose. But you can know with absolute certainty that if you are unwilling to enter the arena in the first place, you cannot win.

CHAPTER TEN

BATTLING BUREAUCRACY

Bureaucracies have befuddled, frustrated, and undermined leaders for as long as the term has been in existence. But although the word *bureaucracy* can give nightmares to business leaders and government officials alike, there's no reason it should instill fear. As with most things, there are ways to get around it. Sometimes it is simply a matter of will.

In 1983, President Reagan asked me to meet with him in the Oval Office to discuss something called the Law of the Sea Treaty. When he had been elected two years earlier, the treaty was on a bureaucratic fast track toward ratification by the U.S. Senate. All the relevant machinery of the U.S. government, including the Departments of State and Defense, favored it. Diplomats had even prepared an elaborate signing ceremony in Jamaica, with more than one hundred nations to be present. All that was required was the President's signature. In short, it was considered a done deal.

In Reagan's view the Law of the Sea Treaty was a power grab by a new international body, accountable to no one, that would dictate to America how we could develop and use the natural resources of the world's oceans. When Reagan said he would not be signing the treaty, the reaction was shock, especially inside the State Department.

Nothing is more obstinate than a fashionable consensus.
—MARGARET THATCHER

That famously independent bureaucracy consists of a cadre of career foreign service officers who tend to be well-educated, intelligent, multilingual, experienced, and dedicated to their work. But over time they can sometimes come to view their responsibility not as representing America to the world, but the other way around. Having served in Brussels as U.S. Ambassador to NATO, I had a good sense of what our foreign service officers experience. When he was Secretary of State, George Shultz had a practice of asking newly confirmed U.S. ambassadors to identify "their country" on a globe in his office. Invariably the newly minted envoys would point to the country where they had been assigned. Shultz would then gently point out that "their country" was actually the United States of America.

Naturally the longer people immerse themselves in another nation's culture, forming close relations with its leaders and citizens, the more likely they are to reorient their thoughts accordingly. There's a word for this: It's called *clientitis.* Bureaucrats can develop a similarly shortsighted view of whose interests they are there to represent. Sometimes it's not their proper bosses, whether it be the democratically elected president of the United States or the CEO selected by a corporation's board of directors.

It is no small matter to throw a wrench into the gears of any large organization, even if you are the nation's chief executive. So when President Reagan stopped the rush to ratify the Law of the Sea Treaty, it had a cost. Reagan accomplished something many leaders don't even attempt. He stood up to a permanent bureaucracy and prevailed.

But a bureaucracy, above all, endures. If defeated today, it lies in wait to win tomorrow. To this day, some three decades later, bureaucrats are still working to get that treaty approved.

---

*If you are going to sin, sin against God,
not the bureaucracy. God will forgive
you but the bureaucracy won't.*

—Admiral Hyman Rickover

My first clash with bureaucracy as an executive occurred as the new director of the U.S. Office of Economic Opportunity in 1969. When I toured the OEO building for the first time, I noticed that more than a few offices had admiring posters of Che Guevara in their cubicles. These were not likely to be people automatically prepared to salute the policies of the newly elected President, Richard Nixon.

Years later, at Searle, I led a company that had many fine people but had been committed to a certain way of doing things that, over the decades, led to the company to become a conglomerate with many different businesses under its corporate umbrella. Over the years, the company had acquired dozens of businesses that had little relationship to each other. Some were successful. Some were underperforming. Management and bureaucracy at Searle had grown to oversee all the new activities. It was my task to refocus

Running the Department of Defense is like wrestling with a seven-million-pound sponge.—*Deputy Secretary of Defense David Packard*

the company on its core business of pharmaceutical research and development and to sell off many of the subsidiaries that didn't fit, and to trim back the bureaucracies overseeing them.

Then there was my time at the Department of Defense—the largest bureaucracy in the world, with more than 25,000 people in the Pentagon alone, and some 3 million more military and civilian employees stationed around the world. The bureaucratic forces that buffet the DoD are often referred to as the "Iron Triangle"—comprising the near-permanent civilian and military officials in the Department, the members of the U.S. Congress, and the defense contractor community. From those experiences, I've come to a few conclusions about how to cope with bureaucracy.

*When you're up to your ears in alligators,
it is difficult to remember that the reason you're
there is to drain the swamp.*

One obvious thing to appreciate is that bureaucracies are a fact of life. Every organization that consists of even a few people requires some form of bureaucracy. There's a bureaucracy at IBM, at the University of Chicago, and even in your local church, labor union, or Chamber of Commerce.

But if there are any folks out there who like to think of themselves as "bureaucrats," I haven't met them yet. Midlevel managers in a corporation or the millions of employees in government tend not to introduce themselves by saying, "I'm your local bureaucrat." Indeed, the very word has come to be seen as a pejorative. The fact is, professional diplomats, intelligence officers, and career military personnel are essential to our national security. They deserve our respect and appreciation. Often they too are victims of bureaucracy, especially when they seek to improve systems that do not make the best use of their talents, much less of the taxpayers' money.

There is nothing that confirms the instincts of a resistant bureaucracy more than a leader who attempts something new and fails. It proves the folly of trying something new in the first place and dissuades new leaders from even trying anything similar in the future. Nonetheless, it's worth keeping in mind that those who carry out an organization's day-to-day functions are not villains seeking to thwart a leader's every move, and if you start with that mind-set, you will probably not gain much traction. Opposition to a new approach isn't always the result of a grand conspiracy.

Judge Laurence Silberman's Law of Diplomacy also applies to bureaucracy: "Every government looking at the actions of another government and trying to explain them always exaggerates rationality and conspiracy, and underestimates incompetence and fortuity." When there is resistance, it usually has more to do with inertia than animus.

If you want traction, you must first have friction.
—Admiral Jim Ellis

When someone in an organization tries to fix the problems of inefficiency and red tape, they usually run into people who strongly favor and defend the status quo. Resistance to change is a natural human response. In a company, opposition may come from an employees' union or a group of senior officials wedded to privileges granted in an earlier, more profitable time. Because it can be next to impossible to remove those types, they can develop a degree of insularity from those they are intended to serve. The larger the bureaucracy, the greater the likelihood that there will be little price to pay, if any, for a lack of responsiveness.

Those in bureaucracies grow accustomed to a certain way of doing things, usually dating back to when they first joined the organization, years or even decades in the past. Sometimes their job descriptions suit the way the bureaucracy functioned at an earlier point but might no longer apply to changed circumstances. When confronted with a disconnect between bureaucratic habits and real-world needs, some in a bureaucracy will dig in their heels and work even harder to prevent change—discovering new, previously untapped wells of energy and motivation now directed toward the preservation of the status quo.

Over time the cumulative effect of a resistant bureaucracy is to sap creativity, innovation, and efficiency. The middle level of an organization tends to want autonomy—to continue doing what they are comfortable with and skilled at doing, whether or not those tasks reflect the current needs of customers, management, or the American people. At its worst, it can bankrupt businesses and bog down government agencies to the point of paralysis.

There is nothing more difficult to take in hand,
more perilous to conduct, or more uncertain
in its success, than to take the lead in the introduction
of a new order of things.
—Niccolò Machiavelli

Attempts to curb the "rule of the desks"—the literal translation of the word *bureaucracy*—typically encounter one of the basic laws of physics: For every action there is an equal and opposite reaction. It has bested a good many U.S. presidents and corporate officers alike. When President Harry Truman recognized that Dwight Eisenhower would succeed him in the White House, he reportedly made a grim prediction. "Poor Ike—it won't be a bit like the Army. He'll sit here and he'll say, 'Do this! Do that!' And *nothing will happen.* He'll find it very frustrating."

As he reflected on his own years in the Oval Office, Truman lamented the yawning gap between the perception of being supposedly the most powerful man on earth and the reality: "I sit here all day trying to persuade people to do things they ought to have sense enough to do without my persuading them. . . . That's all the powers of the President amount to."[12]

If you don't like change, you are going to like irrelevance even less.

—*General Eric Shinseki*

The RAND Corporation, a nonprofit think tank that assesses and analyzes various national and international issues, once commissioned a report on what went wrong in the Vietnam War. This was of interest to me, as I had been in Congress when the Johnson administration escalated the conflict, became troubled by its costly and inconclusive trajectory, and witnessed the antiwar protests that consumed Washington, D.C., in the mid- to late 1960s.

The report was written by Robert "Blowtorch" Komer, a career CIA officer whom I would come to know and who had run the civilian-led pacification and development programs in Vietnam. Komer's report, titled "Bureaucracy Does Its Thing," concluded that institutional inertia and a business-as-usual attitude afflicted the diplomatic and defense institutions of the U.S. government. The report faulted national security bureaucracies—particularly the Departments of State and Defense—for an unwillingness or inability to adapt to the requirements of an unconventional guerrilla war in the jungles of Southeast Asia. Among other things, Komer identified a reluctance in U.S. military institutions— oriented at the time to fight a conventional conflict with the Soviet Union in Europe—to change their established ways of operating, and when faced with poor results, to do more of the same, from training to personnel policies to battlefield tactics.

Some of these challenges arose three decades later when the

Department of Defense needed to be reoriented to deal with unconventional and "asymmetric" twenty-first-century security challenges after the attacks of 9/11.

The Pentagon is like a log floating down a river with
25,000 ants on it, each one thinking it is steering.
—Dr. Harry Rowan

For example, the Pentagon, the media, and foreign allies traditionally measured military strength in terms of numbers of things. That was the way it always had been. So when I proposed to relocate some of the U.S. troops stationed in South Korea and Germany, there were howls of protest in those countries as well as on Capitol Hill, even though we were changing to a more capable and responsive posture. We had to shift our thinking and consider outputs (generated combat power and capability), not only inputs (such as numbers of ships, guns, tanks, troops, and planes). Our greater capabilities were made possible by technological and managerial improvements such as precision-guided munitions and information technology. But in 2001, the Department still lagged in reflecting these significant changes.

That outdated mind-set became obvious when the Afghan and Iraq wars laid bare the reality that the U.S. military had to be organized, trained, and equipped for more than one set of tasks. Our country was now dealing with a new set of problems and adversaries—including nonstate terrorist and insurgent groups that operated among civilian populations and did not adhere to the traditional structures or standards of war.

You go to war with the Army you have—
not the Army you might wish to have.

The military procurement system, for example, typically took years to produce a new weapon or piece of equipment, a pace that was clearly inadequate to the changing needs of an asymmetrical battlefield. Our forces were largely organized, trained, and equipped for a conventional battlefield, with well-delineated front lines and relatively safe rear areas. The biggest killers of U.S. troops in Iraq were improvised explosive devices (IEDs)—crude, homemade roadside bombs. The Army and the Marine Corps ground forces were accustomed to moving around behind the leading edge of the battlefield in thin-skinned HUMVEEs—a descendant of the jeep. Once IEDs emerged as a lethal threat the Army scrambled to rush new "up-armored" HUMVEES to the war zone, going from fifteen produced per month to several hundred per month by 2004.

I created a special IED task force to coordinate all the new technologies being developed to better protect our troops from those deadly devices. I brought back to duty a retired general, Montgomery Meigs, to head the new task force. Not worried about promotion or rocking the boat, Meigs could go head-to-head with the forces that were wedded to the status quo, which he did successfully. The existing bureaucracies in the Pentagon and military services were not set up to respond rapidly to urgent battlefield needs, so we had to create new mechanisms to accomplish what we needed to get done and at a faster pace.

> *It is exceedingly difficult for any military*
> *organization to innovate radically—except in wartime*
> *when it is absolutely necessary.*
> —JIM WOOLSEY

Such challenges are not exclusive to government and the military. There will always be circumstances where organizations—public and private—prepared and organized for one set of challenges are urgently required to deal with an entirely new and different circumstance. Despite a pressing need to change, people in a bureaucracy may resist doing things that disrupt their established routines. In the private sector, a company's survival may depend on its ability to change in ways that government does not. Government, after all, can't go broke. But, in both cases the task is to make clear that "business as usual" won't do and press for the adjustments necessary to respond as real-world circumstances require.

How can you as a leader deal with a resistant bureaucracy? A first step is to recognize your limitations. No leader can or should want to try to eliminate bureaucracy altogether. No leader will prevail over it every time. No leader will get everything he or she may want from a deeply embedded bureaucratic culture. Bureaucratic inertia and opposition are facts of life—realities we all have to accept and work to change as much as is possible.

I could as easily bail out the Potomac River with a teaspoon as attend to all the details of the army.

—*Abraham Lincoln*

W hen I arrived at the Pentagon in early 2001 with the explicit mission from the newly elected President to transform the largest bureaucracy in the world, the Department I had left nearly a quarter century earlier was barely recognizable. The Defense Department of the mid-1970s was hardly a lean and mean operation. No government organization of that size ever is, and back then we were still fighting the Cold War. But the Pentagon of the mid-1970s was a model of efficiency and decisive action compared with what I found in 2001. To begin with, the Department was drowning in paper. The congressional legislation that authorized funds for DoD had been a single page back in 1962, the year I was elected to Congress. When I first served as Secretary of Defense in 1975 the number of pages had ballooned to 75. But by 2001, it had exploded to 988 pages, crammed with detailed requirements, prohibitions, and stipulations—as well as stipulations to the stipulations. The Secretary of Defense was by 2001 required to submit 905 separate reports to Congress each year, even though they were rarely read by any members and were produced at considerable cost to the taxpayer—and to the forests of America. The 535 members of the U.S. House and Senate were sending 2,500 to 3,000 inquiries or complaints to the Department—not every year, not every month, but *every week*. I also found a backlog of more than 15,000 security clearances pending. Meanwhile, the size of the active-duty armed forces had declined from 2.1 million men and women to 1.4 million.

Running the U.S. Navy is like punching a pillow all day.
You end up exhausted and the pillow hasn't changed a bit.
—FRANKLIN D. ROOSEVELT

The Department was also burdened by dozens of redundant systems with little or no justification. There were three separate exchange systems, but we couldn't consolidate them without the approval of Congress. There were three different health-care systems and three surgeons general—one for each military service. While civilian control of the military was one of the founding principles of our country, the way DoD was organized and overseen by Congress made it exceedingly difficult for any Secretary to conduct and be responsible for the business of the Department.

Like Gulliver in Lilliput, the Department was held down by tens of thousands of threads, some imposed by Congress and some self-imposed. While no one Lilliputian thread could hold Gulliver down, in the aggregate they made it so that he couldn't move. The combined effect of all the congressionally imposed regulations made the Department so slow, ponderous, and inefficient that what was done was often late and wasteful of taxpayer dollars. The result, not surprisingly, was still more complaints from members of Congress, and more restrictions and more audits, all of which made it even more difficult to deliver good performance.

The only stupidities that are not easily solved are those
created by very intelligent men.
—AMBASSADOR OF FRANCE FRANÇOIS DE ROSE

One way to reform a bureaucracy is to focus a public spotlight on its challenges. In that way the media can be helpful in moving public opinion toward making the needed changes. Going public signals to those in the bureaucracy that you are serious about change by putting your reputation on the line. And it also can help those inside the bureaucracy who are ready for change find the courage to push for reform.

Almost nine months in, I scheduled a speech to several hundred key employees in the Pentagon to outline the challenges I had determined we needed to address. I said in part:

> *The topic today is an adversary that poses a threat, a serious threat, to the security of the United States of America. This adversary is one of the world's last bastions of central planning. It governs by dictating five-year plans. From a single capital, it attempts to impose its demands across time zones, continents, oceans, and beyond. With brutal consistency, it stifles free thought and crushes new ideas. It disrupts the defense of the United States and places the lives of men and women in uniform at risk.*
>
> *Perhaps this adversary sounds like the former Soviet Union, but that enemy is gone: Our foes are more subtle and implacable today. You may think I'm describing one of the last decrepit dictators of the world. But their day, too, is almost past, and they cannot match the strength and size of this adversary.*
>
> *The adversary's closer to home. It's the Pentagon bureaucracy. Not the people, but the processes. Not the civilians, but the systems. Not the men and women in uniform, but the uniformity of thought and action that we too often impose on them.*

Since the Defense Department was established in 1947, it had become tangled in its proverbial anchor chain. Layer upon layer of management had accreted, one on top of the other. Duplicative duties and redundant systems had grown like barnacles on the hull of a ship. Waste had become the norm, even after the sharp budget cuts during the 1990s, which should have left little tolerance for excess. Every dollar spent unnecessarily was a dollar not available for real military needs—training, care for troops and their families, modern weapons, or the development of new technologies. That was why my speech was labeled "From Bureaucracy to Battlefield." We had to find ways to shift our limited resources from unnecessary overhead to the military capabilities necessary to meet the security challenges of the Information Age.

My speech was startling to some. But I was convinced that a public discussion of these problems was the only way to tackle them successfully.

The date of my speech was September 10, 2001. Whatever publicity it generated was rapidly overwhelmed by the terrible events the following morning. Some commenters assumed that the attacks of September 11 and the wars that followed would undermine our transformation efforts. In fact, going on a wartime footing had the opposite effect, providing a new sense of urgency that would have otherwise been considerably more difficult if not impossible to generate.

Corporate leaders have less access to the national press corps than do government leaders. But there are other ways that CEOs and senior managers can utilize the same tactics. They can raise issues and problems before gatherings of divisions, at corporate meetings, or in business-oriented newsletters or other company publications.

Top-down clarity and common understanding create trust, confidence, and unity.

Working successfully with a bureaucracy requires respect for those you work with and an appreciation of human nature. One important aspect is that people pursue their self-interest. So do them the courtesy of explaining that failure to change can pose an even greater peril to them than doing nothing and sticking with the status quo.

Two of the biggest changes I noticed between my service at DoD in the mid-1970s and my return in 2001 were a lack of trust and an erosion of confidence. A number of the best and brightest junior officers had departed in the face of the budget cuts in the 1990s. Those remaining were concerned that their service was undervalued by the nation's political leadership. President Bush, Vice President Cheney, the Chairman of the Joint Chiefs of Staff, and I tried to convey that we would be respectful of the nation's military and their professionalism. The changes we sought to institute would lead to a more effective military, one that would be more relevant to twenty-first-century threats.

The service chiefs understood the goal, at least in principle, some better than others. The Chief of Naval Operations, Admiral Vern Clark, was particularly forward-leaning. Clark radically overhauled the way the Navy deployed the carrier battle groups with what is called the Fleet Response Plan. After Clark's changes, up to eight carriers were available to surge in a contingency, as opposed to only three. This upended years of how the Navy thought about and managed ship deployment cycles, during which most aircraft carriers were effectively off-station and unavailable for two-thirds of their lifetimes.

Another triumph against those wedded to outdated ways of doing things was changing the fundamental building blocks of the U.S. Army. With the leadership of a retired Special Forces general, Pete Schoomaker, who came back in uniform to be Army Chief of Staff, we undertook the most radical reorganization of the Army in modern history. Schoomaker turned massive 15,000- to 20,000-member troop divisions into brigade combat teams containing 3,000 to 5,000 people each. The smaller, more nimble, and more readily deployable units formed self-contained, interchangeable modules. It was this organizational reform that allowed U.S. forces to sustain operations in Afghanistan and Iraq. The creation of brigade combat teams, for example, made possible the 2007 surge in Iraq. Setting aside centuries of Army history and tradition that proudly celebrated the division makeup wasn't easy. Because there existed a relationship of trust and confidence, Schoomaker was empowered to charge ahead even when he encountered resistance from the bureaucracy.

Leadership is by consent, not command. A leader must persuade.

Early on, I called in the civilian and military personnel in charge of language studies to inquire about the foreign languages being taught to DoD military and civilian personnel. It turned out that a large number were studying French, the language of diplomacy until the eighteenth century. More people were learning Korean than Chinese. Only five people in the entire Department were learning Urdu. This made little sense to me.

French would be useful if visiting Paris or Brussels—it would have been handy for me as U.S. Ambassador to NATO—but was not generally needed for national security purposes. We needed many more learning the languages of our competitors and adversaries in areas of the world that were strategically consequential and where conflict was possible.

Not personally knowing what numbers of people we would need to be skilled in the various languages, I asked Undersecretary of Personnel and Readiness David Chu what languages our top experts thought we might need over the next ten to twenty years. What situations were we likely to face and in what areas of the world? The idea was to have the senior leaders—military and civilian—suggest changes in the Department's language priorities. Achieving consent is almost always more effective than issuing commands. Only when people understand the logic behind the changes and "own" the changes that are needed are they likely to put their full effort into implementing new policies.

It is easier to convince someone they're right than to convince them they're wrong.

Moving a bureaucracy cannot be achieved simply by ordering that something be done, even in a military organization. Instead, leadership almost always requires consent and persuasion. The biggest problem with bureaucracies is the certainty that, as Ronald Reagan put it, they are the "closest thing to eternal life on earth." The machinery of an organization outlasts any one leader.

If you order a bureaucracy to do something it doesn't want to do, very often it will ensure that your attempt at change will fail and prove to all that it was right in the first place. Or else it will resort to the tried-and-true tactic of the "slow roll." Because bureaucracies can almost always outlast leadership, they can appear on the surface to be following guidance from the top, but actually be doing only the bare minimum, ensuring that little, if any, change is accomplished.

In the six years of my last tour as Secretary I could probably count on two hands the number of times I issued a direct order other than an explicit command from the President of the United States. It was exceedingly rare. A more effective approach is a form of the Socratic method—asking a series of questions that help to move toward a preferred outcome. That was one of the reasons I sent some twenty thousand "snowflakes" and memos while I was in the Pentagon. Contained in those memos and notes were a great many more questions than instructions. When I made a specific assertion or action it tended to be followed by something like "Would you let me know what's wrong with this?" or "Why isn't this right?" or "What do you think?" It was more time-consuming than issuing orders, but it had a better chance of achieving results.

Find ways to decentralize and reduce staff, without cutting into the thin layer required for you to manage.

Having a single decision-maker at the top can sap creativity and stifle innovation. It is not as effective as developing multiple leadership centers each of which is empowered to take initiative. There may be some who prefer to pass a difficult problem up the chain of command, so they will not be responsible for making a tough decision, but you must see to it that they have the incentive to make those decisions. Encouraging others to step up leads to a considerably more effective outcome.

In the Pentagon, the key to civilian leadership is having capable, Senate-confirmed presidential appointees serving in the key leadership positions. Over the last six years I was there, however, we functioned with an average of more than 25 percent of the forty-nine key senior posts vacant. This was for a variety of reasons—lengthy periods of time to get needed security clearances, long-delayed White House approvals, a U.S. Senate slow to confirm nominees, natural turnover, and the challenge of persuading folks to leave the private sector for government service. Managing the Pentagon without a full slate of Senate-confirmed appointees was like trying to lift one side of a piano with two fingers. Whatever organization you may be managing, it is important to determine what leadership positions are key to achieving your goals and to make sure you have people in those posts who are capable and comfortable with your direction and tempo.

Walk around. If you are invisible, the mystique of your position may perpetuate inaccurate impressions. After all, you may not be as bad as some are saying.

It helps to try to see your organization through the eyes of those who are there to make it work. One of the best ways to do that is to make yourself available to those you don't work with on a daily basis. Chances are that if people have concerns and complaints, they have them for a reason. Their concerns may have previously been ignored by those above them. Find out what people are working on, what their worries are, what they are wondering about, and what ideas they might have. Learning new things and forging new relationships takes time for a leader, but it is well worth it.

Seek suggestions at all levels. When he was chairman of the board at Home Depot, Bernie Marcus used to visit their stores and walk through the aisles to see how things were operating. My former congressional colleague the late Ed Koch rode the subway and walked the streets of New York City when he was mayor, asking a question that became synonymous with his tenure: "How'm I doin'?"

At Searle, a few times every month I would eat in the employee lunchroom instead of at my desk or with senior executives. And at the Pentagon, I walked through the building frequently, ate lunch in the cafeteria, played squash in the athletic facility, and held town-hall meetings where any private or corporal could ask a question or make a comment to the Secretary of Defense. Only if you get out of your office can you find out how the troops actually feel, ask them about their families, and listen and learn.

Trial and error are the essence of discovery. Your organization should be hospitable to both.

Experimentation is not only the essence of discovery; it also can lead to successful business and organizational ideas. The most successful organizations create an environment that is hospitable to risk-taking, innovation, and creativity. When I was in the pharmaceutical industry, many of the company's important innovations came only after trial and error and a series of unsuccessful dead ends, each of which, while considered a "failure" in one sense, led to valuable information that could be studied and learned from. That was true in the discovery of aspartame, which resulted from a combination of trial and error, with a touch of serendipity. It was said that a lab technician working with two amino acids licked his finger to turn a piece of paper and noticed a sweet taste, which is how a product called NutraSweet that revolutionized the food and beverage industry came to be born.

Nothing will ever be attempted if all possible objections must be first overcome.
—Dr. Samuel Johnson

In 1983, President Reagan put forward the idea of a missile defense shield to protect the American people from the Soviet Union's massive nuclear arsenal. His proposal encountered heated opposition from Congress, the arms control establishment, a State Department bureaucracy that did not like facing complaints from other nations, and even from members of the President's own staff. It also generated opposition from fiefdoms within the Department of Defense, whose interests were aligned with more traditional weapons systems and did not want to see funds moved to a new and untested program.

For some two decades, Reagan's dream of an operational missile defense system was just that—a dream. But sometimes the only way to deal with repeated objections is to keep moving forward, even in the face of opposition. So, in 2001, the George W. Bush administration came up with ways around the political, bureaucratic, and legal logjams. First, the President had to step up and withdraw from the 1972 Anti-Ballistic Missile (ABM) Treaty, which prevented the U.S. and the USSR (by then the Russian Federation) from building defenses against ICBMs. The treaty was a relic of the

Cold War, designed to deter nuclear conflicts by institutionalizing the policy of "mutual assured destruction." We became the first administration to commit to actually putting in place a missile defense system—one that could meet the most likely threat of an attack by a rogue state, not an all-protective shield against many hundreds of ICBMs as originally envisioned. We knew we wouldn't start with a perfect system. Instead we adopted an approach from Silicon Valley they call "spiral development."

In the high-tech businesses like computer software, "spiral development" is a tested way to develop more advanced systems. An early version is brought out and released to customers, who then provide feedback that can lead to improvements in the next version. And thus it continues through a series of iterations. Microsoft has had dozens of versions of its Windows software—each new version an improvement, with fixes to the glitches, problems, and capabilities in the previous one. Likewise, Apple is now on its fifth version of the iPhone.

Making perfection the enemy of the good is a favored technique of those in bureaucracies whose goal is to keep things as they are. Instead, despite our many critics, we continued testing and improving the missile defense system rather than waiting until we believed we had a "finished product" that could do everything we wanted. There were a number of tests instantly deemed "failures" by critics in the media and in Congress because the early efforts were, as to be expected, less than perfect. The critics missed the important point: that every "failed" test actually produced useful lessons and data that eventually allowed us to field a credible missile defense capability, with interceptors in Alaska and California that today are capable of preventing rogue-state nuclear blackmail.

Keep in mind the "tooth-to-tail ratio." The tail's only role is to support the teeth.

The "tooth-to-tail ratio" is an important concept for anyone trying to hack their way through a bureaucratic thicket. In the military context, the phrase refers to the number of support personnel ("the tail") required to supply and sustain the troops on the front lines ("the tooth"). A tail too long is a costly and inefficient use of resources for an organization whose primary purpose—indeed its very reason for being—depends on the teeth. The trick is to try to keep the number of support staff as low as possible, yet still enable those on the front line to do their jobs.

Strive to make solutions as self-executing as possible. As the degree of discretion increases, so too do delay, expense, and the size of the bureaucracy.

In 2001, I discovered that of the hundreds of thousands of people at the Defense Department, only 14 percent were directly related to combat operations ("the tooth"). A large majority of the remaining personnel were there as administrative support or involved in activities that had little or nothing to do with warfighting ("the tail"). These were people in activities we could reduce without damaging overall combat capabilities.

Every organization has its frontline personnel, those on the spear point who deliver the value for the organization. The task is to figure out how many people are actually needed to support them and then steadily work to see if that "tail" can be reduced without a reduction in performance.

Reduce layers of management. They put distance between the top of an organization and the customers.

Over time any organization is likely to accumulate more people than it needs. They usually are found toiling in the middle layers, where they busy themselves by overseeing the people below them. Sometimes things can get out of control as the middle gets larger and larger. Before you know it, a whole community of people has been created watching people watch other people watch other people.

This is a phenomenon that is endemic, though not unique, to government. When I came back to the Pentagon in 2001, I asked how many layers of people stood between the Secretary of Defense and a line officer in the field. When I learned the answer, even I was amazed. It turned out that there were seventeen levels of management between the Defense Secretary and that officer.

Most of the officers in between had ten to sixteen years of experience in the military. They were fully capable of making decisions without needing approval at sixteen different levels. More to the point, we knew that al-Qaeda did not have seventeen layers of approval to make a decision. They work in small networks, which allows them to act more quickly than the large and bureaucratic U.S. government. This of course gives the enemy an advantage.

My advice for leaders in any organization is to determine the number of layers between them and those responsible for carrying out the outfit's fundamental tasks. Chances are they will find unnecessary levels of management. Try to reduce them and give them something more productive to do.

Lawyers are like beavers. They get in the middle of the stream and dam it up.

Before I talk about lawyers, full disclosure: I am a law school dropout. I did fine in law school and I enjoyed it, but I decided that a legal career wasn't for me. I may be one of the few people who've worked in Washington, D.C., who came to that conclusion early enough. Or so it sometimes seemed. I'd never seen a place where so many people have law degrees, yet do not practice law or have any interest in doing so. Then there were other lawyers who seemed to repopulate spontaneously. Where you'd find one, you suddenly found several.

It doesn't take a genius to figure out why we have so many lawyers. We live in the most litigious society on earth. When I was on the board of directors of ASEA Brown Boveri, an international power engineering company, the management had to take that fact into account. Often, when they had to build a new facility, they did it outside the United States, and one of the reasons cited was the abandon with which lawyers operate in our country.

In a society as litigious as ours has become, it's natural that leaders have to seek out legal advice. But this reality has drawbacks. One statistic about the Defense Department that stuns me to this day is that the Pentagon has become home to more than ten thousand lawyers. How remarkable is this figure? Well, consider this: The Pentagon has more lawyers than the Department of Justice! Like anybody, lawyers prefer to keep busy. And because the Pentagon is subject to so many lawsuits, many of them frivolous, every level in the Department, up and down the chain of command, is compelled to regularly seek legal advice on issue after issue. One lawyer's advice can be useful. Two lawyers offering advice can sometimes be useful even if contradictory. But ten thousand lawyers—well, there is such a thing as too much of a good thing.

Having too many lawyers can cause problems in any organization. A lawyer's job, by definition, is to advise as to which courses of action are legal. Before long, in the interest of "protecting" the department, lawyers can become barriers against taking action at all.

It helps to have lawyers advising military officials, but I get concerned when lawyers start making decisions for policy-makers or for those on the firing line, rather than giving legal advice to them. If you are in an organization and find lawyers making decisions instead of advising on decisions, then maybe you need to reduce their number. If you really need an army of lawyers for everything your organization is doing, then you may have a different problem.

Sometimes it's necessary to kill a chicken to frighten the monkeys.
—Chinese proverb

When you do need to take on a bureaucracy directly in what will be likely to prove a high-profile battle, think of the line from Napoleon: "If you start to take Vienna, take Vienna." Few who take on and lose a major bloody battle against a bureaucracy have the grit or the strength to attempt it again.

One of our tough bureaucratic battles at the Pentagon centered on the establishment of the National Security Personnel System.

Because of the rules, regulations, and unions, it became difficult for a civilian leader to hire, fire, promote, offer incentives to, or transfer civilian employees. What tended to happen was that when a manager needed to do a specific task they would feel compelled to bring in military personnel or contractors to do the jobs. They did this for the understandable reason that military personnel could be brought in rapidly, and when the job was completed, they could be moved out. The same was true with contractors. But not so with civilian employees.

The result, of course, is a waste of taxpayer dollars. The Department was paying civilian workers, but bypassing them because they could not be effectively managed. Worse, the Department was taking personnel from their military assignments to perform civilian tasks. And the Department was paying contractors to perform tasks that could have been done by the civilian workforce.

Union leaders did not want changes to the existing system they had helped to fashion—and for good reason. The status quo was working fine for them. But in 2005, after a long battle, we finally succeeded in implementing a new National Security Personnel System, which included the common private sector concept of "pay for performance." But it took several years of effort.

While the new system was not everything we wanted, it was a start. To my regret, after I left the Department, that victory was, in large measure, lost. Perhaps others in the department thought the battle won, or perhaps they didn't see the importance of what we were trying to do. For whatever reason, the government unions were able to successfully kill off all the key elements of the new personnel system. Today, the Department is close to being back where it was, and the odds of refighting that battle are much longer. The lesson, of course, is that even when you win a tough battle against the bureaucracy, you can't afford to look away for a second.

As hidebound an organization as the Defense Department could be—and a reader of this chapter could be forgiven for thinking that trying to manage it is a futile task—it must be emphasized that it is populated with truly remarkable people, both military and civilian, millions of them in fact. They are hardworking, resourceful, and dedicated to protecting the American people. The some 2.5 million men and women serving in uniform, each a volunteer, are examples of the dedication and patriotism that well-trained and well-motivated individuals can bring to an organization. As a whole the U.S. military is very likely the most remarkable leadership institution in the world.

CHAPTER ELEVEN

LESSONS FROM THE WORLD'S MOST SUCCESSFUL LEADERSHIP ORGANIZATION

Washington. Grant. Patton. Marshall. Eisenhower. Nimitz. Each was a successful leader. Yet each had a distinctively different personality and style. Contemporaries described George Washington as stiff and ceremonious. Of the low-key Ulysses S. Grant, Lincoln once said: "He makes the least fuss of any man you ever knew. I believe he had been in this room a minute or so before I knew that he was here." Patton, by contrast, was famous for making a fuss. Swaggering, theatrical, and confrontational, Patton inspired great loyalty from his troops yet brought a flood of censure onto himself by berating and slapping a soldier.

George Marshall embodied reserve and formality. The general was reported to have bristled when even the President of the United States called him by his first name. By contrast, one of Eisenhower's distinguishing traits was geniality, which, together with sharp political instincts, positioned him to deal with the out-size egos and national rivalries endemic in coalition warfare.

Admiral Chester Nimitz, who rebuilt the Pacific Fleet after Pearl Harbor, made his way into the U.S. Naval Academy without completing high school. It was not until after he was made a Fleet Admiral (one of only nine men in American history to wear five stars) that Nimitz received his high school diploma. Nimitz confessed to becoming "frightfully seasick" during his first tour of duty and not long thereafter ran his ship aground in Manila Bay, in what would be a career-ending mistake today. He was comfortable leaving much of the glory to the two larger-than-life figures of the World War II Pacific Theater—General Douglas MacArthur and Admiral William "Bull" Halsey.

How then can a single organization take so many different people, with such different personalities, and manage to have them work together as part of a larger whole? Over two centuries, the U.S. armed forces have done exactly that. At its best, they have developed not only remarkable warriors, but remarkable leaders—individuals skillful at making right decisions, even in split seconds, all the while knowing they are most likely working with incomplete, imperfect, and sometimes even inaccurate information, often under the most adverse circumstances.

Consider what an incredible feat that is: Year after year, our military welcomes tens of thousands of recruits, from different areas of our country, with widely diverse backgrounds and levels of education; puts them through a variety of training regimens; and then integrates them into cohesive, functioning fighting units—all in a matter of months. They dedicate their careers—and their lives—to standing post and, when necessary, take on the unwanted, unglamorous, ugly work that is war. The defense of our country and indeed the defense of the free world rest with them.

It is inevitable that when someone seeks to highlight the strengths of an organization, there is always someone around ready to point out its vulnerabilities. And it is true that members of the U.S. military have, like any other entity, experienced poor decision-making, periodic scandal, and even criminality—from the My Lai Massacre in Vietnam to the prisoner abuse on the midnight shift at Abu Ghraib to, more recently, the alleged murder of sixteen Afghan villagers by a U.S. soldier. Thankfully those are rare exceptions.

No matter how a war starts it ends in mud.
It has to be slugged out.
There are no trick solutions or cheap shortcuts.
—General Joe Stilwell

When failure does occur in the ranks of our military, discipline is meted out. When leadership failures occur, they are carefully examined to avoid repetition. But overall, and by almost any measure, the U.S. military remains a highly successful organization that turns young men and women into leaders. As such, our country's armed forces can offer useful lessons for those seeking to be effective leaders in other walks of life.

As mentioned earlier, in late 1941 my father was working for a Chicago real estate firm helping to manage rental properties. Two years later, during World War II, he was the officer of the deck at night aboard an aircraft carrier in a war zone in the Pacific Ocean. How is it possible to take a civilian approaching forty, with ab-

One of the reasons our military has been so successful is that
there is an unmistakable sense of purpose that comes from being part of
something bigger than yourself.

solutely no experience in the military, train him in a matter of months, and then assign him responsibility for the lives of hundreds of men aboard a ship of war?

After the war, my dad was occasionally asked that question. Without a second's hesitation, he would answer, "Chief petty officers." These seasoned sailors are the senior enlisted personnel in the U.S. Navy. As a commissioned officer my dad technically outranked them, yet it was the chiefs who taught him and other green recruits, officers and enlisted alike, much of what they needed to know to successfully perform their duties.

A decade later, as a young midshipman on my first summer cruise on the battleship USS *Wisconsin*, I saw firsthand how complicated a major warship was to operate—how many men were involved, how meticulously orchestrated the procedures were, how even minor pieces of equipment had to pass careful inspection. Even a single-engine aircraft, with only one pilot, depends on a ground and maintenance crew of dozens. I quickly saw the vital role of the senior enlisted leaders, the noncommissioned officers. Called chiefs in the Navy and sergeants in the other military services, they help transform green recruits into reliable, functioning members of an organization that has only a modest margin for error. The chiefs and sergeants are the vital rib cage of our country's armed forces.

In every organization, there are those who may not have the senior rank, but who have been there longer and know the informal as well as the written rules of the road. They have learned the hard lessons and can provide valuable advice to younger aspiring leaders. These individuals represent the institutional memory of an organization. Find those folks, listen to them, learn from them, and give them the respect they merit. You and your organization will benefit greatly.

The tens of thousands of new military recruits and junior officers who come through the training pipeline each year quickly develop an appreciation for formality and precision in dress. Shirts and pants are pressed, shoes polished, and salutes crisp. These young men and women abide by a strict code of conduct that can penalize a number of things that are not illegal in civilian life: slovenly appearance, tardiness, or disregarding a superior's orders.

This regimentation can be misconstrued by those who have not served in the military as excessive attention to detail or a quaint adherence to dated ethical standards. What does it matter, one might ask, if a button is undone, or a rifle isn't held the exact way it should be, as long as you know when and how to use it? Why should anyone care what a soldier wears in combat?

Well, there are good reasons why the U.S. military places a premium on ceremony, standards of conduct, discipline, precision, and punctuality. For one thing, uniforms help members of the armed forces identify each other, which can become difficult in the confusion of battle. Attention to detail in small things, such as keeping pants pressed, means you're more likely to pay attention to detail in larger things, such as keeping the barrel of a rifle clean, or a pilot carefully reviewing the landing checklist.

It is also essential that troops be able to talk to each other and be quickly understood by using the same precise language and frames of reference. An ambiguous order and a vague wave in the direction of the enemy are what reportedly led to the deaths of more than two hundred British soldiers in the infamous 1854 Charge of the Light Brigade. Precision can be lifesaving. One digit off in a latitude or longitude coordinate can result in a bomb dropped on the wrong target, even on friendly forces. A rendezvous does not succeed if a pilot shows up five minutes after the set time.

In boot camp or officer training school, you quickly learn the phrase "No excuse, sir." Punctuality isn't simply a courtesy; it's a necessity when lives can depend on you and others being in exactly the right place at the right time. Military recruits practice the same maneuvers and drills until they are near perfect. They learn to operate as a single body. Recruits learn to march in formation—something they almost certainly will never be asked to do in battle—but the tradition and practice teach them to obey commands and to be part of a broader whole.

In any organization a culture that helps train newcomers and sets clear guidelines for behavior can inculcate teamwork and effectiveness. Some Japanese and South Korean companies conduct regular physical exercises in which everyone participates, from the CEO to maintenance workers. Many organizations establish company guidelines, ethics briefings, or standard operating procedures that employees are required to read and sign so that precisely what is expected of them is clearly understood. Some companies develop brief mottos and themes that are repeated over and over so that all team members are aware of them and understand that their work should reflect the values the company has deemed important. The result is an organization that has developed and sustained a corporate culture that outlasts the individual employee and sets identifiable standards for new recruits.

Don't wait for feedback from superiors, colleagues, or employees.

In a culture that elevates the collective good to the point where members are willing to risk their lives for the mission, the U.S. military also preserves the strengths of individuality, initiative, and personal success. Soldiers, sailors, airmen, and marines are awarded medals for acts of valor and outstanding performance. They are promoted through a set of evaluations and "fitness reports" issued by superiors who critique their performance and systematically offer suggestions to improve leadership abilities as an individual moves through the ranks.

Some military commanders and service chiefs talk to an individual's peers, superiors, and subordinates to learn how that person is seen by the people he or she works alongside as well as those above and below. This can provide valuable insights about a person's strengths and weaknesses before decisions are made about that individual's future. Some human resource departments in the private sector use a similar technique called "360-degree feedback."

Self-evaluations are used not only for personnel, but also after almost every significant training exercise and each real-life operation. The military conducts "after-action reports" and "lessons learned" studies that examine what worked, what didn't, and what might be done better next time. Self-examination and self-analysis are recurrent themes in the military. Even if everything seemed to go well on a particular mission, you might find that happenstance played a larger role than skill. Without an after-action report, you're not likely to learn that.

In every field of endeavor, people wonder how well they are doing and how they can do better. If you are working for people who do little more than thank or compliment you, you may not be learning things that could benefit your performance and your career. A good boss takes the time on a regular basis to make constructive suggestions about an individual's performance.

But employees need not count on that, or wait for it. An employee who wants to improve his or her skills can always ask the boss to sit down with them at least once a year or after a major event for guidance or suggestions. It's worth asking: Are there things I ought to be doing that I'm not doing? Are there things I am not hearing that I ought to be hearing? If you force yourself to go back to examine how well you and your organization performed in a certain effort, you'll be better prepared the next time you're called on to do something similar. An organization that provides that sort of feedback and regularly takes the time to critique its people will improve leadership skills across the board.

Never give an order outside the chain of command and never expect to learn anything up the chain of command.

—Admiral Hyman Rickover

In the immediate aftermath of the September 11 attacks, President Bush ordered all aircraft across the entire country grounded. Any planes that remained in the air after his order had to be considered a possible threat. At some point that afternoon, we were alerted to reports of two airliners that were emitting the code for "hijacked" and heading toward the United States.

In the command center at the Pentagon, I remember thinking about the young military pilots charged with patrolling the newly established no-fly zone over the nation's capital. They were given authority for "weapons hot." In short, they had been issued rules of engagement that permitted them to fire at any aircraft presumed to be hijacked and threatening an important target— even if it could mean killing the one hundred or more American civilians aboard.

We understood the gravity of the decisions that might need to be made by those pilots, some undoubtedly still in their twenties, who might have only seconds to make a choice that could have outsize consequences for our country, with little if any time to seek advice up the chain of command. I wanted to ensure we did our utmost to provide them with the most precise, sensible, and workable rules of engagement regarding how and when to attack an aircraft that appeared to be on course for a target such as the U.S. Capitol or the White House. The Chairman of the Joint

Chiefs, Air Force General Dick Myers, was confident that, even in the face of such a tough call, the pilots wouldn't flinch. They had been trained well and would follow their lawful orders.

It is not that one general is better than another, but that one general is better than two.

—David Lloyd George

The U.S. military requires a hierarchy. The people at the top are there for a reason. Their judgment counts. Their orders must be followed. A clear chain of command encourages cohesion and unity, which are necessary in situations where the better-trained, coordinated, and led force will generally prevail. Every individual in uniform, officer and enlisted, understands well the chain of command, from the President and Secretary of Defense all the way down to the squad level. They know from whom they must take orders and to whom they must give them.

Where there is no continuity there can be no accountability.

Clear lines of authority also help individuals who require guidance to know exactly who to ask and whose instructions to follow. You would not expect or find the same degree of top-down regimentation in civilian organizations—especially as many companies have become less stratified and more casual in recent decades. But the same qualities of esprit de corps, attention to detail, and clear guidance are found in all successful and well-led institutions.

What is notable about the armed forces is that in every case those in the senior ranks of leadership have worked their way up from the lower positions. Every three- or four-star officer once was a junior officer with a single gold bar on his or her collar, and some of the very best senior officers benefited from service in the enlisted ranks before becoming officers. They are particularly well attuned to the circumstances of those under them, more so than some CEOs in private industry.

Interestingly, in recent decades some businesses have endeavored to ensure that their executives learn how their organizations function from the bottom up. JetBlue, for example, has its managers spend time as flight attendants and baggage handlers to help them better understand their business. At L'Oréal cosmetics, employees in the marketing division spend weeks at a time working in shopping malls and other locations where their products are sold over the counter.

There of course is the danger of those at the top getting too involved with the details at lower levels. Today's technologies, with email and other forms of instant communication, can tempt leaders to try to micromanage a company's activities. When I was in the Pentagon, for example, we had the capability to watch on video military operations in Afghanistan or Iraq in real time. I usually declined those opportunities. The problem I saw was having senior officers at the Pentagon, not to mention the Secretary, in the position of second-guessing aspects of an ongoing operation. That is a danger in the military, as it can be in business. Managers need to let the people in the line make decisions, make mistakes, and learn from them—just as many of them did to get where they are today.

It is not the strongest of the species that survives, nor the most intelligent, but the one most responsive to change.

—Paraphrase of Charles Darwin

Leaders who try to impose rigid authority and centralized control from the top can find their organizations becoming unimaginative and inflexible. Indeed, history is littered with examples of militaries that became too wedded to established ways of doing things and found they were not successful in the face of more adaptive and determined enemy forces: the Persians against the Greeks; the imperial British Army in colonial America; the French army against the German military at the onset of World War II; Arab militaries against the Israeli Defense Forces; and, in the early years of the conflict, the U.S. Army in Vietnam.

What sets the U.S. military apart from some other armed forces—and even some American civilian institutions—is that it encourages principled but loyal dissent. In keeping with a culture that promotes independent thinking and individual judgment at multiple levels of command, it devolves responsibility to the lowest level of authority possible. Junior officers and enlisted personnel in their twenties are regularly entrusted with life-and-death decisions as well as with equipment worth millions of dollars. By contrast, the old rigid, top-down Soviet style of command gave those in lower ranks practically no discretion or responsibility, except to do exactly what they were told.

The U.S. military is an extraordinary training ground where

young men and women learn to think on their feet and to understand that at any given moment, circumstances may require them to dramatically adjust their habitual ways of thinking or acting. Invariably members of the military are given significant responsibility at very young ages. They encounter situations that call for independent judgment and even trial and error. This gives them an opportunity to adapt and innovate; indeed it requires that they do so.

Much of the success of the American military has come from this ingrained ability to adapt and innovate. The use of the telegraph to communicate instantaneously across long distances and railroads to move men and supplies helped the Union prevail in the Civil War (the first war in which railroads were used, something encouraged by a former railroad lawyer named Abraham Lincoln). More recently, the merger of special operations forces with CIA operatives and precision-guided munitions from U.S. airpower was a transformative way of fighting in the twenty-first century, toppling the Taliban government and sending al-Qaeda fleeing from Afghanistan.

In business, adaptability is every bit as important as it is in the military. Our free market system is based on competition. The company that delivers a superior product at a lower price can be expected to gain market share—and succeed. But no victory is permanent. Success is almost always ephemeral. Competitors are continuously trying to do things at lower cost. There is no such thing as a permanent competitive edge. Companies that make a practice of rewarding innovation are the ones that succeed. Companies that rest on their laurels decline and eventually go out of business.

Nothing is static. For every offense there is a defense. For every defense there is an offense.

Nearly every organization has competitors, and sometimes even enemies. The best leaders recognize that competition can make their organization better. In the military, the enemy is studied and watched closely. As the saying goes, it is your enemies who make you strong. The weaker opponent has to find the vulnerabilities and weaknesses of the stronger to survive a conflict. Enemies have brains. They work to understand the other side's patterns and procedures and adjust their tactics accordingly.

In 1983, terrorists detonated a truck filled with explosives at a U.S. Marine barracks in Beirut, killing 241 U.S. Marine and Navy corpsmen. Our military's immediate reaction was to try to prevent similar attacks by erecting cement barricades around buildings in Lebanon that were housing Americans. That worked, but the enemy promptly adapted. Their next tactic was to use rocket-propelled grenades (RPGs), lobbing them over the new anti-truck barricades to hit their targets. As a reaction, U.S. and coalition forces hung wire mesh over their embassy buildings, so that when an RPG hit the mesh, it would bounce off. In response the terrorists starting using snipers and remotely detonated explosives to attack soft targets—Americans on their way to and from work. In short, the enemy went to school on us. They fashioned a counter for every counter our forces employed. They knew that the U.S. and allied armies, navies, and air forces could not be defeated on the battlefield, so they chose spectacular asymmetric attacks that would be covered in our press and, they hoped, convince the

American people and their representatives in Congress to withdraw support for the U.S. presence in Lebanon—which is exactly what happened.

A similar situation has been at work in the conflicts U.S. forces have faced in Afghanistan and Iraq. While strong states developed the use of large massed forces, their enemies fashioned unconventional, asymmetric approaches, such as small terrorist cells. Further, the enemy has found ways to use even the instruments of our democracy against us. For example, the enemy stages attacks that are not militarily significant—a bombing of a nightclub or a military post. They do it not because they expect it will defeat our forces on the battlefield, but because they know that the news footage of the carnage they inflict can demoralize our people and their elected representatives, weakening our country's will to persevere.

The hard truth is that it is not possible to defend at every place, against every conceivable type of terrorist attack, at every moment of the day or night. That is precisely why President Bush resolved after the 9/11 attacks that the only way to be successful against terrorists was not simply to try to defend ourselves against them, but to go on the offense—to put pressure on terrorist organizations wherever they were and on those nations that harbored or financed them. To continue with a purely defensive strategy would have required that we change the nature of our open, democratic society. "The purpose of terrorism," Lenin once said, "is to terrorize." It is not to just to inflict casualties and kill, though that is part of it. Terrorists seek to intimidate and alter our way of life. Had we hunkered down in a "Fortress America" police state, the terrorists would have achieved their goal.

When your enemy is making mistakes, don't stop him in the middle.
—*Napoleon Bonaparte*

When al-Qaeda gained control over some Sunni villages in western Iraq for a period, a resourceful group of American soldiers and marines studied how the Sunni tribes were responding to al-Qaeda dominance. Up until then, the Sunnis had been staunchly, in some cases violently, opposed to the Coalition presence in Iraq and to the elected Iraqi government which they had largely boycotted. But al-Qaeda operatives had imposed their oppressive and brutal rule and, as a result, alienated many Sunnis. So our forces reached out to Sunni tribal leaders and worked to win their support. This led to what became known as the "Sunni Awakening" in 2006, which, along with several other key factors, such as the growing size and capability of the Iraqi security forces and the increasing maturity of the Iraqi government, began to turn the tide of the war. With President Bush's courageous decision to send thirty thousand more U.S. troops several months later, al-Qaeda in Iraq was unable to keep the foothold they had before.

The unforgivable sin of a commander is to assume that an enemy will act in a certain way in a given situation

In the business world, studying your competition can mean the difference between success and failure by providing advance clues of their potential innovations that could disrupt your efforts.

Studying the competition can also suggest new techniques that could benefit your company. When I was a member of the board of Sears Roebuck, we took notice of a company that was offering a variety of goods at lower prices. Some seemed unconcerned about the relatively new, rapidly growing company. They didn't see it as a threat to an established firm that had been in business for a century. Any company that sold some of the things Sears sold in the same markets could obviously become a competitor. That competitor was an Arkansas-based company named Wal-Mart.

In the automotive industry, Japanese car manufacturers carefully studied their successful American counterparts for years— looking at what sold, what didn't sell, in other words, what the consumers wanted. Our automotive industry recognized the rise of sales of Japanese cars in the United States and yet for the most part waited too long to adapt. The result is clear to anyone driving down any street or highway today in America. As Winston Churchill put it, "No matter how enmeshed a commander becomes in the elaboration of his own thoughts, it is sometimes necessary to take the enemy into account."

The mission must determine the coalition. The coalition ought not determine the mission.

Some days after September 11, 2001, I was meeting alone in my Pentagon office with Benjamin Netanyahu, who was then a former as well as future Israeli prime minister. We were discussing military and diplomatic efforts that were under way in the wake of the terrorist attacks against America.

We noted that the United States would need a number of different coalitions that could be fashioned for a variety of different challenges, from combating the proliferation of weapons of mass destruction to addressing the problem of piracy, attacking al-Qaeda and terrorist networks, or toppling state sponsors of terror. The historic pattern in the United States had emphasized the need to build the largest international coalition possible, even if that meant allowing the coalition to determine American objectives. As we talked it became clear that America would best not be bound by a single large coalition that would be able to determine what missions would be in our country's best interests.

It was mindless to believe that every country would agree with every mission we determined was in America's best interests. It wouldn't happen. Instead we should determine a set mission, then go out and develop nations that support that mission, rather than the other way around.

People can be divided into three groups: those who make things happen, those who watch things happen, and those who wonder what happened.

—*John W. Newbern*

Not long ago, a mission took place that did not start auspiciously. One helicopter crashed, striking a wall adjacent to the postage-stamp-sized landing zone. Only the skill of the pilots prevented fatalities. But because the attack had been meticulously planned, rehearsed over and over, and a range of conceivable contingencies thought through—including a possible helicopter crash—the operators were able to quickly adapt and ensure that their objective could still be achieved: killing al-Qaeda's senior leader, Osama bin Laden.

The U.S. Navy SEALs are unquestionably among the most skilled warriors in the world. They are so because they go through a demanding selection process and continuous training regimens. Each year, a few thousand individuals are invited to compete for the coveted Trident insignia that SEALs proudly wear on their uniforms. For twenty-four weeks the trainees endure Basic Underwater Demolition/SEAL (BUD/S) School in Coronado, California. They run for miles carrying their boats above their heads. They swim in pounding surf and experience being in a pool with their hands tied behind their backs. They are denied sleep and subjected to the most physically painful and mentally stressful tests imaginable.

The culmination of their six months of training is "Hell Week." They sleep as few as four hours over the course of the week. Throughout "Hell Week" the pace of drills and tests brings a major fraction of the aspiring SEALs to their breaking points. Those remaining are tempted to toss in the towel. While shivering on the brink of hypothermia, they are enticed with blankets, hot coffee, and the promise of being warm again to give up their quest to become a SEAL. In some BUD/S classes, as many as 90 percent of the carefully selected recruits drop out.[13]

Even after a SEAL earns his Trident, the training doesn't stop. Until they retire, SEALs continue with courses designed to further hone their physical and mental skills. While being a SEAL is for only the most exemplary leaders, there are levels of achievement and excellence even within the SEAL community. They continue to go through a sorting process, by which they are continually evaluated and reevaluated. Their performance in combat situations is scrutinized by their fellow SEALs and by their superiors. Those who excel are encouraged to try out for even more elite teams, such as DEVGRU (Development Group), more commonly known as SEAL Team Six.

At first glance, this band of elite troops may not seem to offer much in the way of lessons for the rest of us mere mortals. What makes these special operators exceptional—like their counterparts in the Army's Delta Force, the Air Force combat controllers, and the Marine special operators—is not their brawn. There are several characteristics of the U.S. special operations forces that make them particularly skilled at producing leaders and achieving exceptional results in the most demanding and dangerous conditions.

First, special operators create order out of chaos. The reason they undergo such grueling physical and mental training is that it simulates the stress and disorder of combat. When the bullets start flying, they are less uncomfortable because they have trained so extensively for it. There's stress involved in any position that entails responsibility for others. If you have a team of people who know each other, respect each other, and are fully prepared to tackle crises as they come, your organization is much more likely to weather those challenges. In the military, a commonly uttered phrase is "Train like you fight." Special operations teams train together so that the particular strengths and weaknesses and the role of each team member are well understood by all.

Second, they have a "we" not an "I" mentality. The special operations forces are known as the "silent professionals." They don't brag. They don't seek public recognition. When they receive awards, they tend to acknowledge the roles of others. They are modest, understated, and committed more to advancing the team and the mission than themselves.

Last, special operators thrive in an organization that is flat—

that is, without the same hierarchy and bureaucracy as conventional forces. Every member of the special operations forces goes through the same training, regardless of rank. Given the complexity and challenges of the missions they are assigned, they are given extraordinary latitude to devise their own solutions and the authority to adapt as required on the fly. More often than not, they do not have to seek permission from headquarters to deviate from their plans. There is less red tape and fewer bureaucratic hurdles thrown in their way. A useful lesson for managers is to provide your troops guidance, but then step out of the way and let them do their jobs. If you've picked the right people, and trained them well, chances are they will succeed.

Weakness is provocative. Time and again it has invited adventures that strength might well have deterred.

History teaches that in a dangerous world, where enemies are on constant search for our vulnerabilities, a strong and capable military is essential. They learn to analyze our capabilities, yes, but also to analyze our weaknesses. While weakness is provocative, so too is a perception of weakness. Weakness entices aggressors into doing things that they otherwise wouldn't consider doing. The classic example, often cited by historians, is when Secretary of State Dean Acheson suggested that South Korea was outside of America's defense perimeter in Asia. It left the impression with South Korea's enemies that America might not defend our South Korean ally if attacked. North Korea invaded five months later.

Those who wear the uniform are taught not only to be vigilant, but to be self-aware. This lesson is applicable in many settings. It is rarely useful to lead with one's chin. In business, for example, senior executives would do well to be aware of their organization's vulnerabilities, knowing how and where their competitors might exploit them. It is also important for a company to not send a signal of weakness, or a perception of vulnerability, that might tempt competitors, or even corporate raiders, from doing something to that company that they otherwise might not have considered. A leader's tone and demeanor can do a great deal to symbolize strength and confidence, or weakness and vulnerability. In the military, the hundreds of thousands who serve in our armed forces provide a daunting deterrent to our enemies—and by so doing, they contribute to a more peaceful world.

As you read this, somewhere in the world there are American military men and women who are enduring not only the hardships of being away from their families, but the physical discomfort of being covered in sand or mud, perhaps in punishing heat or frigid cold, dodging gunfire or clearing explosive devices hidden on a foreign road. It calls to mind that when explorer Ernest Shackleton was planning for his expedition to the South Pole in 1914, he put up recruiting posters across London. They read, "Officers wanted for hazardous journey. Small wages. Constant danger. Safe return doubtful. Honor and recognition in case of success." The hundreds of thousands who serve in the U.S. military don't have corner offices. They don't have casual Fridays. They don't get preferred IPO shares of stock if their organization does well. Their salaries are competitive with the private sector, at least compared with the days when America had a military draft, but relatively low given the responsibilities they assume and the unusual risks they face. Yet somehow the military is able to attract, train, and retain hundreds of thousands of America's best leaders and managers.

One of the reasons our military has been so successful is that there is an unmistakable sense of purpose that comes from being part of something bigger than yourself. Every member of our armed forces today is a volunteer. Each made a personal decision to raise his or her hand and say, "Send me." A sense of purpose, of doing something honorable and important, is a powerful motivator in any organization.

In highly successful organizations, whether a Fortune 500 or a start-up company, a nonprofit organization or a sports team, the best members tend not to be driven solely by the money or the benefits or even the recognition. Most go to work and spend a healthy fraction of their waking moments helping their organization because they believe in its overarching mission. The most motivated employees believe in the *why* of what they are doing. When I served as Secretary of Defense, I held town-hall meetings at the Pentagon and at military bases all over the world, where I talked personally with the troops about why their work was so vital and how deeply their fellow citizens and I appreciated the dedication they put into their important duties.

Finding that noble nugget at the core of your enterprise is a sure way to inspire employees to want to do their best, and in so doing, help their organization achieve success. In the pharmaceutical industry, for example, the products that are discovered, developed, and marketed improve, extend, and save human lives. In the media business, the best reporters can uncover wrongdoing, keep the public well informed, and accurately provide the information American citizens need to make decisions about those they support for high office. Sports teams can provide role models for young people and teach them about teamwork and the important relationship between effort and results.

In the case of our military, one of the reasons so many volunteer, serve, and sacrifice is that they do it for each other. In the military, "no man left behind" is a great deal more than a motto. It announces and assures each individual that those in his unit are there for one another. They can know with certainty that if they are wounded or fall in battle, their fellow troops will bring them home. They can confidently take the necessary risks and place trust in the members of their unit because they know that trust is returned. That camaraderie and sense of purpose encourage acts of uncommon valor—troops covering a grenade to shield others, holding positions under withering enemy fire to ensure that others can move to safety, flying a chopper into a perilous hot zone to pick up wounded soldiers, and other acts of self-sacrifice that those in uniform routinely perform.

My wife, Joyce, and I often visited wounded service members at Walter Reed Army Medical Center and Bethesda Naval Hospital. Each time we searched for something we could say to reassure them of our nation's appreciation for their sacrifices. These were young men and women recuperating from losing limbs and other combat wounds. Yet despite those terrible, painful injuries, they still felt an unmistakable closeness to those in their units. Over the course of our visits, the most frequent remark we heard was "I want to get back to my buddies."

During the Korean War, enemy soldiers were amazed at how American troops, even under heavy shelling, would go back out on the battlefield to retrieve and care for their wounded. To this day the Defense Department and the American people send recovery teams to scour the jungles of Vietnam for the remains of those lost in that conflict. In 2003, when President Bush made the decision to go to war in Iraq, one of our priorities was to find the remains of Scott Speicher, a naval aviator whose plane had been shot down back in 1991 during the Persian Gulf War. It was not known whether he had been captured by Saddam's forces or killed when his plane crashed. Twelve years later, U.S. troops patrolling the area in Anbar Province where his plane had crashed sought new leads. After talking with local Iraqis it was determined that Speicher had been killed in the crash and had been buried in the desert. And on August 13, 2009, his remains returned home. In the sadness, there was also a sense of gratitude and closure. America does not leave its men and women in uniform behind.

The lesson is that every organization is, in some sense, a family. A company that has a zero-sum competition among employees, where one person's success is seen as diminishing another's, isn't an environment people enjoy. A healthy corporate culture is one in which colleagues look out for each other and elevate the interest of the team above the individual, where they channel their individual talents into the service of their group's broader goal. They understand that their success is linked to the organization's success. Work to make yours an organization in which people don't feel left behind, one in which there is camaraderie and a sense of team at all levels.

CHAPTER TWELVE

INSIDE THE OVAL OFFICE

Most of the readers of this book are not going to be elected President of the United States. Chances are most will not work or even aspire to work in the White House. But a number of the lessons useful for service in the White House are every bit as applicable to other organizations, even those who work in offices that are not oval. The president is in some ways like a Fortune 500 chief executive officer—except with a considerably bigger job and a much smaller salary.

When I was a youngster in Illinois in the 1930s, I never dreamed I might end up working closely with four U.S. presidents. My first memory of a president is of Franklin Delano Roosevelt, who as commander in chief during World War II seemed like a larger-than-life figure. I assumed he'd be president forever. When he died abruptly in 1945, I was in the seventh grade. With our fathers serving in the war, some of my classmates and I were so stunned and saddened by the news we cried.

As I got older, I realized that presidents are not gods. They are not perfect. They are not indispensable. They are not all-knowing. Presidents make mistakes. Sometimes serious mistakes.

Never say "the White House wants."
Buildings can't want.

This makes the role of the White House staff particularly consequential. They can provide a crucial link between the President and the American people. They can advise and steer a president away from a poor decision, or they can help a president play a hand like a foot. That was one reason I usually took issue with folks who rushed into some meeting with the breathless phrase "the White House wants." A building and even an organization cannot want something. The people who run that organization can. It helps to have that clarification in one's mind, because unlike buildings, people are fallible.

In politics, every day is filled with numerous
opportunities for serious error. Enjoy it.

When I was White House Chief of Staff for President Gerald Ford, I accompanied him on an official visit to Japan. A state visit by the President of the United States is a major event. It takes weeks of planning. It requires sizable resources in terms of staffing, security, communications, and transportation. There is extensive discussion within the State Department and other agencies about what the President ought to say, what he ought not say, what he ought to try to accomplish, and what risks or problems might be expected. As many as one hundred people might travel with the nation's chief executive on such trips. That doesn't include the press, which could also include dozens of people. They travel on Air Force One or a backup plane and need hotel rooms, communication centers, and White House staff to provide information and respond to their questions.

The trip to Japan was Ford's first foray abroad as president, and indeed, the first visit to Japan ever by a sitting president. Not having been elected to the office in his own right, he was being closely watched by the entire world to see how he would handle his new responsibilities. Although his predecessor, Richard Nixon, was at the time held in low regard by many Americans, outside of the country Nixon was considered an impressive, even visionary, foreign policy leader. The unknown Ford inevitably suffered by comparison when it came to global affairs.

For Ford's Japanese visit, we took pains to make sure everything would be perfect. Briefings were readied. The communications team worked with the press. We thought we were ready.

I was in Ford's suite in Tokyo as he was getting ready for his first public event, a public ceremony and meeting with Emperor Hirohito. That was when I learned about a problem. A big one. The tailor who prepared the formal attire required for the elaborate ceremony had made the President's pants several inches too short. At that point there was nothing that could be done. Ford shrugged and went to the event anyway, with trousers that showed a major fraction of his ankles and in full view of the Emperor, the Japanese audience, and world press.

This was an embarrassing mishap with the last emperor in the world. President Ford might well have blown his top —and at me. I was Chief of Staff and as such it could be fairly argued that any mistakes were ultimately my responsibility. That wasn't how Ford thought. He didn't assign blame. He saw a problem, found the best solution he could, and moved on with his life. Other presidents might well have handled that situation differently—and certainly more loudly.

Politics is human beings.

We tend to think of people at the top as different from the rest of us. That's true of CEOs, heads of large nonprofits or other organizations, and especially true of presidents. The President of the United States is many things. He is a symbol of our country. He is also the head of state, the commander in chief, a political leader, and a human being. People can from time to time forget that last one.

Like anyone, a president has instincts and feelings. He enjoys hearing jokes and good stories. He tends not to like being criticized. He worries about his wife and children. He can get angry. He can get down.

The even-keeled Jerry Ford once got so mad in the Oval Office that he hurled a pencil across the room. George W. Bush was bracingly informal and blunt on occasion. Ronald Reagan loved to tell jokes and Hollywood stories that contained kernels of wisdom if one listened closely. I knew a then-future president who became so upset about something he read in the press that he almost unspooled himself in my office, screaming and carrying on about some minor mix-up.

I have been with former President Bill Clinton on several occasions, and you could sense immediately that he thoroughly enjoys being around people. Richard Nixon was not that way. Interaction with strangers did not seem to come naturally. He would periodically abandon the Oval Office for a private room in the Executive Office Building across the street, where he could be alone to think and write. Yet day after day, he did public events even though they were not completely comfortable for him. Nixon was a formidable politician, winning election to the House, the Senate, the vice presidency, and twice to the presidency, on the second occasion by one of the largest margins in American history.

It's easy for anyone working for a powerful boss in a high-stress atmosphere—whether it's a president of a nation, a chairman of a company, or some other leader—to forget that he or she is a human being.

You will have plenty to do without trying to manage the First Family.

The leader of any organization usually has an assortment of relatives, friends, informal advisors, and even hangers-on with varying degrees of competence and ability. For a staff person that can pose a challenge. That is no less true in the White House. How do you handle those folks—who vary in temperament, intellect, and their perception of their own importance? Easy. You don't.

In the Ford administration, there was considerable consternation among some staff members about First Lady Betty Ford. Being the First Lady of the United States has to be a difficult experience. Yes, you live in a large mansion and even host the British royal family for dinner. But you also completely surrender your own and your family's privacy for four to eight years and for some time thereafter. You are expected not to work or to have a life outside of your spouse's. People comment endlessly on your hairstyle and your dress and can be tough about both. It may be the most visible position in the world without a paycheck.

Eleanor Roosevelt once said that as First Lady, "you are no longer clothing yourself, you are dressing a public monument." You are also expected by many to put your opinions in a lockbox and leave them there for the duration.

Betty Ford was a special human being. She was lively, outspoken, and had a sharp sense of humor. She took the conventions attached to the role of First Lady and tossed them out on their ear. She had no problem disagreeing with her husband or saying things considered unusual for a Republican First Lady, such as her vocal support for abortion rights. At first, some were shocked. One person wrote to the White House telling Mrs. Ford to keep her "stupid views" to herself. "You are no lady," the letter said, "First— second—or last." Some of President Ford's advisors worried that Betty's outspokenness would cost the President votes. At some point I was asked what we ought to do about "the Betty problem."

In the first place I didn't think there was a problem. I thought the country was past the antiquated notion that there was something unacceptable about a First Lady with a mind of her own. Further, I thought you'd have to have an extra hole in your head to think anyone could tell that President's wife how she was supposed to behave.

In Mrs. Ford's case, the public turned in her favor. Buttons popped up that read "Let's keep Betty's husband in the White House" and "Re-Elect Betty for First Lady."

I have a feeling that over time the Betty Ford model—strong, independent women with minds of their own—was not only accepted, but favored by the American people. And one day I fully expect we will have a First Gentleman, with his own set of problems and issues. I wouldn't even begin to advise someone how to manage those.

The First Family can have a sizable influence on an administration. Presidential spouses and children can be assets, as President Kennedy's young children were. They can also get into trouble. In every administration I was directly involved in, the President had children who were young adults. Like many in their generation, some enjoyed parties, had boyfriends or girlfriends, and did the various things that kids do. Of course, the only reason anybody cared about what they were doing was their last names. But I don't know anyone with a lick of sense who went up to any President and critiqued his children.

When one of the Ford children said something less than charitable about former President Nixon, violating the guideline set by his father for members of his administration, it was a political embarrassment. But it wasn't for anyone in the Ford White House to say so. Ultimately dealing with him, an immensely likable young man with a right to his own views and a friend of mine to this day, was a task for his father.

The better part of one's life consists of his friendships.

—*Abraham Lincoln*

Any leader needs friends, their important links to the rest of the world. Many corporate leaders, for example, bring in people they've worked with before to help them. As President, John F. Kennedy relied on a group of Boston pols and made one of his brothers, someone he trusted implicitly, Attorney General of the United States. Ronald Reagan had his "California Kitchen Cabinet," which included future Attorney General Ed Meese, among others. The Clintons had their friends from Arkansas and the Obamas a group from Chicago. George W. Bush had some associates from Texas.

Those relationships from time to time led to criticism in Washington, especially from the "experts" who hang around town forever and who can't imagine why a president wouldn't want to toss aside his friends and hire someone like them in their place. Without friends who help them keep their moorings, presidents can lose touch with how the decisions they make in the Oval Office will affect those outside.

In the Ford White House, I encouraged friends of the President who expressed concerns about the administration's actions to meet with him personally so they could deliver their critiques without anyone as a filter. They generally accepted gladly, but it didn't always work out the way I'd hoped. Full of vinegar, they would stride into the White House intending to give the President their complaints and concerns straight. But when they walked into the Oval Office—one of the world's most intimidating offices—they would turn to jelly. Their old friend Jerry was now the President of the United States and the commander in chief of the armed forces.

As often as not, the old friend with his list of complaints and concerns would figuratively kiss the President's ring and tell him what a fine job he was doing. Then, afterward, when out of earshot from the President, they would turn to me and say, "Well, Don, I'm glad I was able to get that off my chest. He needed to hear that."

Don't be consumed by the job.

Coming to work for any organization with a renowned reputation—an Apple or Google, for example—can be daunting. That is even more true when you work in a place like the White House.

One of the ways I kept my bearings while working in the White House was to remember that the person who was elected to office was not me, but somebody else. The President of the United States wins an election and the confidence of a majority of the American people for a reason. But like the commander in chief, a staff member can also be susceptible to being out of touch with those outside the White House. Working long hours for an important person can make it difficult to separate work from the rest of your life. The risk is that you may begin to think you are indispensable to the person you serve. Something has to give in your life—and what usually gives are your family and friendships. Wherever you are, whatever the setting, however important your title, don't let that happen.

Remember you are not all that important.
Your responsibilities are.

Your network is an important part of your life. And that set of relationships was probably a good part of the reason you ended up in the executive suite of your company, at the White House, or even as President of the United States. Eventually a life of missed school functions and family events and other personal milestones takes its toll. They are not things you can get back.

The role of White House Chief of Staff is that of a "javelin catcher."

—Jack Watson, Chief of Staff to President Jimmy Carter

Arguably, there is no more consequential staff position in the U.S. government, perhaps even the world, than the position of White House Chief of Staff. At its core, the job is about making sure the President is able to focus on what is important for the country, that he is prepared, on schedule, and safe. Being Chief of Staff at the White House, as unique a post as it is, has lessons for anyone helping to manage a large organization with a diverse group of employees and clients expecting the best—clients who, in the case of the White House, are the American people.

As with a leader of any organization, there are many more people who decide they "need" to see the President than the President has time to see. There usually exists a diverse staff of self-confident, strong-willed people—each of whom thinks their own priorities must be the boss's priorities, and that their proximity to the boss needs to be maximized.

So a chief of staff sometimes has to intercede. The best way to handle the task is with good humor, patience, and occasionally a firm hand. When those qualities seem in short supply, that probably means you need them even more. In the Nixon White House, H. R. Haldeman and John Ehrlichman became known as "the Berlin Wall," referencing their German-sounding names and the impression that they were keeping people away from the President, especially those who might tell him things he didn't want to hear.

One price of proximity to the President is the duty to bring bad news.

I was often the first staff person Gerald Ford talked to in the morning and the last before he went up to his private quarters in the East Wing for the evening. I heard his complaints about news coverage, or his concerns about policy decisions, or his preferences on matters ranging from a phone call with the leader of China to the scheduling of his haircut.

Because of that proximity, a chief of staff is in the best position to gauge a president's mood, and to sense when is the right time to deliver important information—whether good or bad. A president, like all of us, can balance only so many peas on his knife at one time. There's a time and place for adding to a president's considerable challenges and there are days when delivering bad news is the last thing one should do. But it is those closest to the boss— any boss—who can best sense when those times are.

As chief of staff, I was the messenger of bad news for Ford on many occasions. It could be something like the Dow Jones Industrial Average taking a sharp drop, or some criticism in the papers from a former member of his staff, or actions with more far-reaching implications such as the 1975 seizure of the USS *Mayaguez* in Southeast Asia by the Khmer Rouge. I also was the one who had to deliver the bad news to Ford that Ronald Reagan had declined his offer to serve in his Cabinet. Reagan, of course, decided to challenge Ford for the presidency instead.

My approach as Chief of Staff was to keep an open door for the Vice President and key Cabinet officials. I did not want to be the gatekeeper for people whose counsel and advice the President wanted and needed. When senior officials asked to meet with the President, they could almost always do so. And promptly.

Being Vice President is difficult. Don't make it tougher.

Being the number two person in any organization is not easy. Become too visible and you're seen as stealing the limelight from the boss. Stay out of the headlines and keep your head down and people conclude you aren't doing much. Enthusiastically back the boss's agenda and you risk being considered a yes-man. Be seen as distancing yourself in even the slightest way from the president or his policies and you're an embarrassment or disloyal or both. You can easily become a punching bag for critics, especially those unwilling to take on the boss directly.

Being Vice President of the United States can mean four or eight years of tiptoeing on eggshells or riding a unicycle on a high wire—pick your metaphor.

For reasons I do not fully understand to this day, presidential candidates often have a tough time selecting their vice presidential candidates. While a few picks have proved valuable—like Dick Cheney and, arguably, Al Gore, others—such as John Edwards, Tom Eagleton, and Spiro Agnew—have been lacking and hurt the candidate and his party.

When President Ford asked for my thoughts on his selection of a vice president, what I said back in 1974 seems to hold up pretty well. I suggested that: one, the individual should be capable of being president by virtue of his abilities, experience, and personal characteristics; two, his selection should serve to broaden potential support for the administration in order to facilitate the process of governing; and three, he should be capable of broadening the appeal of the President's party. Leaders should strive to find people with talents that complement theirs, and, if possible, those who can broaden the reach and strength of an organization.

I've known a number of vice presidents and have had frequent interaction with three—Spiro Agnew, Nelson Rockefeller, and Dick Cheney. Each approached his position in a different way. Agnew seemed to spend more time giving speeches and checking the creases in his trousers than expressing interest in Nixon administration policies.

Rockefeller started life as a scion of one the wealthiest families in America. As such he was no doubt accustomed to getting his way. Moreover, before he became Ford's Vice President, he was already a national figure. Posh restaurants served a dish called oysters Rockefeller. He had been governor of New York for fifteen years, had run for president on two occasions, and was widely known to the press and in the country at large. Rockefeller had no doubt that he was every bit as qualified to be president as Gerald Ford—if not more so. In New York, a state known for rough-and-tumble politics, the governor had been the big boss, used to rolling over people. That is what he tried to do as Vice President. This got him crosswise with a number of people in the administration, and, on more than one occasion, the President himself, which made him a liability for Ford and led the President to conclude he had no choice but to drop him from his election ticket in 1976.

You never get in trouble for what you don't say.
—DICK CHENEY'S FAVORITE RULE, ATTRIBUTED TO SAM RAYBURN

*When the President is faced with a decision, be sure he has
the recommendations of all the appropriate people.*

Unlike Agnew, Dick Cheney didn't worry about how well he
was dressed, and unlike Rockefeller, Cheney did not for a moment
see himself as a co-president or even a future one, given his health
and age. Instead he worked quietly behind the scenes to focus on
policy and kept his views to himself, except when he met privately
with the President. Those characteristics made him one of the
most effective vice presidents in history and certainly in my lifetime. It also left him open to criticism because he spent no time
worrying about what the press said about him and made little if
any effort to correct misimpressions. As a result, his accomplish-
ments and contributions to the Bush administration were significant, but little known. That's the way he wanted it. Dick Cheney
was the model of a number two.

The lesson from this is that in any organization you might want to have some sympathy for the person in such a position. Or at least make an effort to see the world from his or her perspective.

As a staff member in any organization, you may encounter people in important posts whom the boss simply does not enjoy, does not want to be around, or, for whatever reason, holds in less than high regard. It is up to those close to the boss to find ways to remedy that, to see that he or she still receives the advice and counsel they need on key decisions.

In the case of the Ford administration, the President simply did not get on well with Defense Secretary Jim Schlesinger, a talented official he'd inherited from the Nixon administration. As a result, he avoided meeting with him. On the other hand, Ford had an excellent relationship with Secretary of State Kissinger. The result was that Ford's decision-making could not help but lean toward the State Department's views over Defense's. That posed a problem for me when it came to issues like arms control negotiations with the Soviet Union.

I knew how vital it was for the President to hear the views of those in the Pentagon. I took every opportunity to urge Ford to meet with Schlesinger, if only over the phone. I also tried to relay Schlesinger's views to the President separately. I knew I wouldn't be doing my job if Ford wasn't hearing all sides of an important national security issue.

This goes for all of us. We all have individuals we prefer over others, and some that we could do without altogether. Know when you have a bias, pro or con, on people or issues, and make the boss aware of it so he can take it into account.

Don't panic. Things may be going better than they seem from the inside.

Working in the White House can be a disorienting experience. In senior staff positions you will become aware of things that only a handful of people in the country may know. When major national or international news made its way to the front page, it often was not news to those of us inside. We had already processed the information, and knew the background and context in a way those on the outside could not.

This can happen in any organization. It is no surprise that what the public may learn through the press can be different from what you know to be true. For example, public coverage of revenues and earnings can be delayed by days, so while your company may have already taken steps to improve the problems in a negative report, analysts and investors may be panicking. By contrast, your company may be the toast of Wall Street in the financial press, but inside, you may be aware that there are challenges ahead that aren't yet known. The gap between those in the know and the outside world can be disorienting. Accept it as a fact of the job. Know that over time, more context and information will become available that will put criticism as well as praise in a more accurate light.

Don't accept the post unless you are free to tell the President what you think "with the bark off."

A president is physically separated from the people he represents most of the time. Aside from constituent mail and rare unscripted public forays, he doesn't get to interact regularly with the people who elected him. That makes it all the more important for his staff to keep him in touch with the views and attitudes of his constituents. My self-appointed role as a sort of "Minister of Candor" with President Ford was made considerably easier by our long friendship. On his first day in office, he said to a small group of us that "I want my friends to give me hell." We all nodded and promised that we would. But who really likes to give a president hell? Especially a friend you like and respect? I did my best. But it wasn't always easy.

In 1975, Ford was in a heated dispute with members of Congress over funding to the South Vietnamese government. The Congress had voted to withdraw U.S. funding, which made it all but inevitable that South Vietnam would fall to brutal communist control. The President was so angry that he did something uncharacteristic. He started questioning the personal fortitude of members of Congress, suggesting that they didn't have the guts to stand up to the communists. That was tough language for the 1970s, though regrettably it has become more routine since. Of course, what a president says sets the tone for the rest of the administration. His words echo right down the line and are repeated and incorporated into the public remarks of other administration officials.

What Ford had said about Congress, I told him, sounded like something LBJ might have said. This was not meant as a compliment, and Ford didn't take it as one. "There is something about that chair," I said, pointing to the one behind his desk in the Oval Office, "that makes presidents begin to act and talk in a way to make them seem tough." As a member of Congress and even as Vice President, Ford might have been able to get away with an angry outburst or the use of some ill-chosen words. But less so as the President. I was concerned about how his anger, however sincere and strongly felt, would come across to the American people. Presidents are expected to be measured in their rhetoric. What people liked about Gerald Ford, in contrast to his immediate predecessors, was that he came across as a warm, decent, honest person.

I reminded the President there are two particularly harmful things for anyone in public life. One is ridicule and the other is being seen as not up to the job. My concern was that angry and blustering comments like that might leave the latter impression. I suggested instead that he use what I called an "Eisenhower-type approach" in dealing with political opponents. Even though Ike was known to have a temper, he rarely if ever was angry in public or called anyone names. Like FDR, he would talk about his opponents more with disappointment or sadness than anger.

Ford was still seething about the issue. "Well, gawl dangit, they did bug out!" he said. But he agreed with my point and appreciated hearing it. It is likely I was of more value to him as an advisor precisely because our long relationship was such that I could tell him what I believed he needed to hear.

Don't automatically obey the President's requests if you strongly disagree.

Not every relationship between a staff member and the boss begins with a personal friendship. Still, the need for candor and forthrightness is important. I had known George W. Bush only slightly before he was president. It was no secret that his father and I were not close. It said something that despite his great respect for his father, the governor was willing to consider me for a position in his presidential Cabinet.

Unlike when I was Chief of Staff for President Ford, I didn't have one-on-one meetings with President Bush every day where I could offer suggestions or advice. Sometimes I would make points to President Bush, in small meetings or in an occasional phone call. More often, I'd send him a short memo. I find that memos work well for leaders who are busy and don't have time for long conversations with everybody. They can read a memo when it is convenient—especially memos that are to the point.

I sent many such notes to President Nixon, who liked reading concise memos. I once advised Nixon against excluding Senator Edmund Muskie, a likely presidential rival, from the signing of the Clean Air Act, saying the unnecessary exclusion might make the President seem petty and unpresidential. I wrote him memos encouraging Republican Party outreach to minorities. I once wrote a strongly worded memo expressing my opposition to any idea of using the Pentagon to spy on U.S. civilians. "There are 150 reasons why it is a bad thing to do under our system of government," I wrote. "The president knows them all."

There were occasions when I disagreed with George W. Bush about something. Shortly after the September 11 attacks, for example, I questioned the President's calling the hijackers "cowardly" in his public remarks. As a former aviator, I didn't consider climbing into the cockpit of an airplane, gripping the controls, and flying it at 500 mph straight into a building an act of cowardice. That was a crucial misunderstanding of the enemy. They weren't afraid and they weren't cowards. They were fanatics, which is quite a different thing. President Bush understood my point, and ultimately agreed with me.

Telling a boss when you believe he or she may be wrong can sometimes save them a good deal of grief. And in some cases it may even save the company.

Of special value to his leadership are the President's words and time. They should be expended with the utmost care.

In our country, we have come to treat presidents as the center of the universe. That impression is perpetuated by the news media, members of Congress, the political parties, and sometimes even presidents themselves. They appear on TV almost every day, opining about this issue or that. They release statements on the deaths of celebrities. They pop up on late-night talk shows with comedians. By doing so, they risk overexposure. This is true not only of the President of the United States, but of leaders of any organization. They tend to get the credit or the blame for their organization when the truth is that almost any enterprise relies on a large cast of contributors, not only the person at the top.

Overexposure can be a danger for any leader—not just politicians. Having one person be the focal point for every decision, every success, and every mistake puts enormous pressure on that leader. It can also hurt the organization by dissuading others from stepping forward and taking ownership of responsibilities that are properly theirs.

One way to avoid overexposure on the presidential level is to limit their public appearances and statements. Few things are more valuable for a president, a business leader, or any top official than the words they utter. What a leader says echoes throughout their organization. It becomes a template for others. A large and varied audience is attentive to what the boss says—whether voters or shareholders, Cabinet members or board members, competitors or enemies—so when a leader does take the podium, try to ensure it is for a compelling reason.

Move decisions out to the Cabinet and agencies.

Another way to broaden responsibility in an organization is to empower subordinates. In the case of the White House, that applies best to members of the presidential Cabinet. President Nixon used his Cabinet exceedingly well. He picked talented individuals with established reputations and ideas, men and women who had experience running something and who could be credible spokespersons. In some Cabinets, by contrast, it is difficult to remember the names of more than two or three out of a total of the fifteen or twenty.

Most organizations have a wealth of talent that can be utilized and deployed to help spread an organization's message and reach out to people far beyond the confines of a corporate boardroom. At a large Fortune 500 company, for example, there are any number of senior executives who can represent the organization publicly and take ownership of an activity. Give them the authority and responsibility to do so.

Strive to preserve and enhance the integrity of the presidency and pledge to leave it stronger than when you came.

When I was in the Boy Scouts, we learned a rule: "Always leave the campground cleaner than you found it." If you find a mess, clean it up, regardless of who made it.

I felt the same responsibility working in government, especially in the White House. The point was driven home to me by a friend named Bryce Harlow, who had advised a number of presidents, beginning with General Eisenhower. He had been around enough years to see the executive powers of the presidency come under assault from various quarters—the media, the Congress, the courts, and the permanent bureaucracy.

In the wake of the Vietnam War and Watergate, the standing of the institution of the presidency was at a modern historic low. Harlow gave me valuable advice in the early days of the Ford administration when he said something to the effect of "The steady pressure by Congress and the courts is to reduce executive authority. Resolve that when you leave the White House, you will leave it with the same authorities it had when you came. Do not contribute to the further erosion of presidential power on your watch."

Enjoy your time in public service. It is likely to be the most interesting and certainly the most challenging experience of your life.

My sense is that the number of talented young people with an interest in public service may not be as high as it was in my younger years. In part this may be because much of what we hear about government is what it's doing wrong.

I enjoyed my time in the private sector. It was challenging, interesting, and rewarding work. But I would have missed a great deal in my life had I not had the experience of serving in government, seeing how it works, coping with its challenges, and trying to make it work better for the American people.

When I was twenty years old and in my senior year at Princeton University, I attended our class banquet. The guest speaker was Adlai Stevenson. The year was 1954. Stevenson, a former Democratic governor of Illinois, had lost his run for president two years earlier in a landslide to General Dwight D. Eisenhower and was preparing to run again in 1956—an election he would also lose to Ike resoundingly.

Despite his misfortune in challenging one of the most popular politicians in modern times, Stevenson was a thoughtful man. He was also modest, telling those in his audience that evening that we were likely to forget him soon after he left the stage. That turned out to be the only inaccuracy in Governor Stevenson's remarks. In fact, the advice he gave those of us about to leave college and venture off into the world has stayed with me for nearly six decades.

Stevenson spoke eloquently about the importance of public service and the responsibility of every citizen privileged to live in our democratic system.

> *For it is to you, to your enlightened attention, that American government must look for the sources of its power. You dare not, if I may say so, withhold your attention. For if you do, if those young Americans who have the advantage of education, perspective, and self-discipline do not participate to the fullest extent of their ability, America will stumble, and if America stumbles the world falls.*

What Stevenson said is as true today as it was then. Possibly even more so.[14]

Despite much of the reporting in the press and the public opinion polling that shows lack of faith in government, there are a great many dedicated men and women in our government, trying to help it function well on behalf of the American people. There are often tough political fights in government. Sometimes your side wins, and sometimes it doesn't. But if you really pay attention to your time in government and get to know the people who devote their lives to it, it's hard not to come away understanding there is a great deal more that unites us as a country than divides us.

If you do choose to enter public service at any stage in your career, I commend you for it. Do it well. Enjoy your service. And don't screw it up!

CHAPTER THIRTEEN

THE CASE FOR CAPITALISM

We often see leaders of corporate America standing beside presidents and members of Congress, smiling in photos. Despite such access, business leaders are sometimes reluctant to take advantage of their opportunities to tell their elected representatives what they need to hear—instead of telling them what they want to hear.

We seldom read about prominent business leaders directly critiquing the actions of the federal government or stepping up to defend the advantages of free markets and the opportunities they create for the American people. I suppose if more business leaders defended capitalism, there might not be quite as many smiling photos with politicians.

Having been in the position of a chief executive officer, I can understand why a businessman might be reluctant to speak out against the actions of federal agencies that have the power to harm their enterprises. By doing so, corporate leaders could expose themselves and their companies to government retaliation—

from the IRS, the SEC, congressional committees, or the many other agencies of the federal government that regulate and oversee their operations. CEOs answer to their boards of directors, to shareholders, and to customers, all of whom have a full range of political views and whose economic interests could be adversely affected by what a corporate executive might say.

But understanding that reticence does not mean supporting it. America's economy was built on fortitude, not fear. And those who made it to the top of our market system often did so the hard way, not by taking the easy way out.

Over the years criticism of business and capitalism seems to have increased. The word *profit* is often used as an epithet. People in positions of influence—academicians, politicians, and Hollywood moviemakers—often disparage the capitalist system. A startling 68 percent of Americans, according to a 2012 poll, said they believe "big business" and the government "work together against the rest of us."[15] A nontrivial number of Hollywood celebrities, elected officials, and even teachers at various levels seem bent on persuading young people that America and the free enterprise system are inherently unfair and corrupt. A 2010 conference on "capitalism on campus" at the Manhattan Institute, for example, found a pronounced bias against the free market system. One speaker noted that many young Americans "have a 'pervasive disdain' for business, an attitude that is inflamed by what they read and hear in their college courses."[16] This is an attitude that those entering the business world, and those already working in corporate America, must be prepared, willing, and able to rebut.

What is taking place today is a more severe and sustained version of an old phenomenon. Even back in the 1950s, when I was an undergraduate in college, some professors made a practice of criticizing and demeaning business, businessmen, and the supposed greed and corruption in corporate America. The suggestion was that there was something illegitimate about working in a corporation. The flip side of that was that those in academia were honorable and devoid of self-interest. I knew differently. After World War II, my father, George Rumsfeld, sold houses. He was as ethical and honorable as any person I have ever known. He never made a great deal of money, but he provided for his family when times were tough. By his words and actions, he taught us the importance of hard work, earning a living, and doing so honorably.

In the 1960s, President John F. Kennedy addressed the U.S. Chamber of Commerce. He said something extraordinary, at least by today's standards:

> *If American business does not earn sufficient revenue to earn a fair profit, this Government cannot earn sufficient revenues to cover its outlays. If American business does not prosper and expand, this Government cannot make good its pledges of economic growth. Our foreign policies call for an increase in the sale of American goods abroad, but it is business, not Government, who must actually produce and sell these goods. Our domestic programs call for substantial increases in employment, but it is business, not Government, who must actually perform these jobs.*

Ironically, Kennedy was considered to be "anti-business." But few politicians today articulate such a powerful, thoughtful, and, I would add, accurate case for our free enterprise system, much less proud liberal Democrats like JFK.

In the 1980s, the Reagan era was derided as "the decade of greed" because President Reagan supported lower tax rates across the board and defended the role of business in America. The hit movie *Wall Street* featured the sinister Gordon Gekko, who was supposed to be representative of American capitalists. More recently, the far-left filmmaker Michael Moore unleashed the ironically titled film *Capitalism: A Love Story*, a homily about the greed and corruption of corporate America. "Capitalism means that a few people will do very well," he asserted, "and the rest will serve the few." Both films, and other anti-business movies that regularly come out of Hollywood, decry a system that runs on "greed."

Well, the capitalist system does indeed run on "greed"—if by greed one means self-interest and a desire to succeed and do well. The Nobel laureate economist Dr. Milton Friedman once was asked in a television interview how he could defend "the greed and concentration of power" of capitalism. His reply is famous and instructive.

> *Tell me, is there some society you know that doesn't run on greed? You think Russia doesn't run on greed? You think China doesn't run on greed? What is greed? Of course none of us are greedy; it's only the other fellow who's greedy. The world runs on individuals pursuing their separate interests.*[17]

It is important to appreciate that self-interest is not the same as selfishness. The desire to pursue one's goals, to do well, and to gain wealth—for your family, and yes, for yourself—is human nature. The quest for profit has contributed to some of civilization's most significant innovations—electricity, the automobile, the airplane, the railroad, the computer, and dozens of pharmaceuticals that improve, extend, and save lives.

> The inherent vice of capitalism is the unequal
> sharing of blessings; the inherent virtue of
> socialism is the equal sharing of miseries.
>
> —*Winston Churchill*

S ome years ago, Dr. Robert Goldwin, the dean of St. John's College in Annapolis, Maryland, and a friend, noted with dismay the preoccupation with the question "What causes poverty?" An international organization was commissioning a panel to look into that very question and asked Goldwin to chair the group. He declined, pointing out that the construct was exactly backward. The question "What causes poverty?" assumed that the natural state of man is to be prosperous and that there were forces in the world that "make" people poor. He pointed out that the opposite is in fact the case. People are naturally poor. The question that needs to be examined, Goldwin concluded, is "What makes people prosperous?"

If any panel of reasonable observers took up that question, the answer would be obvious: the ingenious free market system based on self-interest. America did not become the most successful nation in the world by happenstance—still less through socialism. The streets of America were not paved with gold. There was no recipe or model for instant success. Instead what the first settlers wanted and found, since they first arrived on these shores in the sixteenth century, was opportunity—the opportunity to apply their God-given talents. They worked hard, took risks, and through enterprise, thrift, and grit they achieved. They were followed by their distant cousins who heard about the possibilities offered by America and risked greatly to seek those same opportunities. And generation after generation has benefited ever since.

Underlying most arguments against the free
market is a lack of belief in freedom itself.
—*Dr. Milton Friedman*

The power of free markets is that they do not rely on command or compulsion. Instead, outcomes are the result of the voluntary acts of millions of people, cooperating in the process of exchanging goods and services. Those millions of individuals each day make self-interested decisions about the value of things they buy and they sell, decisions that in the aggregate determine the values of wages and prices better than any central planner, even the most brilliant, could ever conceivably do.

Because only a capitalist system allows individuals to own property and keep the product of their enterprise, individuals in turn have an interest in the laws and regulations that help protect those properties and products. People do not steal from others with abandon, because they learn there are consequences. As my longtime friend the late Dr. James Q. Wilson wrote, "Perhaps the most powerful antidote to unfettered selfishness is property rights." Because a capitalist system creates an environment that is hospitable to effort, risk, reward, and achievement, individual citizens can invest their time and resources to create wealth without fear of it being seized.

Because they have an interest in long-term wealth creation to benefit themselves, their children, and their grandchildren, citizens in a free market system have a stake in their country's success as well. Entrepreneurs and business owners improve the lives of their fellow citizens, who become their employees, their investors, and their customers. As a result, in market economies, more people tend to be prosperous. Even those at the lower end of the economic ladder tend to be considerably better off compared with their counterparts in countries with different economic systems.

More important, no one at birth is doomed or blessed to remain at any particular economic level, whether at the bottom or the top. The poor have a chance to achieve and become wealthy, and the wealthy may lose out and become poor. Walk down a street with retail stores in any American town. Six months later, some fraction of those stores will have been replaced by different stores. In the free market, companies are allowed to go out of business and be replaced by competitors who offer the same or better products at lower prices. Consider my hometown of Chicago. When I grew up in the 1930s and '40s, the major corporations headquartered there included International Harvester, Montgomery Ward, Sears Roebuck, and Marshall Field's. Today the major companies include Groupon, Allstate, Motorola, OfficeMax, and Orbitz. Sixty years from now, they are likely to again be quite different.

The trouble with socialism is that eventually you run out of other people's money.
—*Margaret Thatcher*

The world has tried socialist, communist, command, and other unfree economic systems in which citizens do not own property and everyone supposedly shares in the production of goods and services. The Soviet Union was founded on the idea that everyone would be equal, and that all would share in the bounty. But everyone was not equal. The ruling class lived in luxurious dachas and were driven around in ZIL limousines. The system was rooted in corruption. The communist system—supposedly an ideal—proved to be an utter failure.

Even today, decades after the fall of the Soviet empire, there are still some who believe socialism can work. It has a perverse popularity in parts of Western Europe and even, it seems, among some young Americans who wear Che Guevara T-shirts, major in things like Marxist studies in college, and camp out in cities, railing against Wall Street and corporate America. Even our federal government has an increasing attachment to the idea of an ever-expansive federal government with a responsibility to meet all of its citizens' needs or whims.

People don't spend money earned by others with the same care that they spend their own.

When people spend their own money, they generally behave in a responsible, rational, predictable way. They act in their own self-interest. They do not throw their money around recklessly. They tend to think things through before spending or committing their money. They take care to try to achieve a return on their investments. But when people are dealing with *other people's money*, they behave quite differently.

This problem poses a serious challenge in any large organization—in government, in business, and even in nonprofits. Generally, the bigger the organization, the more difficult it is to get people to treat the organization's money as they do their own. After all, those funds are "other people's money," not theirs.

Not long ago, federal employees in the General Services Administration made headlines for taking what they characterized as "scouting trips" to five-star hotels to organize a lavish conference in Las Vegas. As part of the conference, they charged the taxpayers hundreds of thousands of dollars in expenses that included $6,000 for commemorative coins presented to fellow government employees in velvet boxes . . . $3,200 for entertainment that included a "mind reader" . . . thousands more for iPods, more than one hundred of which disappeared even before being given to the employees. There were mini beef Wellington hors d'oeuvres and $19-per-person "artisan cheese" plates. What led them to spend so lavishly? It was, quite simply, because they were not spending their own money. They were spending "other people's money."

For every instance of out-of-control government spending that whistle-blowers and the media uncover there are many more that are not known. I've observed instances when an office manager with a budget to buy supplies comes back with multiple staplers, file folders, dozens of pens, and reams of paper that are not needed.

If those same managers were buying supplies for themselves at home, were paying for the supplies out of their own pockets, or gave a thought to the cost to taxpayers of just the interest on the dollars that had to be borrowed to purchase those unneeded supplies, we can be sure that the money would have been spent more prudently. When dealing with "other people's money," the pattern is to spend it in ways that we think will make our lives easier or more pleasant—rather than to make prudent cost-benefit decisions to advance the interests of the taxpayers or the company's shareholders—the people who earned the money in the first place.

Treat every federal dollar as if it was hard-earned; it was—by a taxpayer.

When I served in the Nixon administration, I recall a plane being sent across the country to deliver a briefcase to one of the President's top aides. I later discovered that inside that briefcase were the latest copies of *Time* and *Newsweek* and a collection of newspapers. Thousands of dollars were spent to deliver items that would have cost a fraction of that expense had they had been purchased at the local newsstand.

If we look carefully, we can see the phenomenon of wasting "other people's money" at work every day. If as customers, for example, we each were required to pay for the packets of ketchup at the local McDonald's or charged for every napkin used at a Starbucks, I have a sense we would handle them with greater care. Because these items are thought to be "free," as customers we often give them little thought.

In neither the public nor the private sector is there someone standing around, day and night, watching over everyone to make sure they are spending the taxpayers' or shareholders' money wisely. The best you can hope for is to attract and reward people who have that internal gyroscope, and an innate understanding and respect for the value of "other people's money." Leaders need to search for people who instinctively appreciate the wrongness of waste and misuse.

During one of my first meetings with my staff in the Pentagon in 2001, I made a point of discussing matters that might have been seen as minor, considering the challenges facing the Department. But I felt they were important. I advised my staff not to make personal phone calls on government phones, to be considerate of taxpayer dollars, to treat every expenditure as if it came from their own pockets. I asked them to schedule regular briefings with ethics officers and I personally consulted with the senior ethics official to see how we were doing. I wanted to set a tone—early on—to establish a mind-set, to create a culture that emphasized the importance of respecting "other people's money."

Private enterprises tend to be more responsible than government in this regard, particularly in smaller businesses where entrepreneurs personally understand the cost of capital. They tend to manage their receivables, payables, and inventories with care. They have an interest in making sure their dollars are not wasted. Government, for example, owns buildings that are used only a fraction of the time—generally 9 a.m. to 5 p.m. five days a week. If a company invests large sums of money in a manufacturing plant, the owners want to see that that investment earns a reasonable return and would blanch at the idea that that major facility would be used only eight hours a day, five days a week—or less than one quarter of the hours in a week. The cost of the capital investment required causes well-run companies to use employee shifts to get the maximum value out of their facilities. And in a world that functions twenty-four hours a day, seven days a week, and with a federal government racking up trillions of dollars in debt, it might not be a bad idea for government departments and agencies to follow that same practice. Instead of regularly constructing entirely new buildings, at taxpayer expense, for new federal employees, they might begin using shifts to increase the usage of existing facilities beyond the normal eight-hour, five-day workweek.

Understand the Rule of 72.

The combination of money and time is powerful. Having even a modest amount of money working for you every minute of the day and night, seven days a week, year after year, can add up over time to an amazingly large amount because of compound interest. The Rule of 72 is a simple formula used in financial circles to determine how long it will take to double your investment at various rates of growth. It works like this: Take any interest or growth rate and divide it into 72. The resulting number tells you the number of years it will take for your money to double.

Assume, for example, that you save and invest $100 in an account at a 7.2 percent interest rate or an investment that grows at 7.2 percent per year. Dividing 7.2 into 72 gives the number 10, which means that your investment of $100 will double to $200 in 10 years at that interest rate. If you want your money to double in, say, 20 years, you divide 20 into 72, which indicates that you will need a 3.6 percent interest rate. If your goal is to accumulate $100,000, you can use the Rule of 72 to determine how much money you will need to invest each year, at what rate, and for what number of years, to reach your goal. It is fascinating to watch someone's face as he or she does the math for the first time and realizes the truly amazing power of compound interest.

Assume a grandchild is born in 2014. If two grandparents each put $1,000 in trust for the child, the chart below shows what that $2,000 investment will be worth to the child in the years ahead, assuming an annual growth rate of 12 percent—which may sound high today, but it is roughly the rate at which Standard & Poor's index of 500 stocks has grown over the past sixty years. Dividing 12 into 72 tells you that the investment of $2,000 will double every 6 years.

YEAR	CHILD'S AGE	VALUE OF INVESTMENT
2014	0	$2,000
2020	6	$4,000
2026	12	$8,000
2032	18	$16,000
2038	24	$32,000
2044	30	$64,000
2050	36	$128,000
2056	42	$256,000
2062	48	$512,000
2068	54	$1,024,000
2074	60	$2,048,000
2080	66	$4,096,000

Left out, of course, are taxes, which, depending on the nature of the investment, would take out a portion of the value. Still, the numbers are instructive: As the chart shows, $2,000 invested and leaving interest, dividends, and appreciation to compound, will equal more than $4 million by the time child reaches age sixty-six. That's achieved without the gift-givers or the child lifting a finger. Having a relatively modest sum invested is like having a team of people working for you day and night, 365 days a year, and having them turn their earnings over to you. The Rule of 72, the power of compound interest, is not to my knowledge taught in schools as part of a normal curriculum.

The federal government generally should be the last resort, not the first.

One of my former colleagues in Congress back in the 1960s, Representative Tom Curtis of Missouri, pointed out to me that when the federal government steps in to "solve" a problem, it tends to dry up money from private sources, whether entrepreneurs or charitable contributors. He said "public money drives out private money." Or, in other words, government involvement can "bigfoot" others out. People don't like to feel they are paying for something twice, first in taxes for the government to do it and then again in charitable contributions.

Public money drives out private money.
—REPRESENTATIVE TOM CURTIS

A great many people stand ready to help others. That is particularly true here in the United States, where the American people are undoubtedly the most generous on earth. But when government intrudes, that generosity tends to dry up. And unfortunately, when the government spends money it does so less efficiently than if people are spending their own. The lesson is clear that government aid and assistance programs should be a last recourse.

It's not because government is evil, not because government is corrupt, but because it is so difficult to spend federal funds in a way that actually achieves the intended result.

If government can't do government, what makes anyone think government can do business?
—Ace Greenberg

Contributing to the problem of wasteful federal spending is the declining presence of people in public life with business experience. Basic economics doesn't seem to be taught in enough of our nation's classrooms, at least not to any visible effect. High school graduates should have an understanding of supply and demand, or, for instance, how government intervention and subsidies can distort the economy. Democracy succeeds only by the active and informed participation of the broadest section of our citizenry. Too often the backgrounds of the leadership in our nation's capital tilt toward the professions of law and academia. That narrowness of perspective cannot help but skew public policy.

When Franklin D. Roosevelt was president, as many as one-half of his appointees had experience in business. Nearly 60 percent of Ronald Reagan's appointees had a business background. Today business representation in government has dwindled markedly. Only 22 percent of the Obama first-term administration had any experience in business—which the *Wall Street Journal* reported was the lowest level recorded in the last century.

No one benefits from such a serious lack of balance. There are, of course, many individuals with business experience interested in the direction of our country and whether or not government policies and actions are hospitable to investment and job creation. Yet too few are in government, which is a significant problem, since business leaders know better than most how jobs are created and what is necessary to create an environment that is hospitable to job creation and economic growth.

Beware when an idea is promoted as "bold, innovative, and new."

When I was at G. D. Searle, the Carter administration announced it was planning to impose wage and price controls. A decade earlier, President Nixon had named me director of the Cost of Living Council, in charge of the country's wage and price controls (despite my opposition to the controls). I knew that artificially setting wages and prices was harmful to the economy, so we worked to ensure they had as little adverse effect as possible. Because of my personal experience in this area, I felt an obligation to let President Carter know my thoughts about his unfortunate idea of establishing another wage and price control program, which I did.

If more leaders in our free enterprise system do not speak out on the importance of capitalism, members of Congress and executive branch officials with little or no experience in the private sector cannot be expected to do so. To his credit, Apple CEO Steve Jobs appreciated the responsibility he had as a business leader to tell political leaders what might be called "inconvenient truths." In a now-famous meeting with President Obama in 2010, Jobs warned that he might be a one-term president unless he advanced more business-friendly policies. As Jobs's biographer reported, the Apple CEO told the President the truth—namely that because of excessive Washington regulations, it was far easier and more profitable to build a factory in China than in the United States. This was important advice from a corporate leader, particularly one who had largely been supportive of the President.

There is always a well-known solution to every
human problem—neat, plausible, and wrong.
—*H. L. Mencken*

Unless we understand the cause of a problem, we are unlikely
to be able to solve it. The cost of prescription drugs, for example, has been inaccurately cited as a major reason for the steadily rising cost of health care and as one of the reasons one-sixth
of the nation's economy is about to come under the direct super-
vision of the federal government. The truth is that pharmaceuticals make up a small fraction of every dollar spent on health care.
Prescription drug costs are what they are for an understandable
reason. It takes many years to discover, develop, and successfully
bring a new drug to market. In that time, companies may invest
hundreds of millions of dollars in discovery, testing, development,
marketing, and employing the thousands of people necessary to
achieve that success. All of this is done in the hope that a drug
will be able to improve, extend, and even save people's lives, and
yes, also bring a return on that investment to the shareholders. It
would be wonderful if pharmaceutical companies could charge a
dollar for a drug to treat a serious disease, but if a company did that
it would go out of business in short order and there would be no
new drugs or pharmaceutical advances.

Without effective defenders of the private enterprise system, the
American people and the media hear mostly the critics. This can
lead to some strange ideas. A few years ago a survey of American
college professors asked them to rank what nations they believed
were "the greatest threats to international stability." America consistently was number two.[18] That statistic says a great deal more

about that collection of American college professors than it does about the United States.

America is not what is wrong with the world.

In 2002, Joyce and I attended a dinner honoring Kofi Annan, then Secretary-General of the United Nations. Around the table were a number of notable figures—U.S. senators from both political parties, journalists, and diplomats. Several of the guests commented on the terrorists being held at the U.S. military facility on Guantanamo Bay, Cuba, and the supposed injustices they contended were occurring there. The dinner conversation began to center on what is often fashionable in elite circles: what our country, our corporations, our political leaders, our troops, and our diplomats were doing wrong. There was little comment about what our enemies were doing around the world, or what our country was doing right.

I was a member of the Bush administration at the time. Maybe some of the guests expected me to agree. Maybe others expected me to stay silent. I did neither. After I had listened to more than enough, I placed my hand firmly on the table, so firmly that a few of the wineglasses and some of the silverware shook. Conversations stopped.

I rose and found myself saying, "I don't get up every morning and think that the United States of America is what's wrong with the world." Joyce and I excused ourselves and we departed.

What I said that evening I felt deeply. Yes, America has its problems. We are certainly not perfect. But we need to keep things in perspective. (The next day I spoke with our hosts and explained why I had left abruptly; they graciously understood.) But the fact is, too many of us have become accustomed to taking our country to task and measuring it against some unattainable standard, but the truth is that America is not what is wrong with the world.

America is a nation of hope and possibility and opportunity—the nation that millions of people look to as a model. Americans have no reason to feel guilty as a country or society. As the French philosopher Jean-François Revel wisely wrote, "A civilization that feels guilty for everything it is and does will lack the energy and conviction to defend itself." The American people have done more for more people around the world than perhaps any other country in human history—caring for those suffering from earthquakes, tsunamis, and hurricanes; offering a haven for those fleeing persecution; and much more. I believe in our free system of government and our free economy. The proof is there. And I know that many millions of people in our country share my conviction. It is important that more of us say so more often.

For a good many years I have kept close at hand a photograph that I believe tells it all. It is a satellite photo of the Korean peninsula taken at night. I have used this photo time and again as I've traveled the world discussing the truth of the benefits of free economic and free political systems.

The photo shows literally millions of lights all across the Republic of Korea, a capitalist democracy in the southern half of the Korean peninsula—visible evidence of the energy, vitality, and industriousness unleashed by their free market economy. In the totalitarian, communist north, above the demilitarized zone, the photograph shows only a single pinprick of light, at the capital, Pyongyang. The rest of North Korea is in darkness.

Consider that the same people live in the north as in the south. There are the same resources available to the north and south, and the same heritage and culture north and south. Yet the outcomes

Consider that the same people live in the north as in the south.
Yet the outcomes are dramatically different.

are dramatically different. Today South Korea, the small lower half of that peninsula, is the fifteenth-largest economy in the world—dynamic, self-sufficient, prosperous, contributing. This did not come about because its government plans their economy or because a dictator rules everything. South Korea has succeeded and succeeded brilliantly because individuals and entrepreneurs have the freedom to pursue their self-interest—to invest, create jobs, take risks, make mistakes, fail, try again, and achieve. And they have succeeded brilliantly. But in North Korea—where every aspect of life is controlled by the dictatorial central government—the people are starving, literally starving. And its economy is in endless need of international support to keep it from complete collapse.

That image is a powerful visual lesson as to what works and what does not work. Anyone looking for a way to explain the power of capitalism and the failure of socialism need look no further.

CHAPTER FOURTEEN

THE OPTIMISM OF WILL

When I served as the U.S. Ambassador to NATO in the early 1970s, one of my counterparts in Brussels was a distinguished Belgian diplomat, Ambassador André de Staercke. As the dean of NATO's North Atlantic Council, de Staercke had earned the respect of his peers. Then sixty years old, the elegant and worldly ambassador was helpful to me, a forty-year-old American in my first diplomatic post and who was decidedly neither elegant nor worldly.

In earlier days, de Staercke had been a friend of Winston Churchill. During World War II, de Staercke and the British prime minister once flew together over the city of Dunkirk, the site of the famous 1940 battle against the Nazis that led to the desperate evacuation of British forces from the continent of Europe. As Churchill looked down at the fields of green below, he commented, "I'll never understand why the German army did not finish the British Army at Dunkirk."

De Staercke, a pragmatic man, suggested to Churchill that they pose that question to a German officer at the earliest opportunity. Not much later, a German commander who had been captured by the British after the successful Allied invasion of France was asked just that. Why, the commander was asked, did you not finish off the British at Dunkirk when you had the chance?

According to de Staercke, the commander replied, "I had no orders!"

There is no shortage of books that offer lessons about leadership. Learning from the experiences of others is helpful. But at its core, leadership is not about following ironclad rules; it's about one's instincts. Leadership is not composed of a collection of maxims it comes from one's own independent judgment. It is fortunate for the world that the German commander at Dunkirk lacked those qualities. And, for that matter, that Hitler and his generals did not understand the importance of encouraging such qualities in their subordinates.

What one needs in life are the pessimism of intelligence and the optimism of will.
—*Ambassador André de Staercke*

When I was considering a run for president in 1987, I asked some friends and former colleagues for their thoughts and advice. André de Staercke was one of them. He urged me to appeal to the optimistic spirit of America, a country that he revered for its resilience and can-do nature. He sent me the thought above, which I added to my collection of rules. De Staercke hit on an essential element of leadership—the determination to achieve tempered by humility. It is the ability to accept that there is a great deal out there in the world that we don't know and cannot know, as well as things that we think we know but might judge incorrectly. This is a perspective that comes from experience. And from the courage to venture out into the world and make mistakes and, yes, even fail.

I have so often in my life been mistaken that I no longer blush for it.

—*Napoleon Bonaparte*

Few of us move seamlessly through life skipping along the top of the waves from one success to another. Making mistakes is human. Having the courage to try and to risk mistakes distinguishes a leader from the rest. It's easy to look back on things in life that did not work out the way you had hoped and become paralyzed by second-guessing yourself. As John Reid, a distinguished former British defense minister, put it, "Of course with hindsight, everything is perfect. It's the only exact science known to man."

There were any number of things I said or did during my time in public life that in retrospect I would have handled differently. And of course there were mistakes I made as a son, a husband, a father, and a friend. Learning from mistakes is important. So too is the ability to recover from them. The same is true of disappointments.

You pay the same price for doing something halfway as for doing it completely, so you might as well do it completely.
—PRESIDENT NIXON TO HENRY KISSINGER

Like anyone I've had my share of failures and disappointments over the years. At the time some of them seemed monumental. In the Navy, for example, I was not assigned to single-engine aircraft in 1956 despite my every effort. That major disappointment contributed to my decision to give up a career as a Navy pilot. At the age of twenty-eight, I managed a congressional campaign in Ohio for a man I greatly admired, and was heartbroken for him when he lost by less than one switch vote per precinct. In 1965 in the Congress I lost an election for a leadership position as chairman of the Republican Policy Committee, by one vote. I tried to run for the 1988 Republican nomination for President of the United States, but failed to raise the money needed to be competitive. Each of those setbacks and disappointments changed my trajectory, as they tend to do for anyone. I tried to learn from them, avoid wallowing in regret, and then get on with life.

Then there were the mistakes, miscalculations, and disappointments of more recent vintage, some of which occurred during the conflicts in Afghanistan and Iraq. In the fog of any war, miscalculations are of course inevitable. So is the grim reality that in any military conflict a number of Americans in uniform will not survive it.

Unquestionably the hardest task as Secretary of Defense was that I had to make decisions that I knew would mean that young men and women would almost certainly not return home. I also knew that no matter how many precautions we took, there would be civilians who would be killed. All of those who served, sacrificed, and perished, and the many loved ones they have left behind, remain in my thoughts and prayers.

I have benefited enormously from
criticism, and at no point have
I suffered a perceptible lack thereof.
—*Winston Churchill*

With mistakes come criticism. Handling criticism is an essential part of leadership. Criticism is not always bad, in that it can help identify problem areas that can cause you to recalibrate and improve future decisions. But criticism isn't always good, either.

If you do almost anything in your life, especially if it is something new or different or controversial, you can be certain that someone, somewhere is not going to like it. You almost certainly will be second-guessed, mocked, or scolded. And sometimes the criticism won't come at you directly but through intermediaries or as unattributed quotes in newspaper articles or business journals.

Dogs don't bark at parked cars.

—Wyoming saying as quoted by Lynne Cheney

At the Pentagon, there was no shortage of decisions I made that rattled a few cages and made some folks unhappy. Some of those decisions turned out to be based on poor information, others simply misjudgments. And some were excellent decisions and the critics were later proven wrong, and still more that may yet be proved wrong. It is no secret which of those situations I preferred. Might I have approached some of those decisions differently, knowing what I know now? Of course. Do I regret having given them a try? Certainly not.

It is difficult to name any leader who was spared criticism. Consider the exceptional viciousness leveled at President Abraham Lincoln. There were large groups of people who hated him to his dying day; some even celebrated his assassination. Critics called him an ape, a dullard, a fool, a backward hick, "an awful, woeful ass," and an "obscene clown." If that's the kind of treatment as historic a leader as Lincoln received, there's little hope for anyone in public life to emerge unscathed.

Know that the amount of criticism you receive may correlate closely to the amount of publicity you receive.

In the 1970s, Joyce and I spent some time with Ethel Kennedy, the widow of former Attorney General Robert Kennedy. We often played tennis together on Sunday afternoons. One weekend Joyce and I had been invited to visit the Kennedy compound in Hyannis Port, Massachusetts. As it happened the Kennedy family was in the middle of a media firestorm focusing on some antics by two Kennedy children. Joyce and I heard about it on the radio while driving to the Kennedy home.

When we arrived in Hyannis Port, we expressed our sympathy to Ethel, suggesting that the only reason it was news at all was the prominence of their family.

Ethel said, "Look, our kids have the benefit of being part of the Kennedy family, but they also have the burden. That's life. It's a fair trade." It was a refreshing attitude, and I never forgot it.

Keep your sense of humor.

Ahealthy sense of humor and humility can help when you are receiving criticism. At the Pentagon I kept some cartoons on a wall in my office. They included many that made fun of me, which helped to keep life in perspective. As the years went on, the number of cartoons grew. I occasionally called to mind the well-known comment by President Harry Truman, "If you want a friend in Washington, buy a dog." After a couple of decades in Washington, I added what *New York Times* columnist and friend Bill Safire called the Rumsfeld corollary: "Better get a small dog, in case it turns on you, too."

It also helps to keep life in perspective by recognizing that many things tend to lessen in importance over time. When I served in the Nixon administration, I joined the President and other members of his Cabinet for a meeting at the Presidio in San Francisco. The meeting was held to discuss the vast property holdings of our federal government and what might be done to improve their management. When we took a break for lunch, we walked out of the building where we had been meeting, down a path toward a dock where a boat was waiting to take us on a tour of the harbor. Because the President was there, a large number of people had gathered to try to catch a glimpse of him.

As Mr. Nixon passed by, we could hear people in the crowd along the walkway applaud and say excitedly, "There's the President!" When other senior officials passed by, folks called out, "There's the Vice President" or "There's Secretary of Interior Wally Hickel." I was the lowest-ranking member of the Cabinet and at the very end of the line, but as I passed by I heard someone say,

"There's Don Rumsfeld." I smiled, amused by the thought that nobody—not a single soul—had said a word about the tall, lanky man I was talking with as we walked down the path. His name was Charles Lindbergh.

Only a few decades earlier my companion that day had been one of the most famous men in the world. His photo alone was front-page news. He was the aviation pioneer who, at the age of twenty-five, became the first man in history to fly nonstop across the Atlantic Ocean from New York City to Paris. His family had been the topic of national news after his son had been kidnapped from their home in what was dubbed "the crime of the century." His reluctance to see the United States enter World War II had won him millions of followers, while others had denounced him for it. At one point a famous dance—the Lindy—had been named for him.

For me, a former naval aviator, visiting with a man once considered the world's most famous pilot was a special moment. Yet as the two of us continued walking toward the dock, well behind President Nixon, not a single person recognized Lindbergh, pointed him out, or whispered his name. That somebody would call out my name and not his as we walked along was instructive. Fame, as it is said, is fleeting. What matters in the end is what you have when fame is gone—hopefully a strong and loving family, friends, your own sense of integrity, and a feeling that you have contributed.

In addition to the ability to trust your instincts, to accept and learn from criticism, and to keep life in perspective, leadership sometime profits from still another intangible: providence or old-fashioned good luck.

As a midshipman on the USS *Wisconsin* in 1951, I watched in amazement as that great, powerful battleship, one that had been part of the bombardment of Japan during World War II, pulled loose from its moorings and became stuck in the mud on the New Jersey side of the Hudson River. The crew tried everything to get the ship free. At one point a dozen or so tugboats tried to push it free. It wasn't until someone organized the tugboats and had them work together that they managed to push the *Wisconsin* free from the New Jersey shore. Or so I thought.

Years later, I was talking with the Chief of Naval Operations, Admiral Elmo Zumwalt. I told him that story about my time on the USS *Wisconsin* and explained that I related that story as a way of demonstrating what could be accomplished when people worked together. To my surprise, he revealed that he'd been the navigator on board that ship that day. He told me that my recollection essentially was correct except in one respect. He said it wasn't the tugboats alone that freed the great battleship. What saved the Navy from total embarrassment was that as all the tugboats pushed together—the tide came in. Ever since Zumwalt told me that, I have related a more complete version of that story. It is a reminder that even with the best of efforts, with everyone working together, we can all benefit from a little help from the Lord.

We cannot ensure success, but we can deserve it.
—George Washington

I have now lived more than one-third the life of our country. This suggests that, while I'm getting up there in age, our nation is still quite young. There have been fourteen Presidents of the United States during my lifetime, and I've had the good fortune of meeting eleven of them and of working with four. In my lifetime alone, our country has been through a great depression, a world war, a cold war, and many other conflicts and crises. Our nation has seen prosperous times and lean times. And throughout it all, the United States has never been anything but a leader for good in the world.

Patriotism is not short, frenzied outbursts of emotion, but the tranquil and steady dedication of a lifetime.
—ADLAI STEVENSON

In 1954, as I sat with my college classmates listening to Adlai Stevenson, America was entering a new era. We were at the inflection point moving from the post–World War II period into the early days of the Cold War. Television had just become a household fixture. For most of their news, people read their daily newspapers and the weekly magazines.

Today newspapers are becoming obsolete, some of the major newsmagazines have stopped production in print, and television now has hundreds of channels that can be watched almost anywhere, not only from a set in the living room. Many years ago I flew aircraft in the U.S. Navy that were gleaming, new, and state-of-the-art. Today they dangle as antiques from the ceilings of museums.

Our country has become more populous and more diverse, but we remain in essence the same people. As so many times before, a new generation of Americans has been blessed to live in this special country, with a compassionate and hopeful people, in a land of second and third and even fourth chances. Before these United States no nation on earth had a practice of selecting as our leaders individuals who were not blue-bloods or part of a genealogical lineage or necessarily even among the elite. Our constitution was drafted by farmers, and writers, and tradesmen, people rich and poor, from north and south. We've made mistakes, we've been counted out, but we have persevered and our people have prospered.

Some look at our nation with a measure of skepticism. Politics is corrupt, some say. Government doesn't seem to work. There are elements in our modern culture that promote gratuitous violence and horror. From time to time we see a lack of civility in debates and public dialogue.

But while not untrue, that is not America at its core. Even when our country may seem to be going in a wrong direction, as it has several times over my lifetime, we've always managed to right ourselves before it was too late.

The world is run by those who show up.

The American people have sound inner gyroscopes and centers of gravity. Given sufficient information, the American people usually find their way to right decisions. Or, as the famous observation attributed to Winston Churchill goes, "Americans will always come to the right decision after exhausting all the alternatives."

The twentieth century was called "America's century." An era in which the world was enriched by American leadership. I know that there are people these days who ask if there will be another American century, and whether the era of great American leaders is over. Don't you suppose in earlier eras in our country people asked those same questions? Then, as now, the great leaders were there in the wings. We didn't yet know their names. In some cases they were people making meager wages posted in dry, unpleasant military bases across the country. They moved their families every few years, and brought their children up in difficult circumstances.

It was not until we were attacked in World War II, when the need was urgent, that the American people discovered that the great leaders were there, and, in fact, they had been there all the time. Imagine our country's great good fortune that individuals of character, stature, and dedication rose out of that difficult and thankless environment. And when the call came, there among that anonymous group were a Marshall, an Eisenhower, a Bradley, a MacArthur, an Arnold, and a Nimitz who stepped forward to serve in uniform. And there were civilians who stepped forward, as well—a Roosevelt, a Truman, a Vandenberg, a Stimson, a Nitze.

Many of those leaders had a special appreciation for our country because they saw it from a different perspective. America was one nation among many when a global conflict started. But when that war was over, they helped America become one of the greatest nations in history.

One of the great blessings of my life has been the opportunity to experience America from a different perspective. When I was serving as the American Ambassador to NATO, I lived with my family for a period outside of the United States. For the most part the Europeans I encountered back then looked upon America with respect. They remembered those who twice sailed across the ocean to help to free their continent from tyranny. They remembered a nation that stood strong for noble ideals, even if sometimes its leaders failed to meet them. There were those I met who wanted their daughters to come here so that their grandchildren would be blessed with American citizenship. The privilege of being an American is as great today as ever.

America will always be a beacon of hope to the world as long as there are young men and women capable and willing to lead. I have every confidence they are out there. And I have every confidence that when the time comes they will rise to the challenge of their generation as so many others have before them.

Make no mistake—these leaders won't perform perfectly. Sometimes they'll fall flat on their faces. But they'll get up again, brush off the dust, and keep at it. Harry Truman used to talk about an epitaph he saw on a tombstone in Arizona. According to Truman, it read: "Here lies Jack Williams. He done his damnedest." When you think about it, that's pretty much all we can ask of any leader. If one day you are able to look back on your career and say pretty much the same thing, then count yourself blessed. Because yours was a job well done.

ACKNOWLEDGMENTS

This book has been almost eighty years in the making. Its contents are owed to some of the most brilliant men and women of the last century, some of whom I had the great privilege of working with at various points along the way. Among them, no one is more responsible for convincing me to take those pieces of wisdom and put them into one document than Gerald R. Ford, the thirty-eighth President of the United States.

When I had the idea of turning Rumsfeld's Rules into a book, I turned to two young writers who helped me on my memoir and who have been invaluable through the publication process. Keith Urbahn and Matt Latimer of Javelin have helped me organize my collection of rules and transform them into a narrative. Without their talent, good humor, patience, and drive, this project would have been a considerably more daunting undertaking. My editor at HarperCollins, Adam Bellow, and associate editor Eric Meyers have been sources of excellent editorial feedback and counsel in the whirlwind process to complete this book. I am also grateful to Linda Figura, Bridget Sedlacek, Elizabeth Kuhn, Sarah Conant, and Remley Johnson in my office, and to interns Ellen Christiansen and Nicholas Miknev. All of them have helped keep this enjoyable project on track.

Acknowledgments

I have also benefited from a group of candid readers who have reviewed drafts of these chapters and offered helpful suggestions. They include Torie Clarke, Larry Di Rita, Bruce Ladd, Jean Edward Smith, and Marin Strmecki. Others have reviewed parts of the manuscript and I am grateful for their insights as well: David Chu, Doug Feith, Jim Denny, Bill Gallagher, and Admiral Ed Giambastiani.

The reader who has offered the most bracingly candid advice has to be my closest advisor over six decades, Joyce Rumsfeld.

My thanks to you all.

APPENDIX A:
RUMSFELD'S TIMELINE

1932	Born, Chicago, Illinois
1946–50	New Trier High School
1950–54	Princeton University (B.A.)
1954	Married Marion Joyce Pierson
1954–57	United States Navy service as a naval aviator, a flight instructor, and an instructor of flight instructors
1957–75	U.S. Naval Reserve
1957–59	Administrative Assistant for Congressman David Dennison (R-OH)
1959	Staff Assistant to Congressman Robert Griffith (R-MI)
1960–61	Broker, A. G. Becker & Co. investment bank, Chicago
1962–69	Elected to U.S. House of Representatives from Illinois's 13th Congressional District; reelected 1964, 1966, 1968

Appendix A: Rumsfeld's Timeline

1969–70	Director, Office of Economic Opportunity, Assistant to President Nixon, Member of the President's Cabinet
1971–72	Director, Economic Stabilization Program, Counselor to the President, member of the President's Cabinet
1973–74	U.S. Ambassador to NATO, Brussels, Belgium
1974–75	White House Chief of Staff under President Gerald R. Ford
1975–77	Thirteenth U.S. Secretary of Defense; awarded the Presidential Medal of Freedom
1977–85	CEO, President, G. D. Searle & Co.
1982–83	Special Presidential Envoy for The Law of the Sea Treaty under President Ronald Reagan
1983	Special Presidential Envoy to the Middle East under President Ronald Reagan
1988–2001	Board member, Chairman, Gilead Sciences, Inc.
1990–93	CEO, Chairman, General Instrument Corporation
1998	Chairman, U.S. Ballistic Missile Threat Commission
2000	Chairman, U.S. Commission to Asses National Security Space Management and Organization
2001–2006	Twenty-First U.S. Secretary of Defense
2007–	Chairman, Rumsfeld Foundation
2011	Author, *New York Times* bestselling memoir *Known and Unknown*

APPENDIX B:
RUMSFELD'S RULES
(UNABRIDGED)

ON BUSINESS AND MANAGEMENT

What you measure improves.

That which you require be reported on regularly will improve, but only if you are selective. How you fashion the reporting system announces your priorities and will set the institution's priorities.

If you can't measure it, you can't manage it. (Peter Drucker)

A's hire A's. B's hire C's.

Don't avoid sharp edges. Occasionally they are necessary to leadership.

If you are not being criticized, you may not be doing much.

Dogs don't bark at parked cars. (Wyoming saying as quoted by Lynne Cheney)

The road you don't travel is always smoother. (Representative Duncan Hunter Sr., R-CA)

Know your customers!

Develop a few key themes and stick to them. It works. Repetition is necessary. "Quality." "Customers." "Innovation." "Service." "Safety." You pick them!

Test ideas in the marketplace. You learn from hearing a range of perspectives.

Beware when an idea is promoted as "bold, innovative, and new." There are some ideas that are "bold, innovative, and new" but are also foolish.

Trust your instincts. Success depends, at least in part, on the ability to "carry it off."

When starting at the bottom, be willing to learn from those at the top.

If you are lost—"climb, conserve, and confess." (U.S. Navy SNJ Flight Manual)

Beware of the argument that "this is a period for investment; earning improvements will come in the out years." The tension between the short term and long term can be constructive, but there will be no long term without a short term.

Too often managers recommend plans that look like a hockey stick. The numbers go down the first year or two and then go dramatically up in later years. If you accept "hockey stick" plans, you will find they may be proposed year after year after year.

The worst mistake is to have the best ladder and the wrong wall.

If you don't know where you're going any road will get you there. (Paraphrase of Lewis Carroll)

You will launch many projects but have the time to finish very few. So think, plan, develop, launch, and tap good people to be responsible. Give them authority and hold them accountable. Trying to do too much yourself creates a bottleneck.

There is nothing more difficult to take in hand, more perilous to conduct, or more uncertain in its success, than to take the lead in the introduction of a new order of things. (Niccolò Machiavelli, *The Prince*)

Plan backward as well as forward. Set objectives and trace back to see how to achieve them. You may find that no path can get you there.

Don't "overcontrol" like a novice pilot. Stay loose enough from the flow that you can observe and calibrate.

What we anticipate seldom occurs; what we least expected generally happens. (Benjamin Disraeli)

If you don't want to believe it, there is no body of evidence that cannot be ignored.

Big (and bad) things can start from small beginnings.

It is not the strongest of the species that survives, nor the most intelligent, but the one most responsive to change. (Paraphrase of Charles Darwin)

If you don't like change, you are going to like irrelevance even less. (General Eric Shinseki)

Where there is no continuity there can be no accountability.

Nothing will ever be attempted if all possible objections must be first overcome. (Dr. Samuel Johnson)

Nothing is more obstinate than a fashionable consensus. (Prime Minister Margaret Thatcher)

Lawyers are like beavers. They get in the middle of the stream and dam it up.

Have a deputy and develop a successor.

Never hire anyone you can't fire.

Leave all options on the table. Taking options off the table demystifies the situation for the competition.

Never assume the other guy will never do something you would never do.

It is possible to proceed perfectly logically from an inaccurate premise to an inaccurate and unfortunate conclusion.

When you initiate new activities, find things currently being done that can be discontinued—reports, activities, etc. It works, but you must encourage, persuade, or force institutions to do it.

Keep in mind the "tooth to tail ratio." The tail's only role is to support the teeth.

Nothing ages so quickly as yesterday's vision of the future. (Richard Corliss)

Don't automatically fill vacant jobs. Leave some positions unfilled for six months to see if they are needed.

There are a great many people who have the ability to review something and to make it better, but there are precious few able to identify what is missing.

Reduce layers of management. They put distance between the top of an organization and the customers.

Sometimes it's necessary to kill a chicken to frighten the monkeys. (Chinese proverb)

Appendix B: Rumsfeld's Rules (Unabridged)

I am unable to distinguish between the unfortunate and the incompetent, and I can't afford either. (General Curtis LeMay)

Luck is what happens when preparation meets opportunity. (Seneca)

The first consideration for a meeting is whether to call one at all.

The last consideration for a meeting is "What have we missed?"

Don't allow people to be cut out of a meeting or an opportunity to communicate because their views may differ.

When negotiating, never feel that you are the one who must fill every silence.

In unanimity there may well be either cowardice or uncritical thinking. (Marion J. Levy Jr.)

If you can find something everyone agrees on, it's wrong. (Representative Mo Udall, D-AZ)

You can't reason a man out of something he did not reason himself into.

Nothing betrays imbecility so much as insensitivity to it. (Thomas Jefferson)

Trial and error are the essence of discovery. Your organization should be hospitable to both.

Top-down clarity and common understanding create trust, confidence, and unity.

Don't wait for feedback from superiors, colleagues, or employees. Ask them if there are things that you are not doing that you ought to be and also things that you are doing that you ought not to be.

Appendix B: Rumsfeld's Rules (Unabridged)

If a problem has no solution, it may not be a problem, but a fact, not to be solved, but to be coped with over time. (Shimon Peres)

If a problem cannot be solved, enlarge it. (Dwight D. Eisenhower)

With most problems, one learns 80 percent of what can be known relatively rapidly, but the remaining 20 percent can take forever.

Most people spend their time on the "urgent" rather than on the "important." (Robert M. Hutchins, former president, University of Chicago)

If you expect people to be in on the landing, include them for the takeoff.

Encourage others to give their views, even if it may ruffle some feathers.

New ideas often receive a negative reaction at the outset, regardless of their value

Avoid making a poor decision simply because the best option is presented by someone who may rub you the wrong way.

If a plan cannot be explained clearly enough to be well understood, it probably hasn't been well enough thought through.

This strategy represents our policy for all time. Until it's changed. (Marlin Fitzwater)

If you don't know what your top three priorities are, you don't have priorities.

The inherent vice of capitalism is the unequal sharing of blessings; the inherent virtue of socialism is the equal sharing of miseries. (Winston Churchill)

Underlying most arguments against the free market is a lack of belief in freedom itself. (Dr. Milton Friedman)

People don't spend money earned by others with the same care that they spend their own.

It's well worth understanding the Rule of 72 and the power of time and money.

Find ways to decentralize and reduce staff, without cutting into the thin layer required for you to manage.

Prune—prune businesses, products, activities, and people. Do it annually.

People think focus means saying yes to the thing you've got to focus on. But that's not what it means at all. It means saying no to the hundred other good ideas that there are. (Steve Jobs)

If you want traction, you must first have friction. (Admiral Jim Ellis)

People do better in staff jobs if they have had operational experience, and vice versa. It helps to look at things from the perspective of others.

Don't let the complexity of a large company mask the need for better performance. Bureaucracy can become a conspiracy to bring down the big. You may need to be large to compete on the world stage, but don't allow size to mask poor performance.

The way to do well is to do well.

Résumés should not require a decoder ring.

Mistakes in hiring are the employer's error, not the employee's.

Operations drive out planning.

Perhaps the most powerful antidote to unfettered selfishness is property rights. (Dr. James Q. Wilson)

When one starts building a temple unto oneself, it's the beginning of the end.

To see which direction things are moving in, apply the "gate test."

An excellent organization chart with poor leadership won't work; an imperfect organization chart with good leadership will.

ON SERVING IN GOVERNMENT

Public servants are there to serve the American people and our nation. Serve them well!

The federal government generally should be the last resort, not the first. Determine if a proposed program can be better handled privately, by a voluntary organization, or by local or state government.

Treat every federal dollar as if it was hard-earned; it was—by a taxpayer.

It is difficult to spend "federal [that is, taxpayer] dollars" in a way that achieves the intended result.

Congress, the press, and the federal bureaucracy too often focus on how much money is expended, rather than on whether or not that money actually achieves the intended result.

Public money drives out private money. (Representative Tom Curtis, R-MO)

Strive to make solutions as self-executing as possible. As the degree of discretion increases, so too do delay, expense, and the size of the bureaucracy.

Presidential leadership needn't always cost money. Look for low- and no-cost options. They can be surprisingly effective.

Stubborn opposition to proposals often has no basis other than the complaining question, "Why wasn't I consulted?" (Senator Daniel Patrick Moynihan, D-NY)

If in doubt, don't. If still in doubt, do what's right.

When you're up to your ears in alligators, try to remember that the reason you're there is to drain the swamp.

If you do something, somebody's not going to like it.

People are policy! Without the best people in place, the best ideas don't matter. (Dr. Ed Feulner)

Every government looking at the actions of another government and trying to explain them always exaggerates rationality and conspiracy, and underestimates incompetence and fortuity. (U.S. Circuit Court Judge Laurence Silberman's Law of Diplomacy)

You begin when you're least capable and most popular, and you end when you're least popular and most capable. (Former Prime Minister Tony Blair)

People will always forgive you for being wrong. But they won't forgive you for being right. (Robert Bartley, editor, *Wall Street Journal*)

In tough jobs, the days are long and the years are short. (Former Secretary of State George Shultz)

Appendix B: Rumsfeld's Rules (Unabridged)

The United States is a rich country. Not rich enough to do everything, but rich enough to do everything important. (Dr. Herb Stein)

When running a U.S. federal government agency, the two key rules are: overinform and never surprise. (John Robson)

The statesman's duty is to bridge the gap between his nation's experience and his vision. If he gets too far ahead of his people he will lose his mandate; if he confines himself to the conventional he will lose control over events. (Henry Kissinger, *Years of Upheaval*)

The two most important rules in Washington, D.C., are: Rule One: "The cover-up is worse than the event." Rule Two: "No one ever remembers the first rule."

Government does two things well—nothing and overreact.

Bureaucracy is nature's way of bringing down old empires (and organizations) so new ideas can replace them.

The trouble with socialism is that you eventually run out of other people's money. (Former Prime Minister Margaret Thatcher)

You never want a serious crisis go to waste. (Rahm Emanuel)

In Washington, D.C., the size of a farewell party may be directly proportional to an honoree's new position and his or her prospective ability to dispense largess. (Devon G. Cross)

If you want to have a friend in Washington, D.C., buy a dog (President Harry S. Truman). The Rumsfeld corollary is: Get a small dog, because it may turn on you.

Of course, with hindsight, everything is perfect. It's the only exact science known to man. (John Reid, former Secretary of State for Defense, United Kingdom)

Appendix B: Rumsfeld's Rules (Unabridged)

If government can't do government, what makes anyone think government can do business? (Ace Greenberg)

Washington, D.C., is sixty square miles surrounded by reality.

ON POLITICS AND CONGRESS

Politics is human beings; it is addition, not subtraction.

The three rules of politics: if you run, you may lose; if you tie, you do not win; and, most importantly, you can't win unless you are on the ballot.

In politics, every day is filled with numerous opportunities for serious error. Enjoy it.

The winner is not always the swiftest, surest, or smartest. It's the one willing to get up at 5 a.m. and go to the plant gate to meet the people.

Disagreement is not disloyalty. (Curtis E. Sahakian)

When someone says, "I don't know much about politics," zip up your pockets.

The oil can is mightier than the sword. (Senator Everett McKinley Dirksen, R-IL)

In politics, you must march toward the sound of gunfire.

Remember where you came from.

The difference between the executive branch and the legislative branch is that the executive branch has the data and Congress traffics in it. (Doug Necessary)

Members of the U.S. Congress are not there by accident. Each managed to get there for a reason. Learn what it was and you will know something useful about them, about our country, and about the American people.

Hold still, little fishy, I's just goin' to gut you. (Congressman Howard Smith, D-VA, describing a "perfecting amendment")

ON THE PRESS

Trust leaves on horseback but returns on foot.

Avoid both infatuation with or resentment of the press. They have their job to do and you have yours. (Joyce Rumsfeld)

You never get in trouble for what you don't say. (Dick Cheney's favorite rule, attributed to Sam Rayburn)

Don't do or say things you would not want to see on the evening news.

Arguments of convenience can lack integrity and often come back to trip you up.

People respond in direct proportion to the extent you reach out to them. (Vice President Nelson Rockefeller)

There is often a great deal more certainty in the public debate than information and data are available to support.

As for what is not true, you will always find abundance in the newspapers. (Thomas Jefferson)

It would be a strategic error to assume that everyone in the press is seeking the truth. (General Pete Schoomaker)

Let your words be as few as will express the sense you wish to convey and above all let what you say be true. (Stonewall Jackson)

A lie travels halfway around the world before the truth gets its shoes on. (Mark Twain)

The least understood risk for a politician is overexposure.

Sunshine is a weather report—a flood is news. (Attributed to Reuven Frank, NBC News)

May the words I utter today be tender and sweet, for tomorrow I may have to eat them. (Representative Morris "Mo" Udall, D-AZ)

There are really only three responses to questions from the press: "I know and will tell you"; "I know and I can't tell you"; and "I don't know." (Dan Rather)

Don't accept an inaccurate premise in a question. Rephrase it if necessary.

You're either a target or a source. (Columnist Robert Novak)

Not all negative press is unearned. If you're getting it, see if there's a reason.

Nothing proves more persuasive than a clearly stated fact.

With the press there is no "off the record."

Those who know, don't talk. Those who talk, don't know. (Lao Tzu)

You can wreck any story if you check the facts. (An anonymous Chicago reporter)

Great events and personalities are all made small when passed through the medium of this small mind. (Winston Churchill)

Appendix B: Rumsfeld's Rules (Unabridged)

SERVING IN THE WHITE HOUSE

Don't accept the post unless you have an understanding that you are free to tell the President what you think "with the bark off."

Visit with your predecessors from previous administrations. They know the ropes and can help you see around some of the blind corners. Try to make original mistakes, rather than needlessly repeating theirs.

Don't speak ill of your predecessors or successors. You didn't walk in their shoes.

Your performance will depend on the people you work with. Select the best, train them, and support them. When mistakes happen, and they will, give better guidance. If errors persist, help them move on. The country cannot afford amateur hour in the White House.

A president needs multiple sources of information. Avoid excessively restricting the flow of people or ideas to the President. If you overcontrol, it will be your "regulator" that controls, not his. Only by opening the spigot fairly wide, risking that some of his time may be wasted, can you let his "regulator" control.

In the execution of presidential decisions work to be true to his views in both fact and tone.

Know that the White House staff and others in the administration will be likely to assume that your manner, tone, and tempo reflect the President's.

Learn to say "I don't know." If used when appropriate, it will be often.

Bad news does not get better with time. If you foul up, tell the President and correct it fast. Delay only compounds the problem.

Don't automatically obey the President's requests if you disagree or suspect he hasn't considered important aspects of the issue. Go back and tell him.

Walk around. If you are invisible, the mystique of the office may perpetuate inaccurate impressions about you. After all, you may not be as bad as some are saying.

Leadership is by consent, not command. To lead, a president must persuade.

Be precise. A lack of precision can be dangerous when the margin of error is small.

Preserve the President's options. He will need them.

It is easier to get into something than to get out of it.

Amid all the clutter and despite the static, set your goals, put your head down, do the best job possible, and let the flak pass as you work toward them.

Never say "the White House wants." Buildings can't want.

You will have plenty to do without trying to manage the First Family. They are likely to do fine without your help.

Make important decisions about the President's personal security yourself. He can overrule you, but don't make him the one who has to counsel caution.

Don't blame the boss. He has enough problems.

Being Vice President is difficult. Don't make it tougher.

You and the White House staff must be—and be seen to be— above suspicion. Set the right example.

The role of White House Chief of Staff is that of a "javelin catcher." (Jack Watson, Chief of Staff to President Jimmy Carter)

Don't begin to think you're the President. You're not.

Strive to preserve and enhance the integrity of the presidency and pledge to leave it stronger than when you came.

See that the President, the Cabinet, and the staff are informed. If they are cut out of the information flow, their decisions may be poor or not confidently or persuasively implemented.

If in doubt, move decisions up to the President.

When you raise issues with the President, try to come away with both that specific decision and a precedent.

When the President is faced with a decision, be sure he has the recommendations of all the appropriate people.

If a matter is not a decision for the President, or you, delegate it.

Give your staff guidance against which to test their decisions. Otherwise their actions may be random.

One price of proximity to the president is the duty to bring bad news. You fail him and yourself if you are unwilling to do so.

Of special value to his leadership are the President's words and time. They should be expended with the utmost care.

Move decisions out to the Cabinet and agencies. Strengthen them by moving responsibility, authority, and accountability in their direction.

If you are working from your inbox, you are working on other people's priorities.

Think of dealing with Congress as a "revolving door." You will need to go back to today's opponents for their help tomorrow. The President will need a member's support on some issue, at some time, regardless of their philosophy, party, or positions on other issues.

Work continuously to trim the White House staff from your first day to your last. All the pressures are to the contrary—particularly during election season.

People around the President often have sizable egos before entering government, many with good reason. Their White House positions will do little to moderate their self-images.

"Responsibilities abandoned today will return as more acute crises tomorrow." (Gerald R. Ford)

Enjoy your time in public service. It is likely to be the most interesting and certainly the most challenging experience of your life.

Don't think of yourself as indispensable or infallible.

Remember you are not all that important. Your responsibilities are.

"The cemeteries of the world are full of indispensable men." (Charles de Gaulle)

Be able to resign. It will improve your value to the President and do wonders for your performance.

Don't be consumed by the job.

When asked for your views, by the press or others, remember that what they really want to know are the President's views.

Most of the fifty or so invitations you receive each week come from people who are inviting the President's Chief of Staff—not you.

If you doubt that, ask your predecessor how many invitations he received after he left.

Know that the amount of criticism you receive may correlate closely to the amount of publicity you get.

Don't panic. Things may be going better than they seem from the inside.

Keep your sense of humor. "The higher a monkey climbs, the more you see of his behind." (General Joe Stilwell)

FOR THE DEPARTMENT OF DEFENSE

The legislative branch is in Article I of the Constitution; the executive branch is Article II. That is not an accident.

Speed kills. It creates opportunities, denies the enemy options, and can hasten his collapse.

Nothing is static. For every offense there is a defense. For every defense there is an offense.

The President of the United States is the commander in chief. Both military and civilian leaders need to understand civilian control, and be respectful of it.

Weakness is provocative. Time and again it has invited adventures that strength might well have deterred.

Si vis pacem, para bellum. (If you wish for peace, prepare for war.) (Latin proverb)

To be prepared for war is one of the most effectual means of preserving peace. (George Washington)

You go to war with the army you have—not the army you might wish to have.

It is not that one general is better than another, but that one general is better than two. (David Lloyd George)

The mission must determine the coalition. The coalition ought not determine the mission.

War is a series of catastrophes that results in a victory. (Georges Benjamin Clemenceau, seventy-second Prime Minister of France)

Thinking about conflict today, it is more like a rheostat, not a light switch—on for war—off for peace. Many of our rules and policies are not aligned with this. (General Pete Schoomaker)

The Secretary of Defense is not a super-general or admiral. His task is to exercise leadership and civilian control over the department on behalf of the commander in chief and the country.

How does the military successfully recruit, organize, train, and equip tens of thousands of men and women year after year? The answer: chief petty officers and master sergeants.

When reducing staff at the Pentagon, don't cut into the very thin layer that is required for civilian control.

No matter how a war starts it ends in mud. It has to be slugged out. There are no trick solutions or cheap shortcuts. (General Joe Stilwell)

Manage the interaction between the Pentagon and the White House. Unless you establish a relatively narrow channel for the flow of information and "tasking" back and forth, the relationship can become chaotic.

If you are going to sin, sin against God, not the bureaucracy. God will forgive you but the bureaucracy won't. (Admiral Hyman Rickover)

I could as easily bail out the Potomac River with a teaspoon as attend to all the details of the army. (Abraham Lincoln)

Normal management techniques do not always work in the Department of Defense. When pushing responsibility downward, be sure not to contribute to centrifugal forces that tend to pull the services apart. What cohesion exists in DoD has been painfully achieved over decades; don't do anything to weaken it.

Establish good relations between the Departments of Defense and State, the National Security Council, CIA, and the Office of Management and Budget. You'll need them.

Avoid public spats. When a department argues with other government agencies in the press, it reduces the President's options.

Develop a good working relationship with the chairman and members of the Joint Chiefs of Staff and the combatant commanders. They are almost always outstanding public servants. In time of crisis, those relationships will be vital.

The task is to create trust and confidence, unity of effort at the top, to enable and empower the combatant commanders.

If you get the objectives right, a lieutenant can write the strategy. (General George C. Marshall)

The unforgivable sin of a commander is to form a picture—to assume that an enemy will act in a certain way in a given situation—when in fact his response may be altogether different. (Napoleon Bonaparte)

Plans are worthless, but planning is everything. (General Dwight D. Eisenhower)

Appendix B: Rumsfeld's Rules (Unabridged)

No plan survives first contact with the enemy. (Helmuth von Moltke the Elder)

No matter how enmeshed a commander becomes in the elaboration of his own thoughts, it is sometimes necessary to take the enemy into account. (Winston Churchill)

What design would I be forming if I were the enemy? (Frederick the Great)

When working with senior enlisted personnel or a senior officer, know that they have achieved their position by demonstrating world-class capabilities to the benefit of our country. While you may be working with them in an area outside their expertise, value them for what they can and do contribute.

He who defends everywhere, defends nowhere. (Sun Tzu)

In the long run it is inevitable that the party which stays on the defensive will lose. (Frederick the Great)

When asked, "Who do you consider to be the greatest generals?" Napoleon responded, "The victors."

In war, one tank too many is a great deal better than one tank too few.

There is a difference between force and power. You generally need force in situations where you haven't marshaled sufficient power to shape events. (Admiral Arleigh Burke)

We need to win the savage war of peace. (Rudyard Kipling)

Belief in the inevitability of conflict can become one of its main causes. (Thucydides)

I don't mind generals planning for the last war, so long as they are all on the other side. (Rear Admiral Arthur Cebrowski)

The only thing harder than getting the . . . military to adopt a new technology is getting them to give up an old one. (Former NASA Director Dr. William Graham)

Never give an order outside of the chain of command and never expect to learn anything up the chain of command. (Admiral Hyman Rickover)

Try to select Chiefs of Staff of the military services who have previously served as a commander or deputy commander of a combatant command. Joint experience balances lingering service-centricity.

It's a whole lot like listening to a cow pee on a flat rock. It just doesn't matter. (General T. Michael "Buzz" Moseley, commenting on the numerous retired military officers and pundits who criticized the Iraq war plan "they had never seen")

There is only one thing worse than fighting with allies, and that is fighting without them. (Winston S. Churchill)

If Americans had listened to some European leaders during the past fifty years, we would still be in the Soviet Union. (Vaira Vike-Freiberga, former President of Latvia)

We [IRA terrorists] only have to be lucky once; you will have to be lucky always. (Note to Margaret Thatcher from the Irish Republican Army)

The challenge in an insurgency is that the insurgents don't have to win, they just have to not lose. (General George Casey)

In an era when weapons are increasingly lethal, if the enemy has already attacked, the defender may have started too late.

There lies at the heart of deterrence . . . an inescapable paradox: the more seriously the possessor is believed capable in extremis of using the armory, the less likely it is that others will cause or allow circumstances to arise challenging its use. The converse is also true. (Sir Michael Quinlan)

It is exceedingly difficult for any military organization to innovate radically—except in wartime when it is absolutely necessary. (Former CIA Director R. James Woolsey)

In war—unity. You can deal with the past later. It never runs away. It is the future we must affect. (President Shimon Peres, on his support for the Prime Minister of Israel)

This war isn't like the last war, and it isn't like the next war. This war is like this war. (Admiral Vernon Clark, Chief of Naval Operations)

With too much authority to the warfighter, it is like a peewee soccer game—everybody chases the ball, it doesn't advance the ball, and it leaves the rest of the field open for unpleasant surprises. (General Larry Welch)

Too often military (and civilian) officials are not in their assignments long enough to discover the mistakes they've made and learn from having to clean them up.

You get what you inspect, not what you expect.

The Pentagon is like a log floating down a river with 25,000 ants on it, each one thinking it is steering. (Dr. Harry Rowan)

Transformation begins with thinking. (Admiral Vernon Clark)

In war the weaker side can often adapt faster than the stronger side. Size and strength can be cumbersome and lead to complacency, while vulnerability leads to fear, and fear is a powerful motivator.

For almost twenty years we had all of the time and almost none of the money; today we have all of the money and no time. (General George C. Marshall during World War II)

Running the U.S. Navy is like punching a pillow all day. You end up exhausted and the pillow hasn't changed a bit. (Franklin D. Roosevelt)

Running the Department of Defense is like wrestling with a seven-million-pound sponge. (Deputy Secretary of Defense David Packard)

When your enemy is making mistakes, don't stop him in the middle. (Napoleon Bonaparte)

Europe is always right, but always late—Stalin, Hitler, Saddam, and Iran. (Shimon Peres)

Everyone told Lincoln not to engage in a civil war. If he had agreed, there would be no United States of America. (Shimon Peres)

Lawfare has become another dimension of warfare. (John Yoo)

At the top there are no easy choices. All are between evils, the consequences of which are hard to judge. (Secretary of State Dean Acheson)

Every war is going to astonish you in the way it has occurred and in the way it is carried out. (Dwight D. Eisenhower)

The inevitable never happens. It is the unexpected always. (John Maynard Keynes)

Freedom is the sure possession of those alone who have the courage to defend it. (Pericles)

Generals never lose a war in their own memoirs.

The strength of terrorists today is the weakness of the international community. (Shimon Peres)

No people in history have ever survived who thought they could protect their freedom by making themselves inoffensive to their enemies. (Dean Acheson)

It is axiomatic that the probability of leaks escalates exponentially each time a classified document is exposed to another person. (Former CIA Director Richard Helms)

Dictators ride to and fro upon tigers which they dare not dismount. And the tigers are getting hungry. (Winston Churchill, *While England Slept*)

The best service a retired general can perform is to turn in his tongue along with his suit and to mothball his opinions. (General Omar Bradley)

An appeal to force cannot, by its nature, be a partial one. (General Dwight D. Eisenhower)

Precision weapons require precision intelligence. (Admiral Dave Jeremiah)

The more we do something, the better we get at it. But the more we do something and the better we get at it, the less likely it will need to be done . . . because the enemy has a brain.

Space is more than just another higher hill. (General Ed Eberhart)

In revolutions, the characteristics are: there are winners; there are losers; and there is pain.

We never go final; we just run out of time to make more changes. (Doug Necessary)

The perfect battle is the one that does not have to be fought. (Sun Tzu)

ON INTELLIGENCE

There are known knowns: the things you know you know. There are known unknowns: the things you know you don't know. But there are also unknown unknowns: the things you don't know you don't know.

When you know a thing, to hold that you know it, and when you do not know a thing, to allow that you do not know it; this is knowledge. (Confucius)

Many intelligence reports in war are contradictory; even more are false, and most are uncertain. (Carl von Clausewitz)

Tell them what you know. Tell them what you don't know. And, only then, tell them what you think. And, be sure you distinguish among them. (Colin Powell)

Know what you do not know. Those who think that they know, but are mistaken, and act upon their mistakes, are the most dangerous people to have in charge. (Prime Minister Margaret Thatcher)

The only thing that should be surprising is that we continue to be surprised.

The absence of evidence is not necessarily evidence of absence; nor is it evidence of presence.

Some of it (what you can see), plus the rest of it (what you can't see), equals all of it. (Baldy's Law)

First reports are often wrong.

Appendix B: Rumsfeld's Rules (Unabridged)

No one ever sees successful camouflage.

Warning time not used is wasted time. It's like runway behind a pilot. (General Lee Butler)

The wind through the tower presages the coming of the storm. (Chinese proverb)

Hire paranoids. Even though they have a high false alarm rate, they discover all plots. (Dr. Herman Kahn)

It is easier to convince someone they're right, than to convince them they're wrong.

A sample of one from a homogenous population is sufficient. (Dr. Herman Kahn)

Oh, really. What do you suppose was his motive? (Talleyrand at the Congress of Vienna, on learning the Russian ambassador had died)

The intelligence community is a collection of feudal baronies. (Admiral David Jeremiah)

In this post–cold war world, intelligence is not just bean counting—we need to know cultures and intentions. (General Chuck Horner)

If it were a fact, it wouldn't be intelligence. (Former CIA Director General Michael Hayden)

ON LIFE (AND OTHER THINGS)

You can't pray a lie. (Mark Twain, *Huckleberry Finn*)

It takes everyone to make a happy day. (Marcy Rumsfeld, age seven)

Appendix B: Rumsfeld's Rules (Unabridged)

It is quite true what philosophy says: that life must be understood backwards. But that makes one forget the other saying: that it must be lived—forwards. (Søren Kierkegaard)

Certainty without power can be interesting, even amusing. Certainty with power can be dangerous.

It is not because they are difficult that we do not dare things; rather they are difficult because we do not dare them. (Seneca)

The most important things in life you cannot see—civility, justice, courage, peace.

The Lord doesn't require us to succeed. He just expects us to try. (Mother Teresa)

He who cannot change the very fabric of his thought will never be able to change reality. (Anwar Sadat)

Persuasion is a two-edged sword—reason and emotion, plunge it deep. (Dr. Lew Sarett)

Patriotism is not short, frenzied outbursts of emotion, but the tranquil and steady dedication of a lifetime. (Governor Adlai Stevenson)

Your best question is often why.

Don't be afraid to see what you see. (President Ronald Reagan)

Proper preparation prevents poor performance.

The art of listening is indispensable for the right use of the mind. It is also the most gracious, the most open, and the most generous of human habits. (Attributed to Dr. R. Barr, St. John's College)

In writing if it takes over thirty minutes to write the first two paragraphs select another subject. (Raymond Aron)

Learn from those who have been there.

You can't recover the fumble unless you're on the field. Get out there. (Tim Russert Sr.)

Discipline yourself and others won't need to. (John Wooden)

Whatever you are, be a good one. (Abraham Lincoln, county champion wrestler)

Once you've wrestled, everything else in life is easy. (Dan Gable)

If doesn't go easy, force it. (My dad's assessment of my basic operating principle at age ten)

Put yourself in the other person's shoes.

In sports as in life, keep something in the tank.

You always have two choices: your commitment versus your fear. (Sammy Davis Jr.)

When married, always have six months of your current salary in the bank. With that you will have the ability to leave any job at any time and never feel pressure to do something you do not think is appropriate. (Joyce Rumsfeld's father, Red Pierson)

One of the benefits of pessimism is that you are probably right more often than you are wrong, and when you are wrong, you are pleased. (George Will)

What one needs in life are the pessimism of intelligence and the optimism of will. (Belgian Ambassador to NATO André de Staercke)

When you're in a bind, create a diversion. (Alf Landon)

In life, as in gymnastics, never let go of one ring until you have a good grip on the next one.

You never know which twist is the one that will open the jar—just stay with it. (Tim Russert Sr.)

The world is run by those who show up.

You can learn something from everyone—from a five-year-old to a head of state. Listening is important. (Dr. Robert Goldwin)

What's the difference between a good naval officer and a great one? Answer: about six seconds. (Admiral Arleigh Burke)

First law of holes: If you get in one, stop digging. (Denis Healey)

Talent hits a target no one else can hit. Genius hits a target no one else can see. (Arthur Schopenhauer)

The reason I don't worry about society is nineteen people knocked down two buildings and killed thousands. Hundreds of people ran into those buildings to save them. I'll take those odds every [expletive deleted] day. (Jon Stewart)

The potential of anything is the most important thing about everything. (Hernando de Soto)

If you wish to study painting, do it in the winter, when the trees are bare and you can see the structure. (Chinese saying, per Shimon Peres)

Behold the turtle. He makes progress only when he sticks his neck out. (James B. Conant)

When drinking the water, don't forget those who dug the well. (Chinese proverb)

The harder I work, the luckier I am. (Stephen Leacock)

Read no history: nothing but biography, for that is life without theory. (Benjamin Disraeli)

Appendix B: Rumsfeld's Rules (Unabridged)

History will be kind to me, because I will write it. (Sir Winston Churchill)

But I am me. (Nick Rumsfeld, age nine, on receiving advice from his parents)

You learn in life that there are few plateaus; you are going either up or down.

If you're coasting, you're going downhill. (L. W. Pierson)

Explanations exist; they have existed for all time; there is always a well-known solution to every human problem—neat, plausible, and wrong. (H. L. Mencken)

Simply because a problem is shown to exist it doesn't necessarily follow that there is a solution.

The only stupidities that are not easily solved are those created by very intelligent men. (Ambassador François de Rose)

If you think you have things under control, you're not going fast enough. (Mario Andretti, racecar driver)

Clearly, a civilization that feels guilty for everything it is and does will lack the energy and conviction to defend itself. (Jean-François Revel)

To be absolutely certain about something, one must know everything or nothing about it. (Olin Miller)

The better part of one's life consists of his friendships. (Abraham Lincoln)

You get to do what you want to do only when you no longer want to do it.

When you're skiing, if you're not falling you're not trying.

The test of a first-rate intelligence is the ability to hold two opposed ideas in the mind at the same time, and still retain the ability to function. (F. Scott Fitzgerald)

Men count up the faults of those who keep them waiting. (French proverb)

It is seldom that liberty of any kind is lost all at once. (David Hume)

History marches to the drum of a clear idea. (W. H. Auden)

I have benefited enormously from criticism, and at no point have I suffered a perceptible lack thereof. (Winston Churchill)

I do not at all resent criticism, even when, for the sake of emphasis, it for a time parts company with reality. (Winston Churchill, House of Commons, January 22, 1941)

Demographics is destiny. (Auguste Comte)

Civilizations die from suicide, not murder. (Arnold Toynbee)

When Dr. Johnson defined patriotism as the last refuge of a scoundrel, he was unconscious of the then undeveloped capabilities of the word *reform.* (Senator Roscoe Conkling)

America is not what is wrong with the world.

I have so often in my life been mistaken that I no longer blush for it. (Napoleon Bonaparte)

You pay the same price for doing something halfway as for doing it completely, so you might as well do it completely. (President Nixon to Henry Kissinger)

What should they know of England who only England know? (Rudyard Kipling)

It is difficulties that show what men are. (Epictetus)

Appendix B: Rumsfeld's Rules (Unabridged)

You never really lose until you quit trying. (Mike Ditka)

Following the path of truth is sometimes difficult, but never impossible. (Pope John Paul II)

What you see is what you get. What you don't see gets you.

We cannot ensure success, but we can deserve it. (George Washington)

Victory is never final. Defeat is never fatal. It is courage that counts. (Sir Winston Churchill)

All generalizations are false—including this one.

If you develop rules, never have more than ten.

NOTES

1. Robert A. Caro, *The Years of Lyndon Johnson: The Passage of Power* (New York: Knopf, 2012), p. 224.

2. Donald Rumsfeld to President George W. Bush, "Predicting the Future," April 12, 2001. Available at www.rumsfeld.com.

3. Donald Rumsfeld, "Iraq: An Illustrative List of Potential Problems to Be Considered and Addressed," October 15, 2002. Available at www.rumsfeld.com.

4. Jonathan Aitken, *Charles W. Colson: A Life Redeemed* (New York: Doubleday, 2005), p. 167.

5. Robert L. Jervis, *Why Intelligence Fails: Lessons from the Iranian Revolution and Iraq War* (Ithaca, NY: Cornell University Press, 2010).

6. Thomas Schelling, foreword, in Roberta Wohlstetter, *Pearl Harbor: Warning and Decision* (Stanford, CA: Stanford University Press, 1962).

7. Dana Priest and William Arkin, "A Hidden World Growing Beyond Control," *Washington Post*, July 19, 2010, p. A1.

8. Ron Nessen, *It Sure Looks Different from the Inside* (Chicago: Playboy Press, 1978), p. 110.

9. Rumsfeld voting record, "Defense Authorization, FY 1966—HR 12889," 89th Cong., 2d sess., March 1, 1966.

10. RedState.com, "Documenting Bob Woodward's 'State of Denial.'"

11. Donald Rumsfeld, "Discussions with Russia," July 12, 2001. Available at www.rumsfeld.com.

12. Quoted in Peter Rodman, *Presidential Command* (New York: Knopf, 2009), p. 5.

13. Eric Greitens, "The SEAL Sensibility," *Wall Street Journal*, May 7, 2011.

14. The entire Stevenson speech can be found at www.rumsfeld.com.

15. Rasmussen Reports, "68% Believe Government and Big Business Work Together Against the Rest of Us," February 2011.

16. Marilyn Fedak, introduction to "Capitalism on Campus: What Are students Learning? What Should They Know?" Center for the American University, Manhattan Institute, University Club, New York, October 2010.

17. *The Phil Donahue Show,* date unknown, is available online at http://www.youtube.com/watch?v=E1lWk4TCe4U.

18. Gary A. Tobin and Aryeh Weinberg, "A Profile of American College Faculty: Political Beliefs and Behavior."

ABOUT THE AUTHOR

DONALD RUMSFELD has been an American government official and businessman. Rumsfeld served as CEO of two Fortune 500 companies and as the thirteenth and twenty-first Secretary of Defense.